URBANIZING
CITIZENSHIP

Thank you for choosing a SAGE product! If you have any comment, observation or feedback, I would like to personally hear from you. Please write to me at <u>contactceo@sagepub.in</u>

—Vivek Mehra, Managing Director and CEO,
SAGE Publications India Pvt Ltd, New Delhi

Bulk Sales

SAGE India offers special discounts for purchase of books in bulk. We also make available special imprints and excerpts from our books on demand.

For orders and enquiries, write to us at

Marketing Department
SAGE Publications India Pvt Ltd
B1/I-1, Mohan Cooperative Industrial Area
Mathura Road, Post Bag 7
New Delhi 110044, India
E-mail us at <u>marketing@sagepub.in</u>

Get to know more about SAGE, be invited to SAGE events, get on our mailing list. Write today to <u>marketing@sagepub.in</u>

This book is also available as an e-book.

URBANIZING CITIZENSHIP

Contested Spaces in Indian Cities

Edited by
Renu Desai
Romola Sanyal

⑤SAGE www.sagepublications.com
Los Angeles • London • New Delhi • Singapore • Washington DC

First published in 2012 by

SAGE Publications India Pvt Ltd
B1/I-1 Mohan Cooperative Industrial Area
Mathura Road, New Delhi 110 044, India
www.sagepub.in

SAGE Publications Inc
2455 Teller Road
Thousand Oaks, California 91320, USA

SAGE Publications Ltd
1 Oliver's Yard
55 City Road
London EC1Y 1SP, United Kingdom

SAGE Publications Asia-Pacific Pte Ltd
33 Pekin Street
#02-01 Far East Square
Singapore 048763

Published by Vivek Mehra for SAGE Publications India Pvt Ltd, typeset in 10/12 pt Adobe Garamond by Diligent Typesetter, Delhi and printed at Chaman Enterprises, New Delhi.

Library of Congress Cataloging-in-Publication Data Available

ISBN: 978-81-321-0730-9 (HB)

The SAGE Team: Neelakshi Chakraborty, Aniruddha De, Vijay Sah and Rajender Kaur

The cover photograph is by Javed Iqbal and is reproduced by permission.

Contents

Part 1: Governance and Citizenship in the Neoliberal City

Part 2: Protest and Claims-making in the Indian City

List of Tables and Figures

TABLES

FIGURES

Foreword

The essays in this pioneering volume make the case that Indian cities have become the most salient sites for emerging formations of Indian citizenship. They do not argue that the nation is irrelevant; they do not dispute that the village remains crucial to India's political imagination. But they show that India's vibrant cities are not only the stage but also the script for developments in citizenship that challenge assumptions of both national and rural formulations of political membership. These findings are important on several counts. It has often been noted that for several generations, India's social thinkers, politicians, and artists—its elites generally—thrived in the era of nationalism since Independence not by imagining an Indian urban future but by focusing on what would make rural India modern. The studies in this volume show that the struggle for India's modernity is now dramatically urban as both middle and lower classes define their stakes in the future through competing claims to city spaces.

Urbanizing Citizenship demonstrates, moreover, that these conflicts are well understood as engagements of citizenship. Though they bear a family resemblance to those analysed in classic Western social theory, they are also distinctive in their conjunctions of protest and negotiation between residence-based organizations and government. These distinctions occur, however, in the context of the kinds of intense urbanization, democratization, globalization, and neoliberal economic restructuring that characterize much of the global South in the last half-a-century. Thus, in accounting for contemporary developments of Indian cities and citizenship, the volume also suggests how this understanding transforms conceptualizations of both that remain anchored in North Atlantic and classical history and culture. One of the striking ways in which these essays invert the traffic of 'North–South' theorization (often colonial in origin) is to use theories and research developed to analyse cities and citizenship in other regions of the global South (especially Latin America) to interrogate Indian conditions. In doing so, they realize an important but rarely achieved 'South–South' dialogue. This critical and cross-pollinating inquiry makes *Urbanizing Citizenship* of real comparative value to researchers like me who work on similar issues in different places.

A key innovation of this volume is to use the emerging concept of urban citizenship to analyse a variety of specific cases of conflict over urban spaces and resources. The authors see these conflicts as collisions of multiple and often contradictory claims, identities, and differences that both shape and are shaped by the commitments residents make to the city as their political community of belonging in their daily lives. These commitments in conflict make the city an arena of citizenship change—an arena where national citizenship is reconfigured as its substance, practices, meanings, institutions, and publics become reshaped through conflicts over the terms and aspirations of urban life. There may be some hesitancy in the essays to define why this shaping constitutes an urban citizenship. If so, it is no doubt because, after several centuries in which the nation has triumphed over the city worldwide as the primary domain of political membership, urban citizenship typically has no formal definition in national constitutions and is only recently being reinvented as both practice and analytic.

Nevertheless, the meaning of urban citizenship that threads through the volume is clear: it refers to the city as its primary political community for an agenda of rights-claims that address city living as its substance. It applies when residents—rich and poor—mobilize not primarily as nationals, but as urban residents who legitimate their demands on the basis of their sense of stakes in the city—of making, contributing to, and appropriating it—even when, as some cases in the book illustrate, that sense of legitimation also promotes nationalist and exclusionary constructions of (Hindu) politics. Where it appears, urban citizenship typically recalibrates the national by generating new kinds of public participation, conceptions of rights, notions of belonging, and uses of law outside the kinds dictated and formalized by the State.

Most of the case studies in this volume distinguish between the formal and substantive aspects of this citizenship and analyse urban conflicts in relation to the particular combinations of both that define their terms of engagement. Formal refers to the status of membership in the political community and its criteria; substantive to the distribution of rights, duties, and resources this formal status entails and people deemed citizens actually exercise. Using the analytic of formal and substantive has several important advantages. It corrects the biases and inaccuracies of the classic 'civil society/ political society paradigm' that divides citizenship into dichotomous camps of the included ('proper citizens' within civil society, generally the rich, who supposedly have lawful property relations with the state) and the excluded (always populations of the poor outside civil society, who cannot be viewed analytically as 'legitimate citizens' and whose politics cannot be understood in terms of citizenship because they generally live and work illegally). Often confusing folk and analytic concepts, this paradigm precludes the existence of citizenship outside the frame of the nation-state and its structure of law. Thus, it analytically forecloses the development of other kinds of publics and conceptions of belonging and rights attached to them.

Certainly, poor urban Indians have been forced into segregated and illegal conditions of residence, estranged from law, and funneled into labour as servile workers. Certainly, they have been excluded from resources and denied rights. But these discriminations result not from their exclusion from citizenship itself, as the civil society paradigm typically assumes, because overwhelmingly, they already are citizens: they are formal members of the politically democratic Indian nation-state who exercise this status minimally by voting. Rather, these Indians are discriminated against because they are certain kinds of citizens, with particular distributions of disadvantages. The important questions to ask, therefore, as these essays do, are what kinds of citizens are they, what is the relation between the formal and substantive aspects of their citizenship, and how does the application of a particular type of citizenship generate their discriminations. In these terms, moreover, the volume shows that all citizens, rich and poor, are simultaneously populations with substantive attributes defined and managed by technologies of government administration.

By analysing the complexities of formal incorporation and substantive distribution, the urban citizenship paradigm thus avoids reducing politics to dichotomous and homogeneous categories. Rather, it highlights the simultaneities of actually lived politics and the superimpositions of the city in their unevenness and heterogeneity. As the studies in Urbanizing Citizenship demonstrate, citizenship mobilizations produce new equalities and new inequalities. They generate new publics and new segregations, new modes of association and new modes of violence. Citizen participation both empowers and fragments, identifies and differentiates. This volume is especially welcome in showing that right-to-the-city movements are not only organized by the lower classes and around socially progressive issues. The upper classes also use right-to-the-city arguments to advance their interests, and all classes may do so for objectives that are nativist, racist, and segregationist. In India, as elsewhere, both upper and lower classes develop competing right-to-the-city movements: the poor primarily to avoid eviction, legalize their housing, and partake in the urban economy; the rich to have a pollution-free environment cleared of slums and pavement dwellers, secure public spaces, and centrally located land for real-estate development befitting their commitments to globalized economies and lifestyles.

By focusing its attention on conflicts of cities and citizenship, and by doing so in ethnographic detail, *Urbanizing Citizenship* challenges a set of naturalized, gendered, and dichotomous analogies that has characterized both urban and political studies. These assumptions associate the middle classes with a masculinized exercise of rights, citizenship, powers of protest, and the associational life of civil society, and the lower classes with a feminized cooperation (and its chain of negotiation, cooptation, and resignation), patronage, and the disciplined subjectivities of political society. The essays in this volume complicate these assumptions to the point of shredding them. They are able to do so not only because cities and their social relations have profoundly changed in the developing world with the extraordinary urbanization, democratization, and neoliberalization of the last 50 years—so much so that the object of study requires a different kind of theorization to account for its complexities. They are also able to do so because the lens of urban citizenship they employ shows that the political sphere of urban India emerges from the lived conditions of city life without heeding the dichotomous conceptualizations of Western social thought that divide the social universe into public and private, state and family, *polis* and *oikos*, secular and religious, rule of law and lawlessness, juridical and biological, and so forth. Rather, it reveals that conflicts over the meanings and practices of citizenship are found in every corner of Indian cities and get conceived in terms of both the mundane aspects of residential life (plumbing) and the dramatic (eviction). The leaders of these conflicts are the barely citizens of the poor—women, manual laborers, squatters, pavement dwellers—as well as the resplendent citizens of the upper classes. Out of their contestations over the quality of their lives and nature of their citizenship in Indian cities, a vast new urban India emerges.

James Holston
Berkeley, California
January 2011

Acknowledgements

This book has its genesis in a discussion that we had in spring 2008 about our mutual interest in South Asian urbanism. Not only were we carrying out research in different Indian cities ourselves, but we were also excited by the ethnographies on contemporary urban India that some of our other colleagues were doing. Finding ourselves in a moment when urban debates were becoming increasingly important both in India and at a global scale, we organized a one-day symposium at the University of California, Berkeley, on cities and citizenship in South Asia. Most of the scholars who presented their research at the symposium were completing their doctoral dissertations and collectively their papers covered a gamut of urban processes, revealing the diversity and richness of processes of urban citizenship in Indian cities and posing challenging questions for urban studies. Following the symposium, we therefore decided to bring together a selection of the papers along with some invited contributions in an edited volume. We have a number of people to thank for the success of this endeavour.

First, our deepest thanks goes to the Center for South Asia Studies (CSAS) at the University of California, Berkeley, particularly its Chair, Professor Raka Ray; Vice-Chair, Dr Sanchita Saxena; and Program Director, Puneeta Kala, for giving a home to the symposium and providing us with logistical and financial help both through the event and with the production of the book. This book project would not have materialized without their encouragement. We would also like to thank the Department of Architecture and the Doreen B. Townsend Center for the Humanities at UC Berkeley for co-sponsoring the event with CSAS. Several others have helped us develop this project intellectually. Mrinalini Rajagopalan generously gave her time towards brainstorming and drafting out the symposium's call for papers. Professor Ananya Roy gave us advice on the theme and intellectual aim of the symposium. Professor Nezar AlSayyad, who has been a mentor to us, gave us advice on the symposium as well as the book. Professor Jenny Robinson and three anonymous reviewers gave us useful feedback on the book that helped us develop the project further. Professor James Holston, whose book *Cities and Citizenship* (1999) provided us with the inspiration for the symposium, has been with this project from the very beginning.

Both he and Professor Janaki Nair have very kindly agreed to write the Foreword and Afterword, respectively, for this book. Asher Ghertner generously gave us useful feedback on our introduction chapter. Nisha Ravindran copyedited the entire book manuscript during its initial preparation. Saurja Sen volunteered many hours to help us edit and format the entire book manuscript. A number of people at SAGE India have been very supportive and helpful at various stages of the book's publication. In particular, we would like to thank Dr Sugata Ghosh, Vice-President of Commissioning, Elina Majumdar, Commissioning Editor, and Aniruddha De, Editor. Our sincere thanks go to all these people for their time and energy towards this project.

We are grateful to Javed Iqbal for granting permission to reproduce his photograph from Ganesh Krupa Society, Golibar, Khar East, Mumbai, on the cover of this book. Residents of this neighbourhood have seen brutal slum demolition drives over the past year and have engaged in a protracted struggle against a developer who has sought to acquire their land through fraud and against state authorities who have often colluded with the developer. Their organized struggle as well as their ordinary everyday lives, both of which are captured in Javed's photograph, stake a claim to the city in numerous ways, showing both the fragility and the promise of the city as a site of citizenship for many urban residents.

Finally, and most importantly, we would like to thank our contributors for their work on this project and their immense patience through the long process of realizing an edited book. They have been an intellectually stimulating group for us to work with and we are delighted that they gave us this opportunity to bring their work into an edited volume.

Chapter 1

Introduction

Urbanizing Citizenship: Contested Spaces in Indian Cities*

Renu Desai and Romola Sanyal

The last 20 years of liberalization of India's economy has brought about profound changes to its urban areas. Paralleling this has been a rise in academic interest in the 'urban' as a legitimate site of scholarship and concentrated attention (Prakash 2002). This recent scholarship rather than exploring the city as a modernist space and an emblem of progress and development explores its contradictions and complexities. Studies in this vein have examined the politics of identity, evolving socio-economic inequalities, and the shifting relationship between the state and the citizens and their implications for democracy, civil society, and secularism. Questions of citizenship have lurked through all of these writings in different ways. This volume attempts to take these discussions further and uses ethnographies of the urban to reflect on the dynamics and emerging forms of urban citizenship.

Over the past several years, scholars have pointed out that in South Asia there has been theoretical anxiety and ambiguity with the city. Gyan Prakash (2002) has argued that until recently 'the urban' was marginalized in the imagination of modern India as it was the village that was seen as its authentic heart. Others have argued that in the nationalist imagination the city was seen either as a symbol of modernization and development (under the Nehruvian approach) or as an 'inappropriate historical trajectory for Indian modernity' (Rao 2006: 226). This is because unlike in the West, where the experience of modernity with its associated promises of freedom and equality was linked with the urban, here it was linked to the nation-state

---

* We would like to thank Asher Ghertner for his valuable comments on an earlier draft of this chapter.

(Rao 2006). This not only led to an anti-urban bias in development agendas in the post-Independence period, but also shaped Indian scholarship, even as urbanization continued apace. As Janaki Nair writes, the city has only recently become 'a legitimate object of attention, investigation and research, and as a site that recasts the meanings of citizenship, democracy, and indeed modernity in contemporary India' (Nair 2005: 1).

Despite the ambivalent location of 'the city' within historical discourses in South Asia, urban environments have been important and their relationships to their inhabitants have evolved over time. In many of the larger cities, squatters, for example, have come to expect certain rights to resettlement (however tenuous and imperfect) when evicted from their 'illegal' settlements. Such expectations have developed over time through everyday urban practices and government policies as well as through activist interpretations of legal and constitutional rights (Ramanathan 2006). Such practices, policies, and expectations indicate that ideas of urban citizenship present in different cities are constituted by their histories. With the nation-state liberalizing and evolving, these relationships are also changing. Thus, the 'urban turn' is not only significant for the study of South Asia, but also for exploring the historiography of South Asian cities and the ways in which people have laid claims to them.

Today, Indian cities provide a rich tapestry of urban politics (see, for example, Hansen [2001] on Mumbai, Nair [2005] on Bangalore, and Roy [2007] on Calcutta). The development of India's democracy as a result of colonial legacies and post-colonial struggles has given rise to particular cultural and political communities and ideas of democratic rights in Indian cities. Certainly, the politics of religion and secularism are products of colonial and post-colonial governmentalities (Hansen 1999). The rise of Hindu nationalism and the shift from Nehruvian developmentalism to a liberalizing economy in the 1990s began to transform the relationship between the state and its citizens in crucial ways (Ray and Katzenstein 2005). This has been reflected in the ways in which urban crises and development are managed and mediated by the state. Cities in India thus mirror the uneven and varied landscape of neoliberal interventions and post-colonial formations, providing key sites for analysing citizenship in the subcontinent. They are spaces in which identity, politics, and power are shaped and re-shaped through multiple negotiations and contestations that are rooted both in historic legacy and contemporary challenges.

Urban citizenship as a conceptual framework allows different case studies to reveal the varied and changing dynamics of politics and belonging in the Indian city across space and time. What emerges is not only how the role of the city has changed discursively and politically within the larger nation-state, but how it is also evolving for its own citizens in different cities. This conceptual move is important both because the city in India has emerged as a legitimate site of scholarship and because it is a key site of experimentation with urban and social forms and practices, and a signifier therefore of things to come.

The 'urban turn' in India has moreover come at a critical time when the geopolitical landscape is also being reconfigured due to rapidly shifting power relations and financial crises. Although notions of 'First World' and 'Third World' were problematic earlier, now it seems impossible to categorize countries as such. The language of 'emerging economies' used to describe Brazil, China, India, and Russia attempts to capture shifting power structures in the world, but even these are contested and inadequate. Within urban studies, there have been several attempts by scholars to rank cities in the world, particularly through economic criteria (Beaverstock, Taylor, and Smith 2000; Friedmann 1986; Sassen 1991). But such rankings fail to recognize the different ways in which cities in the world connect up and are 'globalized', particularly cities in the global South that host largely informal economies (McFarlane 2006; Robinson 2006). Existing systems for ranking and ordering cities, such as global city or world city models, are furthermore unable to capture the complex geographies within cities. 'First World' cities often have 'Third World' spaces within them and vice versa. In Brazil, for example, the enclaves of the very wealthy stand cheek by jowl with the *favelas* of the very poor (Caldeira 2000). Such geographies have interesting parallels with urban India. Those who insist on adhering to these dichotomous categories or using other fixed and hierarchical categorizations thus run the risk of inadequately theorizing and imagining the urban.

In response to this enduring North–South division and hegemony of Western urban theory, there is a growing recognition among scholars that cities in the global South are far more generative of urban change and innovation than previously thought/theorized, and that these cities are indeed in productive conversations with cities in the global North (rather than acting as mere foils to them). As cities in Africa, Asia, and South America continue to grow at a rapid pace, many scholars have called for new geographies of urban theory (Robinson 2006; Roy 2009). They have argued that the alternate understandings of urbanization and urban theories that these cities present us with can successfully 'provincialize' (Chakrabarty 2000) the dominance of Euro-American discourses. For example, writing on African cities, Abdoumaliq Simone argues that contrary to 'being marginal to contemporary processes of scalar recomposition and the reimagination of political communities, African cities can be seen as a frontier for diffuse experimentation with the reconfiguration of bodies, territories and social arrangements necessary to recalibrate technologies of control' (Simone 2004: 2). He refers to the interest the EU has in the apparent ungovernability of cities such as Lagos and Kinshasa and what the ongoing survival of people living there might have to say about the future of urban governance in general.

Similarly, while concerns about global poverty have often produced discourses of crisis and anxiety centred on megacities of the global South and specifically on the 'slum' (Davis 2006), Vyjayanthi Rao's essay on 'Slum as Theory' shows how such analytical constructions are debilitating and how reading the 'slum' from categories imposed from elsewhere (and thus seen through a lens of crisis, emergency, the future, empire, and so forth) can be deeply problematic (Rao 2006). 'Slum as theory,' she notes, 'becomes an important point of departure precisely because it is located in the interstices of a whole range of mutations whose specificity is no longer locatable within singular frameworks' (Rao 2006: 232). Moreover, the site itself is constituted through the relationships between the politics of location and the politics of empire, the nation, and the global. But even as scholars have challenged such readings of crisis by making visible the dynamic social and economic spaces of the 'slum', Ananya Roy (2011) cautions us about the limits of this 'subaltern urbanism' and its often celebratory narratives of slum entrepreneurialism and subversive political agency. She urges us towards alternative concepts that might disrupt the very dualities of slum/suburb, formal/informal, and legal/illegal. This is a project that has broad repercussions for theorizing the urban more generally. These evolving debates illustrate not only the limits of current epistemologies of the urban, but also point to how the global South is fundamental to reshaping critical urban theory.

The 'urban turn' has also come at a crucial time when development policy initiatives and practices (like academic scholarship) are increasingly grappling with the complexity of the global South. While the United Nations Millennium Development Goals (MDGs) emphasize 'problems' in developing countries and advocate for an 'eradication of slums', the UK's Department for International Development (DFID) approaches issues of development from a seemingly more nuanced perspective. The DFID's country plan for India, although advocating the United Nation's language of a 'fight against global poverty', recognizes at least three faces of India and outlines a strategy for 'working with Global India', 'supporting Developing India', and 'assisting Poorest India' (DFID 2008). While such an overview of India is somewhat facile, it is a step towards recognizing the ways in which the country simultaneously provides important international aid and creates valuable knowledge, while itself addressing acute poverty and deprivation amongst its people.

But such vast inequalities also create challenges for policy and practice. Thus, while there has been a turn in India towards decentralization in urban governance and a call for citizen participation, this has often become an avenue for the middle classes and elites to capture more political space and expand their claims on the city (Zérah 2009). Cities are thus reshaped in accordance with the needs and interests of the upper classes rather than the poor who make up over half the urban population in most places. Projects that specifically call for the participation of the urban poor also pose a challenge. International development organizations, governments, and local non-governmental organizations (NGOs) working in many countries including India have increasingly recognized that policies and projects are doomed to fail unless local communities are involved in their conception and execution. Yet participatory methods themselves are messy and can fail to account for differences such as age, gender, class, and caste during implementation. As a result, there have been critiques about participation and the way it has largely failed to bring about meaningful social change due to its inability to engage with issues of power and politics, or because of the way in which participation itself has been corrupted (Cooke and Kothari 2001). Other scholars argue that participatory development can be successful if people are included as equal and creative partners and if participation itself is conceptualized as a radicalized form of citizenship (Hickey and Mohan 2005; McFarlane 2008).

The challenges to policy and practice are likely to only increase. Although only 30 per cent of India's population currently resides in urban areas, UN projections estimate that 55 per cent of the country's population will be living in its cities by 2050. According to UN Habitat reports, the mega urban regions of India, although decelerating in their growth rates, have expanded through sub-urbanization and satellite cities.[1] Urban corridors are developing between metropolitan cities such as Mumbai and Delhi (UN Habitat 2008a). Contrary to many other Asian and African examples, much of India's urban growth is taking place in intermediate cities such as Pune, Jaipur, Indore, Cochin, and Jabalpur. India also faces important environmental challenges to its cities due to climate change (UN Habitat 2008b). In addition there is an urgency among UN institutions, international and multilateral development organizations, and affiliated NGOs to meet the MDGs, which involve addressing questions of access to adequate

housing, security of tenure, urban infrastructure (especially water and sanitation), and environmental sustainability. Various issues related to these
pose complex challenges for governments, policy makers, NGOs, and local
communities, and policies often have unanticipated outcomes. What may
seem like technocratic urban planning is, in fact, intimately intertwined
with urban politics. If India's urban challenges are to be addressed, the
evolving politics of urban space must be brought to the centre of urban
research agendas. This volume attempts to do this through the framework
of urban citizenship.

In the next section, we discuss some of the citizenship debates, the
concept of urban citizenship, and its analytical utility for studying Indian
cities. The chapters in this collection use the lens of urban citizenship to
explore diverse urban processes such as urban renewal, participatory slum
resettlement, municipal reforms, city imagineering, urban environmentalism, squatting politics, forms of urban protest, and civil violence. In the
following section, we discuss the contributions of these chapters by focusing
on two themes: (*a*) urban governance and (*b*) urban protest and claims-
making, and their implications for urban citizenship in India. We also discuss the conversations that these chapters generate with each other and with
other urban scholarship. We conclude with some brief reflections on the
volume's contributions and on the Indian urban condition.

CITIZENSHIP AND THE CITY

The notion of the city as a site of citizenship has a long history going back
to the ancient Greek city-state or *polis*, ancient Roman cities, and medieval
European cities. The word 'citizen' itself derives from the Anglo-French
citizein which derives from *cité* or the city (Bennett et al. 2005: 29). Most
debates around citizenship in the contemporary city are, however, embedded in more recent histories. Over the 19th and 20th centuries citizenship
came to be defined around the world as membership in a larger national
political community which delineated a range of rights and duties for its
members.[2] In his seminal essay 'Citizenship and Social Class', T.H. Marshall (1950) analysed how citizenship in Britain came to be defined by an
expansion of rights, from civil rights which are the bundle of rights necessary for individual freedom that emerged in the 18th century, to political
rights which originated in the 19th century and guaranteed participation
in the exercise of political power as a voter, to social rights which made
possible the attainment of a modicum of economic welfare and security in
the 20th century (Shafir 1998: 14). Although the relevance of Marshall's

analysis of progressively expanding formal citizenship rights has been questioned in non-British contexts, it has served as an important starting point for thinking about the evolution of citizenship rights in different national contexts, including the history of struggles for rights and their emerging configurations (Shafir 1998).

Within the Indian context, the articulation of citizenship has been complex and shifting. Following the formation of the Indian nation-state in 1947 and under the Nehruvian developmental state, a certain configuration of civil, political, and social rights was enshrined in the Indian Constitution to realize a secular, socialist, and democratic India. These included seven 'fundamental rights' enforceable in a court of law: the rights to equality, freedom, property, freedom of religion, constitutional remedies, the right against exploitation, and cultural and educational rights.[3] In addition, the Constitution listed a range of 'directive principles' that instruct the state to 'promote the welfare of the people by securing and protecting as effectively as it may a social order in which justice, social, economic and political, shall inform all institutions of the national life'.[4] These include principles that direct the state to secure for all citizens the right to an adequate means of livelihood, humane conditions of work, the right to a living wage and a decent standard of life, and so forth. Unlike the fundamental rights, these principles are not enforceable in the courts; rather, they are meant to guide the state in the framing of laws and policies.

Colonial legacies as well as capitalist development and socio-political transformations in the post-Independence period meant that many of these fundamental rights have been protected more in theory than in practice for majority of India's citizens. Similarly, the directive principles have not always steered the framing of laws and policies and have rarely guided implementation. Beginning in the mid-1980s, with the development of public interest litigation and an activist interpretation of the Indian Constitution, the courts in India became important arenas of social struggle, with lawyers and judges broadening the meaning of particular fundamental rights and linking them to the directive principles to expand the rights of marginalized groups (Cassels 1989). However, while establishing important case law/precedents, this judicial activism was not always successful in expanding people's rights in practice. Thus, various social inequalities have remained entrenched and have mutated into new forms. As a result, there have been profound disjunctions between the formal (legal) aspects and the substantive aspects (that is, the rights that are actually realized in practice) of citizenship in India.

Indeed, disjunctions between the form and substance of national citizenship have often been the norm rather than the exception around the world. Although formal citizenship in the nation might extend the same set of formal rights to all its citizens, the contours of substantive citizenship have usually been inflected by class divides, and are often also racialized, ethnicized, and gendered in various ways.[5] Feminists have furthermore critiqued the universalist assumptions of liberal citizenship, proposing alternate conceptions such as differentiated citizenship which would be sensitive to class, race, gender, sexuality, and culture, and which would incorporate different groups through a recognition of these social differences (Young 1998).[6] In recent decades, as a result of political-economic transformations at the national and global scales, the disjunctions and uneven contours of citizenship have taken on new forms, further calling into question conceptions of citizenship. Scholars have argued that citizenship has been re-scaled, re-territorialized, and re-oriented because of the changing role of the nation-state, unprecedented levels of migration, the emergence and consolidation of supranational structures, and the rise of new discourses of belonging and identity (Holston and Appadurai 1999; Purcell 2003). Transnational citizenship (Bauböck 1994), global citizenship (Urry 2000), and flexible citizenship (Ong 1998) are some of the concepts that have attempted to capture the new forms and practices of contemporary citizenship. It is in this context that the notion of urban citizenship has also emerged.

In one of the first attempts to develop the idea of the contemporary city as a key site of citizenship, James Holston and Arjun Appadurai (1999) pointed to the particularities of cities—as spaces concentrating diversity, difference, opportunity, and conflict—and the social, cultural, and spatial practices that constitute and negotiate citizenship at the urban scale. In turning to the city as the site of citizenship, their approach emphasized the lived space of both the uncertainties of citizenship and the emergent spaces of citizenship, both expansive and restrictive. Locating urban citizenship in the context of late 20th century political-economic transformations, they furthermore argued that cities were challenging, diverging from, and even replacing nation-states as the important space of citizenship. Over the past decade, the body of scholarship on urban citizenship has steadily expanded as scholars have examined citizenship in relation to diverse urban processes in the context of globalization and its discontents.[7] We briefly discuss four approaches or analytics (which are not mutually exclusive) that we propose are of relevance for studying urban citizenship in Indian cities, particularly for the discussions that unfold in this collection.

Focusing on the increasingly fragmented and divided landscapes of urban citizenship in cities around the world, Nezar AlSayyad and

Ananya Roy (2006) have proposed 'medieval modernity' as an analytic to think about the configurations of power, territory, and citizenship in the modern city. This is not just another vocabulary for thinking about sharpening urban polarization and exclusion as AlSayyad and Roy also draw attention to the potentials and paradoxes of urban spaces. Rather, by proposing 'medieval' as a transhistorical analytical category, they provoke us to think about the 'fragmented domain of multiple and competing sovereignties' (AlSayyad and Roy 2006: 12) in the modern city which have resonances to medieval forms of power and organization. This involves different territorialized forms of power, association, and patronage forged through actors like the state, international development institutions, NGOs, religious organizations, and private resident associations, which produce and compete in urban spaces like the gated enclave, the squatter settlement, and the urban refugee camp. Their approach opens up an important way to think about the citizenships emerging in various sites across the differentiated space of the Indian city, and how these might be crucially shaped not only by state–citizen relations but by a range of territorialized power relations and sovereignties.

A second analytic that is useful is Teresa Caldeira and James Holston's notion of 'disjunctive democracy'. Although their focus is on democracy in Brazil, it is clear that their ideas have emerged from their research on Brazilian cities, specifically São Paulo, at a time of Brazil's transition to a democracy (Caldeira 2000; Holston 2008). They argue that the development of citizenship in democracies—in all democracies, and not only Brazil—is 'never cumulative, linear, or evenly distributed for all citizens, but is always a mix of progressive and regressive elements, uneven, unbalanced, and heterogeneous' (Caldeira and Holston 1999: 692). This is what they call 'disjunctive'. Thus, at any one moment citizenship may expand in one area of rights while contracting in another, and thus democracy is always in a process of 'becoming and unbecoming, often confusing and unstable' (Caldeira and Holston 1999: 717). Here, democracy and citizenship are obviously viewed as extending beyond political rights to include social, economic, and cultural spheres of life. The notion of 'disjunctive democracy' clearly has significance for thinking about India's democracy as well, and it can provide a particularly powerful analytic to think through the ways in which Indian cities are shaped today by processes of polarization, fragmentation, and violence on the one hand, and by gains made by various marginalized groups on the other, thus leading citizenship rights to 'expand and erode in complex arrhythmic ways' (Holston and Appadurai 1999: 15).

A third analytical approach has been to think through the ways in which urban social movements and other forms of subaltern agency shape cities and expand citizenship rights in the city. Practices of claims-making that challenge the elite production of the city by subverting dominant forms of control or through the production of new forms of knowledge from below have thus been conceptualized as 'insurgent citizenship' (Holston 2008) and 'deep democracy' (Appadurai 2001). This is a departure from the perspectives of scholars like Partha Chatterjee (2004) who argues that the state views and responds to marginalized groups as 'populations to be managed' as opposed to 'proper citizens' with legitimate claims, and thus squarely locates the politics of the urban poor in a separate domain of 'political society' as opposed to 'civil society'. While Chatterjee's analysis provides important insights into the political calculations of the state vis-à-vis marginalized groups, it stops short of seriously analysing the numerous ways in which these groups negotiate their claims to the city. Nonetheless, these contrasting perspectives raise important questions about the relationships between the state and subaltern groups; about the nature of subaltern agency; and whether, when, and how subaltern practices challenge the elite-making of the city. Indeed, recent writings on African cities raise challenging questions around the agency of urban subalterns. These writings explore the deep uncertainties of African urban life, the incessant improvisation and provisionality, calculations, and risks that urban residents engage in, and the shifting topographies of possibilities and closures that this continually creates (Simone 2004, 2008). Ananya Roy argues that these 'Africanist debates about agency, subjectivity, and politics defy the easy categorizations of power and resistance' (Roy 2009: 827). 'Under conditions of crisis,' she writes, 'the subaltern subject is simultaneously strategic and self-exploitative, simultaneously a political agent and a subject of the neoliberal grand slam' (Roy 2009: 827). Roy's reflections suggest that we need to be more attentive to the ways in which the urban poor and working classes participate in the shaping of the city and urban citizenship.

Finally, various scholars have approached questions of urban citizenship through Henri Lefebvre's concept of the 'right to the city' (Lefebvre 1996), that is, the right of all urban inhabitants to participate directly in the production of the city and shape it in ways that fulfill their needs and have meaning for them. The concept has been catalyzed to trace how the exclusionary city is produced and to simultaneously reclaim the city for urban inhabitants increasingly dispossessed and disenfranchised by neoliberal processes (Fawaz 2009; Harvey 2008; Mitchell 2003). It has also been mobilized to think about more inclusive ways of producing the city (Purcell

2003), including through the arenas of everyday life (Gilbert and Dikeç 2008). The 'right to the city' has, moreover, provided an important lens for thinking about the rights of all urban inhabitants, regardless of their citizenship in the nation-states in which cities are invariably located, thus bringing to the centre the rights of illegal immigrants, asylum-seekers, and so forth.

What is shared across many of these discussions, implicitly or explicitly, is the way in which the right to the city is inextricably linked to the very form, space, and meaning of the city. Urban citizenship understood in these ways is thus a productive lens for interrogating the mutual constitution of citizenship and urbanism in India. As Indian cities have come to be situated within transnational flows of capital, ideas, images, and people, the lens of urban citizenship opens up productive ways of interrogating emerging urban reconfigurations and their politics. While the Indian nation-state certainly remains the source of formal citizenship, old and new contradictions in Indian cities mean that there are new and deepening disjunctions between formal political membership (and the rights this entails) and what this actually guarantees or even makes possible in people's everyday lives. While those at the lowest rung of the urban economy have always been denied many of their 'fundamental rights' in practice, economic liberalization and the world-class and bourgeois city visions that it has fuelled has led to further erosions of these rights, often in extremely violent ways. In recent years the courts have also increasingly taken a revanchist stand vis-à-vis the urban poor, reversing its earlier stance which had recognized their claims (Ramanathan 2006). Furthermore, elite non-citizens including many members of the Indian diaspora have been able to access and appropriate city resources in ways that were not easily possible before the 1990s. As concentrations of diversity, inequality, and competing interests, Indian cities are also marked by deep anxieties about difference, some of which have coalesced into chauvinistic regionalisms and nationalisms. Here, the lens of urban citizenship is useful for thinking about the profound implications of these processes for the interplay of urban and national belonging. Simultaneously, NGOs and grassroots organizations have been carving out new spaces of negotiation with the state, whose implications for inclusive citizenship seem to be mixed.

In this book, we approach urban citizenship through the broad definition put forth by James Holston (2009: 12): 'A citizenship that refers to the city as its public sphere and to rights-claims addressing urban practices as its substance—claims concerned with residence, neighborhood life, infrastructure, transportation, consumption and so forth.' We also emphasize the ways in which citizenship and cities are mutually constitutive. Thus, we see the city not as a container in which citizenship is realized or denied, but rather we emphasize the ways in which citizenship rights and a sense of belonging to the city and/or nation are realized or denied through the reshaping, regulation, and governance of urban space and resources, and through contestations over urban space and resources. Ultimately, top-down and bottom-up processes and their interplay shape substantive citizenship, practices of citizenship, and citizen subjectivities and identities.

CONVERSATIONS

This book brings together research on Ahmedabad, peri-urban Bangalore, Calcutta, Delhi, Mumbai, and Varanasi, and examines a range of processes: city imagineering and place marketing, urban renewal, participatory slum resettlement, municipal reforms, urban environmentalism, squatting politics, forms of protest, and civil violence. Each of the chapters situates itself in and poses questions for particular debates on the city and citizenship as it grapples with specific urban processes in different Indian cities. Collectively, the chapters demonstrate how struggles around citizenship are situated in particular constellations of the local, regional, national, and transnational. Together, they also reveal the multiple arenas and practices through which citizenship and urbanism are co-constituted.

We organize the book into two parts, investigating urban processes and emerging citizenships in Indian cities through two sets of practices: urban governance, and protest and claims-making. Part 1, 'Governance and Citizenship in the Neoliberal City', focuses on practices of restructuring urban space and modes of governance in the context of intensifying inter-urban competition and neoliberal urban reforms. By examining governance practices around particular urban projects, this section interrogates the links between projects linked to global city-making; the role of the state; the ways in which elites, NGOs, and marginalized groups are incorporated into these projects; and the implications of these for the city and urban citizenship. Part 2, 'Protest and Claims-making in the Indian City', examines practices of protest, claims-making and even violence, through which diverse groups negotiate access to the state and urban resources. By examining the acts, strategies, and outcomes of these practices, this section interrogates how urban citizens, particularly those who are excluded from formal structures of governance, attempt to negotiate with the state and claim a right to the city, and the implications of this for citizenship and the city. The separation between governance and protest/claims-making is not always clear-cut, and as some of the chapters show, opposition and protest sometimes shape practices of governance. In the following section, we turn to a discussion of the individual chapters and the conversations they generate with each other and other urban scholarship.

Governance and Citizenship in the Neoliberal City

Following the Indian government's New Economic Policy of 1991 which initiated a process of economic liberalization, Indian cities have increasingly become more globally oriented, witnessing various related projects of urban transformation. Theoretical perspectives on the restructuring of governance and urban space have analysed 'neoliberal' transformations such as the emergence of 'urban entrepreneurialism', the shift from 'government' to 'governance', the rescaling of the state, the 'roll-back' of the state from certain arenas and its 'roll-out' in others (Brenner and Theodore 2002; Harvey 1989; Peck and Tickell 2002) and the emergence of spatial and neoliberal governmentalities (Robins 2002; Rose 1999). Although theoretical perspectives articulated through the experiences of one context might not easily translate to another, like many other cities around the world, Indian cities have become 'strategic targets for an increasingly broad range of neoliberal policy experiments, institutional innovations and politico-ideological projects' (Brenner and Theodore 2002). This has significant implications for the ways in which Indian cities are being re-imagined, developed, and governed and for urban citizenship. The four chapters in Part 1 interrogate practices through which governance, urban space, and citizenship in Ahmedabad, Mumbai, and peri-urban Bangalore are being transformed in the context of particular projects linked to global city-making and neoliberalization.

Entrepreneurial strategies to attract capital, jobs, and tourists have emerged in many cities around the world in the context of the coercive power of inter-urban competition. Renu Desai's chapter, 'Entrepreneurial Urbanism in the Time of Hindutva: City Imagineering, Place Marketing and Citizenship in Ahmedabad', examines some of these strategies in the particular social and political context of Ahmedabad. Desai shows how entrepreneurial strategies of city imagineering and place marketing emerged following a brutal state-supported anti-Muslim pogrom in Ahmedabad, and the rest of Gujarat, in 2002. Interrogating the images and narratives constructed through these strategies, Desai shows how they have been crucial in creating a discursive shift away from the city and region as violent and unsafe to the city and region as a culturally dynamic and developmental space. She argues that in doing so, these narratives have involved a 'politics of forgetting' and a 'politics of erasure and denial' vis-à-vis the experiences of marginalized groups, thus reproducing the patterns of material and symbolic exclusion inscribed through Hindutva politics. The rehabilitation of the city's and region's image has moreover served to legitimize and reproduce the political power of an illiberal regime. Desai argues that these practices furthermore participated in attempts to articulate an urban citizenship amongst Ahmedabad's religious majority that folded into each other the politics of Hindu nationalism and Hindu identity, pride in regional Gujarati identity, and civic pride in an entrepreneurial Ahmedabad. In numerous ways then, Desai shows how exclusionary urban citizenships based on class and religion are produced through entrepreneurial governance. The links between the city, governance, and exclusionary citizenships based on religion have also been explored by scholars working in other contexts of religious and ethnic nationalism such as Israel/Palestine. Oren Yiftachel's concept of urban ethnocracy, which refers to an urban regime in which a dominant ethnic group appropriates the city apparatus to buttress its domination and expansion (Yiftachel 2006), can potentially open up productive ways of examining some of these processes in Indian cities even though there are differences between the two contexts.

In many cities around the world, entrepreneurial strategies have involved the design of urban mega-projects to attract global investment and facilitate global-city formation. Existing literature emphasizes the ways in which the governance of these elite-driven projects disenfranchise and further dispossess marginalized groups. Liza Weinstein's chapter, 'Democratic Urban Citizenship and Mega-project Development in Globalizing Mumbai', complicates this perspective by examining the Dharavi Redevelopment Project (DRP)—a US$2 billion housing and infrastructure mega-project designed to transform Mumbai's largest slum settlement into a multi-use, mixed-income township and attract global real-estate investment into India's commercial capital. She argues that the global orientation of the project itself led to a more inclusive planning process. In a regulatory context that is perceived to be cumbersome, overly bureaucratic, and corrupt, international development firms have generally found it financially unviable to invest in Mumbai's land markets. As a result, in order to encourage foreign investors and global real-estate developers to put in bids for the project, the state and DRP administrators attempted to avoid negative publicity for the project and smoothen its implementation; these attempts included efforts to create a receptive local community by engaging them in the planning process. Tracing the conflicts that emerged and the state's increasing and unprecedented engagement with the local community between 2004 and 2008, Weinstein conceptualizes this as facilitating a democracy through co-optation, arguing that this form of democratic urban citizenship is not the product of high liberal ideals but emerged in response to practical, and largely material, considerations. She further argues that this citizenship is inherently uneven as the planning process was opened only to those groups within Dharavi with symbolic power and the political resources required to oppose the project and generate negative publicity. Here, symbolic power and political resource—and thus opportunities to make citizenship claims and carve out a space in DRP's planning process—were crucially linked to class, caste position, and historical claims on space.

Sapana Doshi's chapter, 'The Politics of Persuasion: Gendered Slum Citizenship in Neoliberal Mumbai', also investigates new modes of governance and their articulations of citizenship in the context of urban renewal projects involving informal 'slum' settlements. Studying participatory slum resettlement under the Mumbai Urban Transport Project (MUTP), a World Bank-funded infrastructure expansion project with over 20,000 project-affected slum households, Doshi's chapter seeks to address some key silences in the literature on citizen mobilization in working-class neighbourhoods of post-colonial cities. These silences concern the social differentiation within such neighbourhoods and whether and how citizen mobilizations within them enable or challenge market-oriented projects of urban transformation. Doshi explains that spatially produced, overlapping, and hierarchical axes of difference—including gender, ethnicity, and class—shape slum dwellers' political subjectivities. By analysing the citizenship discourses and mobilization processes that constituted resettlement under MUTP, she shows how participatory gendered citizenship was mobilized and harnessed. This, she argues, created new configurations of responsibility and community solidarity through a 'politics of persuasion' through which resettlement was managed. Non-governmental organizations and women slum leaders played a crucial role in these practices. Doshi further argues that such governance processes involving participatory citizenship have been deeply contradictory. While, on the one hand, they enabled a space of citizenship and negotiation for evictees, on the other, they facilitated slum clearance and resettlement. Examining the highly uneven experiences among resettled women, Doshi demonstrates how gendered forms of participation and citizenship carved out a space for women slum leaders to play empowered roles in what are usually top-down elite-driven projects, but also reinforced already existing socio-economic inequalities amongst slum residents. She ultimately argues that it is precisely the 'spatialized production of difference along multiple axes that has formed the basis of hegemony and consent to neoliberal redevelopment'.

These two chapters on 'slum' redevelopment and resettlement in Mumbai open up challenging questions for urban debates on the implications of entrepreneurialism and neoliberalism for the urban poor and disenfranchised. Scholars have conceptualized these processes as involving 'accumulation by dispossession' (Harvey 2003) and as producing revanchist cities (Smith 1996) and carceral geographies (Davis 1998). These perspectives have also been echoed in the scholarship on Indian cities, which has revealed that poverty and informality have been increasingly criminalized, leading to increasing exclusions and evictions (Banerjee-Guha 2009; Baviskar 2003; Bhan 2009; Ramanathan 2006). On the other hand, some scholars have also studied new modes of governance that seek to create spaces of participation for the urban poor in India. Some have celebrated the democratic potential of NGOs and grassroots movements to carve out a space for the urban poor to participate in shaping urban agendas (Appadurai 2001). Others have launched a critique of the ways in which these modes of governance involve a 'managerial vision of participation' (Zerah 2009) or discipline the urban poor rather than supporting their struggles over rights to housing or their self-realization (Harriss 2007). These latter critiques are important and the chapters by Weinstein and Doshi do not contradict them, but they also show how these processes, in certain contexts, might be more complex and contradictory than all these perspectives allow for. They show how the neoliberal restructuring of governance and urban space often works through difference, leading simultaneously to participation, empowerment, cooptation, and dispossession, with uneven effects on different marginalized groups. Their chapters challenge the homogenization of the 'urban poor' and 'slum dwellers' and reveal the different and even competing practices and possibilities of citizenship within these groups.

Malini Ranganathan's chapter, 'Reengineering Citizenship: Municipal Reforms and the Politics of "e-Grievance Redressal" in Karnataka's Cities', explores a very different kind of participatory process. She examines an e-governance project which has introduced computerized complaint management or what she refers to as 'e-grievance redressal'. The project seeks to improve urban service delivery in Bangalore and other cities in Karnataka by restructuring the ways in which complaints about municipal services are made, recorded, and responded to. The project is part of broader municipal reforms introduced in the name of 'good governance', an agenda that revolves around enhancing the transparency, accountability, and efficiency of governments as well as promoting citizen participation and empowerment.

Ranganathan argues that under the e-grievance redressal system, social citizenship is assuming contractualized forms with citizens no longer considered passive recipients of welfare and entitlements but called on to play a more proactive role through contracts between individual customer and service provider. She contrasts this with the ways in which social rights such as access to urban services are negotiated by residents and civic associations of the informal city in the realm of 'political society' and on the basis of moral solidarity rather than on legal grounds, thus making collective complaining the norm. Ranganathan argues that, in this context, the contractualization of social citizenship by e-grievance redressal undermines collective struggles and has socio-economic and gender biases. Her chapter also discusses the introduction of e-governance as reflecting the increased influence of the corporate sector in urban policy-making and how this has been made possible by the rescaling of the state in Karnataka with greater centralization around international loans and urban reforms. The stakes of Ranganathan's research are high as Nirmala Nagara, the project under which the e-grievance redressal system has been designed and implemented, is currently the largest project for municipal e-governance in the world and its e-governance initiatives are being scaled up to other cities across India.

Together, the four chapters in Part 1 thus reveal a multitude of state and non-state actors who participate in urban governance, their vectors and territories of influence, and the implications for urban citizenship (Kumar's chapter on Delhi in Part 2 also contributes to these explorations in some key ways). They show how the governing of urban space, resources, and residents—be it through the remaking of the city's image (Desai); displacement, resettlement, and redevelopment (Weinstein and Doshi); or emerging technologies for better service delivery (Ranganathan)—shapes substantive citizenship (both in symbolic and material terms) along the axes of class, religion, ethnicity, caste, and gender. While Weinstein's and Doshi's chapters reveal the ways in which certain developments in Indian cities are opening up possibilities of expanded citizenship, their chapters also reveal the limits of this expansion and even suggest that these expansions might be predicated on simultaneously restrictive forms of citizenship. Although Desai and Ranganathan's chapters focus on very different urban processes, both deconstruct state and elite discourses and practices to reveal the restrictive citizenships they construct and how these are based on particular ways of seeing, manipulating, and transforming the city.

Protest and Claims-making in the Indian City

Urban spaces have historically been the sites in which multiple and often contradictory claims to space, identity, and rights have collided. This, according to James Holston and Arjun Appadurai, is what makes the city the arena in which national citizenship is recalibrated (Holston and Appadurai 1999). Shifts in political and economic policies over the past few decades have had profound effects on the rights and privileges of different social groups, creating new forms of conflict. For David Harvey (2008), periodically through history the city as a site for building elite spaces has eventually collided with the spaces of the poor and this has ended in revolt. His analysis of urban processes as now being controlled by a small elite bemoans the fact that localized social movements in different parts of the world are not converging into a single unified global struggle against finance capital. This view is generally dismissive of the varied dynamics and concerns of localized social movements in different parts of the world. Yet, grappling with the city in the global South requires a recognition of these smaller moves, negotiations, and alliances that form to challenge the status quo and stake claims to urban rights and resources. Challenges asserted by subaltern classes do not exclude confrontation, but the dynamics of protest and claims-making in urban India reveals that confrontation is part of a larger toolkit of strategies that the urban poor draw upon to exercise their rights. The state in India also responds to these strategies in diverse ways, from cooptation (as Weinstein's and Doshi's chapters in Part 1 show) to suppression to tactical indifference. Processes of economic liberalization, identity politics, and changing urban vulnerabilities have also led to changing dynamics of protest and new ways of staking claims to urban space and resources, involving elites and middle classes as well as the urban poor and working classes. The four chapters in Part 2 examine diverse practices of protest and claims-making in the context of Delhi, Varanasi, Mumbai, and Calcutta. They reveal how the changing politics of protest and negotiation and the shifting relationships between different class and religious groups as well as between the state and these groups shape the urban environment.

Sunalini Kumar's chapter, 'Clean Air, Dirty Logic? Environmental Activism, Citizenship, and the Public Sphere in Delhi', raises questions about the changing nature of the urban public sphere and the class specificities of those who are able to define what constitutes the 'public sphere'. Indeed, the public sphere has rarely ever been truly public. Don Mitchell argues that in the United States, the right to speak has often been undermined by restrictions of where one can speak (Mitchell 2003). In India too, the right to protest has always been regulated and often crushed, whether this was by the British in colonial India or later by the Indian government (Kumar 1993). However, public protests on city streets and in its public spaces have often played an important role in shaping the 'public sphere' and 'public debate'. This has, however, been changing in New Delhi and Sunalini Kumar's chapter reveals this through a study of the Compressed Natural Gas (CNG) conversions in its public transport. She examines how the judiciary, the English-language media, scientific and technical organizations, and the middle classes emerged as important actors in the framing of the public debate around questions of urban pollution and health at the expense of the working classes whose livelihoods it largely affected. By creating a particular discursive space, these actors cast their middle-class claims as being in the public interest, and thus compelled the Delhi government to act in their favour. Thus, 'public health' was linked to a narrow concern with air pollution, and the right to 'public' health came to be pitted against the right of the working classes (owners and operators of autorickshaws and taxis that came under the ruling) to participate in the urban economy. Kumar's analysis echoes arguments by Usha Ramanathan (2006) who has pointed to the hypocrisy of the judiciary when it evokes a notion of the 'public' to protect the right of the propertied classes to 'public space' and in the process denies the poor access to land for shelter. However, Kumar further draws out the role of numerous actors and the discursive space they created to articulate their claims and shape the city. This involved, for instance, the use of scientific and more specifically technical imaginary in the CNG case which 'allowed the complex social, economic, political, and ecological problem of air pollution to be whittled down to a neat, convenient *technical* solution'. In this context, the subaltern voices of the working classes who were affected by the judiciary's CNG ruling had little opportunity to effectively challenge it. Such manipulations through the shaping of particular discourses (also see Ghertner 2008 for an analysis of the new legal 'nuisance' discourse that has facilitated slum demolitions in Delhi) complicate struggles over the right to the city by those who live literally and metaphorically on the margins.

Jolie Wood's chapter, 'Who Operates and Who Agitates? A Class-wise Investigation of Contentious Action and Citizenship in Varanasi, India', continues this discussion of different forms of protest and claims-making. She examines four different occupational groups in Varanasi and how they make demands on the state in different ways. She points out that contrary to established discourse on civil society which sees its members as engaging with the state in an orderly, rational, and contained manner, the middle-class occupational groups exhibited tendencies towards more contentious and public forms of protest. She shows how the urban provides an ideal setting for such forms of public protest. Furthermore, increasing urbanization is also changing associational forms in Varanasi. Thus, many occupational associations are no longer coterminous with caste due to various factors pressuring the urban economy, including higher in-migration, the emergence of new economic opportunities, and the formation of new alliances and solidarities. She also shows how lower-class occupational associations, such as those of boatmen and weavers, which would normally be seen as contentious protestors have instead approached the government through more formal, institutionalized forms of claims-making such as making appeals to district- and state-level administrative officials, voting in elections, and using the judicial system to stake their claims. Wood's argument echoes the findings of James Holston (2008) who shows how *favela* dwellers in Sao Paolo, Brazil, have used the legal system against itself to stake claims to urban spaces and rights to citizenship, thus resorting to institutionalized forms of negotiation with the state rather than contentious action against it. Her findings and analysis run in the face of the broader arguments made by theorists such as Partha Chatterjee (2004) and John Harriss (2006) about the politics of the poor and middle classes in urban India based on their research in other Indian cities. Wood thus challenges Partha Chatterjee's assertion that civil society in India is a closed, modern, bourgeois fraternity of citizens that excludes the poor whose engagement with the state constitutes a separate realm of action, 'political society', and comprises more contentious and politicized actions. She instead argues for a broader and more inclusive definition of civil society and urges us to accept that civil society is inherently political and, therefore, also revisit our assumptions about the relationship between civil society and civility.

Together, these two chapters reveal the diverse practices through which different class groups make claims and the ways in which the state responds to these class practices. Contrary to what emerges in Kumar's chapter, Wood shows how middle-class occupational groups in Varanasi did not pressure the state in a rational and contained manner but frequently through disruptive contentious practices, and this was also crucial to their success. While Kumar's chapter shows that the working classes were unable to influence the 'public debate' and the judiciary ruling on CNG in Delhi, Wood shows how lower-class occupational groups in Varanasi are often able to compel the state to respond to their demands, sometimes through public protest and frequently through less contentious forms of making claims. One reason for this difference in how the state has responded to poor and working-class groups in Delhi and Varanasi might be that as a much smaller city and with a very different history, deep class conflicts over the city have not emerged in Varanasi as they have in Delhi. Thus, Wood mentions that the state has often responded to the claims of the boatmen community and not enforced the bans on fishing and motor-boats even though the river has been designated as a wildlife sanctuary. One cannot help but wonder then whether the state's response might change as Varanasi grows and other rationalities begin to influence decision-making around the urban environment. Moreover, Delhi is an exception among Indian cities by virtue of being the nation's capital, and the state at multiple levels is more deeply invested in 'showcasing' it than in any other Indian city. Comparisons with other Indian cities might be fruitful in revealing the ways in which Delhi's exceptional status complicates poor and working-class politics in this city.

Jaideep Gupte's chapter, 'Linking Urban Vulnerability, Extralegal Security, and Civil Violence: The Case of the Urban Dispossessed in Mumbai', looks at a different kind of urban negotiation. Over the past two decades, Mumbai in particular has become a site in which violence has been depicted and studied, largely due to the 1992 riots and the subsequent tensions between Hindu and Muslim communities. While many, such as Thomas Blom Hansen (2001) and Roma Chatterji and Deepak Mehta (2008), have focused on the ethnic dimension of this violence and its role in shaping urban spaces (also see Mehta 2004), Gupte approaches the issue of violence from a perspective of urban vulnerability and infra-power. Quoting Hansen, he defines infra-power as 'non-obvious, non-formal, and often ephemeral forms of organization, knowledge, connections, solidarity, and mythology that organize and weave together urban localities'. He argues that in a context of inadequate state provision of security against various kinds of vulnerability, the physical perpetration of violence opens up access to forms of infra-power through which people secure their day-to-day needs and counteract vulnerability. Here, physical perpetration of violence might be seen as an urban survival strategy for the more vulnerable sections of the urban population. Indeed, can we see violence as a legitimate means of laying claim to the city? Gupte's chapter can moreover be seen as drawing together two somewhat distinct bodies of literature on urban violence and enclaves. On the one hand, scholars have tried to understand the agency of those who participate in violence in response to ethnic and racial marginalization and uneven access to resources (Amin 2003; Hansen 2001). On the other hand, scholars have discussed the links between the rise of extra-state actors such as the Hezbollah, Al Gamaa al Islamiyya, and drug gangs that control large parts of cities to neoliberal restructuring and the withdrawal of the state from providing public services (AlSayyad and Roy 2006). Gupte's chapter links people's participation in urban violence to the role played by extra-state actors. He raises important concerns about the evolution of extra-state actors and networks that organize and control urban space and challenge state power and legitimacy. Gupte proposes that addressing the causes of urban vulnerabilities may be one way to stem the tide of violence in urban India.

Romola Sanyal's chapter, 'Displaced Borders: Shifting Politics of Squatting in Calcutta', continues to examine questions of urban vulnerability by examining the changing history of protest in Calcutta (now known as Kolkata). Like Kumar's chapter on Delhi, it examines the ways in which marginalized groups are able to engage the government in the contemporary Indian city. It specifically looks at squatting and the particular history of Calcutta in relation to its large and continually increasing refugee population. In the aftermath of the partition in 1947, Calcutta became home to thousands of East Bengali refugees coming over the border from newly founded (East) Pakistan. In the climate of fear and uncertainty, refugees forcibly occupied land around the city and, though faced with severe responses by the government, nevertheless prevailed in holding on to their hard-fought assets. Sixty years later, refugees continue to trickle across the vast India–Bangladesh border. Sanyal shows, however, that their practices have changed significantly from a direct confrontation with the government to a squatting practice akin to what Asef Bayat (2000) has called the 'quiet encroachment of the ordinary'. She observes that since 1972, people seeking asylum from Bangladesh in India are no longer treated as refugees, even if their situations demand such recognition. As economic and environmental crises in Bangladesh coupled with state policies have pushed thousands of people over the border, be they Hindu, Muslim, or tribals, in India an increasing concern over national security, particularly in relation to the 'Muslim question', has resulted in more stringent border controls by the Indian state. Such security policies have spilled over into the urban environment, affecting those who come illegally across the border, and compelling them to secure housing through covert means and hiding in the urban milieu of the city. Sanyal argues that in recent years the consolidation of an Indian identity has been possible through the marginalization and condemnation of the stateless body in the national space of India, particularly its cities. This is a case in which the body of the refugee and the body of the informal squatter are condemned to a 'state of exception' (AlSayyad and Roy 2006). The chapter uses squatting as a lens of interrogation to understand the shifting politics of nationalism and its consequent outcomes for space and citizenship in Calcutta.

Gupte and Sanyal's chapters show how profound vulnerabilities amongst certain groups of residents and migrants in Indian cities shape the ways in which they can negotiate the city and the possibilities for substantive citizenship in such a context. Their chapters also provoke questions about whether subaltern practices in this context—such as the violence as described by Gupte and the squatting practices of today's refugees as described by Sanyal—can be understood as forms of claims-making and enactments of citizenship or whether these are simply daily survival strategies. In what ways do their practices attempt to force open spaces of citizenship in the city, and does this simultaneously draw these subaltern groups into ever-increasing marginalized spaces and fields of action? The two cases also reveal, albeit in quite different ways, how these vulnerabilities and practices of negotiation are linked to religious and ethnic politics.

CONCLUDING REFLECTIONS

The chapters in this volume reveal the myriad implications of urban processes for urban citizenship and vice versa. Through their ethnographies and histories of the urban, they unsettle theories generated in the Euro-American context to show how urban citizenship might be differently practiced, understood, and reconfigured within the Indian context. The conversations generated between ethnography/history and theory in each chapter raise many possibilities for reshaping epistemologies of the urban. Collectively, the chapters interrogate a range of spaces in the city—such as the squatter settlement, the slum resettlement site, the refugee colony, the poor and working-class *mohalla* or urban 'neighbourhood, the city street, and the urban mega-event—as sites of emerging citizenships in Indian cities. These are certainly not bounded spaces, and are shaped by various constellations of the local, regional, national, and transnational. The chapters show how each of these spaces is made and transformed through particular spatial imaginaries and modes of control, regulation, and governance, as well as in many cases through different forms of negotiation and claims-making by subaltern groups. Different actors—including various branches and agencies of the state, political parties, international development institutions, NGOs, private capital, elite and middle-class organizations, and the urban poor and working classes—play a role in shaping these spaces through territorialized relations of power. Moreover, it might be useful to think further about how emerging forms of urban citizenship in Indian cities are shaped by contestations over the different, overlapping urban spaces that people inhabit and traverse, since urban inhabitants certainly dwell in and move across multiple, connected spaces of the city.

But what is the picture of urban citizenship in India that emerges in this collection? As a number of the chapters show, it is certainly true that over the past decade or two, Indian cities have seen intense forms of violence—be it through different projects of neoliberal urban restructuring or through symbolic or physical forms of ethnic/religious violence. This should rightly deepen our concerns about the contradictions of India's 'successful growth story' and the nature of exclusionary citizenships emerging in Indian cities. But as many of the chapters also show, ordinary urban inhabitants are far from passive actors and are continually engaged in struggles over citizenship through myriad ways. The chapters provide a window on to the openings and closings as well as contradictions and paradoxes of the citizenships emerging through these multiple urban arenas and practices. Some of these contradictions and paradoxes might well be the hallmark of neoliberal urbanism in India, though they are likely to also be at the core of the 'disjunctive democracy' (Caldeira and Holston 1999) that India is. Ultimately, this collection calls for more analyses and discussions about the emerging city and citizenship in India, rather than presenting any singular notion of the promises and challenges of its urban condition.

With regard to the urban condition in India, the multi-sited approach of this collection also provokes an understanding of emerging urbanisms in India. Laying the chapters next to each other reveals convergences and divergences in urban practices and processes in Indian cities. This leads us to the question: is there a distinct Indian urbanism? The answer would be a qualified no. The withdrawal of the state has impacted Indian cities in that it has allowed both the rich and middle classes to gain by allowing them to create their own exclusive spaces such as shopping malls, gated residential spaces, and corporate enclaves. Meanwhile its retraction from providing public good has gravely affected the urban poor and working classes who do not have these opportunities of seceding. However, the dynamics of these transformations may differ, depending on the histories of each city. Similarly, the responses to the withdrawal of the state have been varied across different cities and the different politics of each city impacts the ways in which these processes deepen. Thus, while there is congruence between cities in terms of approaching macro-scale issues, both these and grassroots responses have ultimately been informed by specific historical, social, and political factors. This makes the idea of a singular Indian urbanism intriguing but ultimately problematic.

This book provokes discussions on Indian urbanisms through the use of urban citizenship as an analytical framework. Clearly, other frameworks can be deployed within the Indian context to provide useful insights. We have focused on urban citizenship as it provides a powerful lens for interrogating the contradictions and paradoxes of urbanization in India as well as the challenges and possibilities that these processes pose for India's urban future. It also opens up avenues for conversations across regional and disciplinary borders, thus contributing to a reconfiguration of urban studies such that cities in the global South are not viewed as 'aberrations of the model' but rather key partners in growing debates about urbanism and urbanity.

NOTES

1. The numbers for such statistics are also questionable as often urban population counts do not consider many of the urban poor or daily commuters.
2. Debates on citizenship reveal the multiple historical conceptions of citizenship. While the Greek *polis* gave rise to the civic-republican model of citizenship—whose key principle is civic self-rule, and which calls upon citizens to be active participants in processes of deliberation—the experience of the Roman Empire and later liberal Enlightenment thought gave rise to the liberal model of citizenship. The liberal model conceptualizes citizenship as primarily a legal status; here the role of politics is only to protect individual freedoms from the interference by governments and other individuals (Leydet 2006; Shafir 1998). In post-World War II democracies, a liberal-democratic model became dominant which 'imagines that individual political actors agree to a "social contract" with the state in which they consent to be ruled in exchange for certain privileges and protections'; amongst the privileges is an institutionalized say in the decisions of the state through an electoral system (Purcell 2003: 565).
3. Part III: Fundamental Rights, Constitution of India. Various 'Articles' provide elaboration on each of these fundamental rights. Further, the provisions regarding the right to property have been amended several times and in 1978 an amendment removed the right to property from the list of fundamental rights, although a new provision was added elsewhere in the Constitution to protect private property.
4. Part IV: Directive Principles of State Policy, Constitution of India.
5. In certain national contexts, rights have also been formally circumscribed for certain ethnic or religious groups as in ethnocratic states like Israel/Palestine (Yiftachel 2006).
6. This politics of difference argues that although different treatment can produce inequality, equal treatment when it means sameness can discriminate against the kinds of values and identities people find most meaningful.
7. The phrase 'globalization and its discontents' was first used by Saskia Sassen (1998) in a book by the same title to talk about the economic, political, and cultural processes of the late 20th century globalization and the new dynamics of inequality that these processes were engendering.

BIBLIOGRAPHY

Amin, A. 2003. 'Unruly Strangers? The 2001 Urban Riots in Britain', *International Journal of Urban and Regional Research*, 27(2): 460–63.

AlSayyad, N. and A. Roy. 2006. 'Medieval Modernities: On Citizenship and Urbanism in a Global Era', *Space and Polity*, 10(1): 1–20.

Appadurai, A. 2001. 'Deep Democracy: Urban Governmentality and the Horizon of Politics', *Environment and Urbanization*, 13(2): 23–43.

Banerjee-Guha, S. 2009. 'Neoliberalising the "Urban": New Geographies of Power and Injustice in Indian Cities', *Economic and Political Weekly*, 44(22): 95–107.

Bauböck, R. 1994. *Transnational Citizenship: Membership and Rights in International Migration*. Aldershot, UK: Edward Elgar.

Bayat, A. 2000. 'From Dangerous Classes to Quiet Rebels: Politics of the Urban Subaltern in the Global South', *International Sociology*, 15(3): 533–57.

Baviskar, A. 2003. 'Between Violence and Desire: Space, Power and Identity in the Making of Metropolitan Delhi', *International Social Science Journal*, 55(175): 89–98.

Beaverstock, J., P. J. Taylor, and R. G. Smith. 2000. 'World-City Network: A New Meta-geography?', *Annals of the Association of American Geographers*, 90(1): 123–34.

Bennett, T., L. Grossberg, and M. Morris. 2005. *New Keywords: A Revised Vocabulary of Culture and Society*, s.v. 'citizenship'. Malden, MA: Blackwell.

Brenner, N. and N. Theodore. 2002. 'Cities and the Geographies of "Actually Existing Neoliberalism"', *Antipode*, 34(3): 349–79.

Bhan, G. 2009. '"This Is No Longer the City I Once Knew": Evictions, the Urban Poor and the Right to the City in Millenial Delhi', *Environment and Urbanization*, 21(1): 127–42.

Caldeira, T. P. R. and J. Holston. 1999. 'Democracy and Violence in Brazil', *Comparative Studies in Society and History*, 41(4): 691–729.

Caldeira, T. P. R. 2000. *City of Walls: Crime, Segregation, and Citizenship in São Paulo*. Berkeley: University of California Press.

Cassels, J. 1989. 'Judicial Activism and Public Interest Litigation in India: Attempting the Impossible?', *The American Journal of Comparative Law*, 39(3): 495–519.

Chakrabarty, D. 2000. *Provincialising Europe: Postcolonial Thought and Historical Difference*. Princeton, NJ: Princeton University Press.

Chatterjee, P. 2004. *The Politics of the Governed: Reflections on Popular Politics in Most of the World*. New Delhi: Permanent Black.

Chatterji, R. and D. Mehta. 2008. *Living with Violence: An Anthropology of Daily Events and Everyday Life*. London: Routledge.

Cooke, B. and U. Kothari, ed. 2001. *Participation: The New Tyranny?* London: Zed Books.

Davis, M. 1998. *Ecology of Fear: Los Angeles and the Imagination of Disaster*. New York: Metropolitan Books.

———. 2006. *Planet of Slums*. London: Verso.

DFID. 2008. *Three Faces of India: DFID India Country Plan 2008–2015*. Department of International Development, United Kingdom.

Fawaz, M. 2009. 'Neoliberal Urbanity and the Right to the City: A View from Beirut's Periphery', *Development and Change*, 40(5): 827–52.

Friedmann, J. 1986. 'The World City Hypothesis', *Development and Change*, 17(1): 69–83.

Ghertner, D. A. 2008. 'Analysis of New Legal Discourse behind Delhi's Slum Demolitions', *Economic and Politcal Weekly*, 43(20): 57–66.

Gilbert, L. and M. Dikeç. 2008. 'Right to the City and Politics of Citizenship', in K. Goonewardena, S. Kipfer, R. Milgrom, and C. Schmid (eds), *Space, Difference, Everyday Life: Henri Lefebvre and Radical Politics*, pp. 250–63. New York: Routledge.

Hansen, T. B. 1999. *The Saffron Wave: Democracy and Hindu Nationalism in Modern India*. Princeton: Princeton University Press.

———. 2001. *Wages of Violence: Naming and Identity in Postcolonial Bombay*. Princeton: Princeton University Press.

Harvey, D. 1989. 'From Managerialism to Entrepreneurialism: The Transformation of Urban Governance in Late Capitalism', *Geografiska Annaler*, 71(1): 3–17.

———. 2003. *The New Imperialism*. Oxford: Oxford University Press.

———. 2008. 'The Right to the City', *New Left Review*, 53(Sept–Oct): 23–40.

Harriss, J. 2006. 'Middle-class Activism and the Politics of the Informal Working Class', *Critical Asian Studies*, 38(4): 445–65.

———. 2007. 'Antinomies of Empowerment: Observations on Civil Society, Politics, and Governance in India', *Economic and Political Weekly*, 42(26): 2716–724.

Hickey, S. and G. Mohan. 2005. 'Relocating Participation within a Radical Politics of Development', *Development and Change*, 36(2): 237–62.

Holston, J. 2008. *Insurgent Citizenship: Disjunctions of Democracy and Modernity in Brazil*. Princeton: Princeton University Press.

———. 2009. 'Dangerous Spaces of Citizenship', CLAS Working Papers, Center for Latin American Studies, University of California, Berkeley.

Holston, J. and A. Appadurai. 1999. 'Cities and Citizenship', in J. Holston (ed), *Cities and Citizenship*, pp. 1–18. Durham: Duke University Press.

Kumar, R. 1993. *History of Doing: An Illustrated Account of Movements for Women's Rights and Feminism in India, 1800–1990*. London, New York: Verso.

Lefebvre, H. 1996. *Writings on Cities*. Selected, translated and introduced by E. Kofman and E. Lebas. Oxford, UK: Blackwell.

Leydet, D. 2006. 'Citizenship' in *Stanford Encyclopedia of Philosophy*. Available online at http://plato.stanford.edu/entries/citizenship/ (accessed on 10 October 2010).

Marshall, T. H. 1998 (1950). 'Citizenship and Social Class', in G. Shafir (ed.), *The Citizenship Debates: A Reader*, pp. 93–111. Minneapolis: University of Minnesota Press.

McFarlane, C. 2006. 'Crossing Borders: Development Learning and the North–South Divide', *Third World Quarterly*, 27(8): 1413–437.

———. 2008. 'Urban Shadows: Materiality, "The Southern City" and Urban Theory', *Geography Compass*, 2(2): 340–58.

Mehta, S. 2004. *Maximum City: Bombay Lost and Found*. New York: Random House.

Mitchell, D. 2003. *The Right to the City: Social Justice and the Fight for Public Space*. London and New York: The Guilford Press.

Nair, J. 2005. *The Promise of the Metropolis*. New Delhi: Oxford University Press.

Ong, A. 1998. *Flexible Citizenship: The Cultural Logics of Transnationality*. Durham: Duke University Press.

Peck, J. and A. Tickell. 2002. 'Neoliberalizing Space', *Antipode*, 34(3): 380–404.

Prakash, G. 2002. 'The Urban Turn', in R. Vasudevan, R. Sundaram, J. Bagchi, M. Narula, G. Lovink, and S. Sengupta (eds), *Sarai Reader 02: The Cities of Everyday Life*, pp. 2–7. New Delhi: Sarai CSDS and The Society for Old and New Media.

28   *Renu Desai and Romola Sanyal*

Purcell, M. 2003. 'Citizenship and the Right to the Global City: Reimagining the Capitalist World Order', *International Journal of Urban and Regional Research*, 27(3): 564–90.

Ramanathan, U. 2006. 'Illegality and the Urban Poor', *Economic and Political Weekly*, 41(29): 3193–197.

Rao, V. 2006. 'Slum as Theory', *International Journal of Urban and Regional Research*, 30(1): 225–32.

Ray, R. and M. F. Katzenstein. 2005. 'Introduction: In the Beginning, There Was the Nehruvian State', in R. Ray and M. F. Katzenstein (eds), *Social Movements in India: Poverty, Power, and Politics*, pp. 1–31. Lanham, MD: Rowman and Littlefield.

Robins, S. 2002. 'At the Limits of Spatial Governmentality: A Message from the Tip of Africa', *Third World Quarterly*, 23(4): 665–89.

Robinson, J. 2006. *Ordinary Cities: Between Modernity and Development*. London: Routledge.

Rose, N. 1999. *Powers of Freedom*. Cambridge UK: Cambridge University Press.

Roy, A. 2007. *Calcutta Requiem: Gender and the Politics of Poverty*. New Delhi: Pearson Press. (New edition of *City Requiem: Gender and the Politics of Poverty*, Minneapolis: University of Minnesota Press, 2003.)

———. 2009. 'The 21st Century Metropolis: New Geographies of Theory', *Regional Studies*, 43(6): 819–30.

———. 2011. 'Slumdog Cities: Rethinking Subaltern Urbanism', *International Journal of Urban and Regional Research*, 35(2): 223–38.

Sassen, S. 1991. *The Global City: New York, London, Tokyo*. Princeton: Princeton University Press.

———. 1998. *Globalization and Its Discontents*. New York: The New Press.

Shafir, G. (ed.). 1998. *The Citizenship Debates: A Reader*. Minneapolis: University of Minnesota Press.

Simone, A. M. 2004. *For the City Yet to Come: Changing Life in Four African Cities*. Durham and London: Duke University Press.

———. 2008. 'Emergency Democracy and the "Governing Composite"', *Social Text*, 26(295): 13–33.

Smith, N. 1996. *The New Urban Frontier: Gentrification and the Revanchist City*. London: Routledge.

UN Habitat. 2008a. *State of the World's Cities 2008/2009: Harmonious Cities*. London and Sterling: Earthscan.

———. 2008b. *State of the World's Cities 2010/2011: Bridging the Urban Divide*. London and Washington, D.C: Earthscan.

Urry, J. 2000. 'Global Flows and Global Citizenship', in E. Isin (ed.), *Democracy, Citizenship and the Global City*, pp. 62–78. London: Routledge.

Yiftachel, O. 2006. *Ethnocracy: Land and Identity Politics in Israel/Palestine*. Philadelphia: University of Pennsylvania Press.

Young, I. M. 1998. 'Polity and Group Difference: A Critique of the Ideal of Universal Citizenship', in G. Shafir (ed.), *The Citizenship Debates: A Reader*, pp. 263–90. Minneapolis: University of Minnesota Press.

Zérah, Marie-Hélène. 2009. 'Participatory Governance in Urban Management and the Shifting Geometry of Power in Mumbai', *Development and Change*, 40(5): 853–77.

PART I

**Governance and Citizenship
in the Neoliberal City**

Chapter 2

Entrepreneurial Urbanism in the Time of Hindutva

City Imagineering, Place Marketing, and Citizenship in Ahmedabad*

Renu Desai

Entrepreneurial urbanisms have emerged around the world in the context of global and national economic restructuring and intensifying inter-urban competition.[1] Broadly speaking, this has entailed a new mode of urban governance characterized by a shift away from social redistribution to the promotion of local economic development and growth by urban governments, usually in alliance with private capital (Hall and Hubbard 1996, 1998; Harvey 1989; Ward 2003). A wide repertoire of strategies have been deployed towards this end. One set of strategies involve city imagineering and place marketing through practices such as city branding, staging mega-events, and constructing flagship architectural and urban projects. A significant scholarship has explored these practices to reveal the ways in which they re-image and reinvent the city through a conscious manipulation and promotion of urban imageries that are intended to lure capital, jobs, and tourism into the city (for example, Hall and Hubbard 1998; Short 1999; Yeoh 2005). Vale and Warner (2001: xv) have argued that these practices produce representations of the city that construct particular narratives of the potential of the city as a profitable place to invest in, a good place to live and work in, and an exciting place to visit. This chapter examines some of these entrepreneurial practices in contemporary Ahmedabad, India's seventh largest city and the commercial capital of the State of Gujarat.

---

* I am very grateful to Arafaat Valiani, Navdeep Mathur, and Colin McFarlane for reading through an earlier draft and giving me useful feedback, though I have certainly not been able to do justice to all their comments.

The chapter develops three arguments by interrogating the agents that have articulated these entrepreneurial practices, the images and narratives they construct, and their implications for urban citizenship. First, it argues that many of the practices which emerged in Ahmedabad around 2005 were inextricably bound up in rehabilitating the city's and region's image following the Hindutva-driven and State-government-supported pogrom against Muslims in Gujarat in 2002 and the 'crisis of representation' this created for Ahmedabad and Gujarat.[2] In doing so, these practices have successfully created a discursive shift away from the city and region as violent and unsafe to the city and region as vibrant and a space of development. Since the political regime in the State government has remained unchanged, this has served not only to aggressively re-insert the city and region into the capitalist space-economy but also to legitimize and reproduce the political power of this illiberal regime. Second, I argue that the images and narratives that these practices constructed have involved a 'politics of forgetting' (Lee and Yeoh 2004). This has not only been crucial for rehabilitating the city's and region's image but has also served to silently reproduce the patterns of material and symbolic exclusion inscribed in the city through both upper-middle-class politics and Hindutva politics. Third, I argue that these practices, when seen in the broader social and political context, participated in attempts to articulate an urban citizenship amongst Ahmedabad's religious majority that folded into each other the politics of Hindu nationalism and Hindu identity, pride in regional Gujarati identity, and civic pride in an entrepreneurial Ahmedabad. These practices thus participated in the larger re-inscribing of the city as a space of exclusionary citizenship along the vectors of class and religion.

The chapter begins with a discussion of the literature on urban entrepreneurialism and strategies of city imagineering and place marketing, situating the Ahmedabad case study in relation to this. In the next section, I turn to the Vibrant Gujarat events organized by the Gujarat government. Contrary to most urban contexts, city imagineering and place marketing in Ahmedabad has involved what I refer to as a 'promotional coupling of city and region' at least so far as the Gujarat government has been concerned. In this section I therefore examine the ways in which Ahmedabad was imaged and mobilized as part of the larger agenda of promoting Gujarat. I situate these events in the political context in which they were organized and accordingly I analyse the images and narratives they constructed to explore the purposes they served and their implications for urban citizenship. The following section examines the city branding and place marketing initiatives of two groups of social and economic urban elites, the images and narratives they constructed, and the implications for urban citizenship this entailed. In the section following this, I briefly explore alternate images and narratives constructed by marginalized groups that challenged some of these dominant images and narratives and sought to articulate profoundly different forms of urban citizenship. I conclude by bringing together some of the main arguments and their implications for urban citizenship.

This chapter is based on ethnographic research carried out in Ahmedabad over 18 months between 2005 and 2007 for a larger research project on Ahmedabad's remaking in the context of 21st century globalization and Hindutva politics. The arguments that I elucidate here are based specifically on participant observation at the Vibrant Gujarat events, city branding seminars and real estate property shows, and at numerous meetings and demonstrations organized by a grassroots housing movement. They are also based on the collection and analysis of written and visual materials produced between 2003 and 2007 through city imagineering and place marketing practices, as well as newspaper reports on urban issues during this period.

ENTREPRENEURIAL URBANISMS

A large literature has emerged on urban entrepreneurialism and entrepreneurial cities since David Harvey's (1989) seminal piece on the shift in urban governance in Late Capitalism from urban managerialism to urban entrepreneurialism. This literature approaches entrepreneurial urbanisms from various theoretical and empirical concerns. Here, I briefly review three strands of this literature which are relevant to this chapter: debates about the shift from 'government' to 'governance' and the role of governments and private capital in shaping the entrepreneurial city; discussions about the particular narratives and images constructed by city imagineering and place marketing practices; and discussions about the implications of these practices for urban residents.

David Harvey (1989) has emphasized three aspects which together define urban entrepreneurialism: (*a*) a reorienting of the priorities of local governments from provision of welfare and services towards local growth, which results in the pursuit of strategies to enhance inter-urban competitiveness at the cost of social redistribution; (*b*) a shift from 'government' to 'governance' wherein the power to reorganize urban life now lies with coalitions of the local government and the private sector; and (*c*) the speculative nature of the activities of these coalitions. Various scholars have since reminded us that state restructuring, the reorienting of priorities towards growth, and the formation and objectives of coalitions is contingent upon the diverse social and political pressures, institutional frameworks, and policy regimes existing in a given context (Brenner and Theodore 2002; Desai and Imrie 1998; Hall and Hubbard 1998). Thus, while research in a variety of contexts has identified a shift from 'government' to 'governance' and an increasing role played by private capital in the shaping of cities, many scholars have challenged the assumption that this implies less state involvement (Ward 2003) or that this necessarily results in the 'capturing' of the state by private capital (Pow 2002). Proactive government and state entrepreneurship might, in fact, even harness private capital for instrumental and symbolic goals (see Bunnell [2002] on Kuala Lumpur; Pow [2002] on Singapore). In Ahmedabad, the state has often pursued entrepreneurial strategies independently without entering into institutionalized partnerships with private capital. This is not to say that private capital interests do not influence the state and the restructuring of the city. In fact, they endeavour to do so in various ways, some of which are discussed in this chapter. What is also important here is that these entrepreneurial strategies—whether pursued by the state or private capital interests—have instrumentally and symbolically often reproduced the power of the existing political regime in Gujarat.

Moreover, existing literature reveals that entrepreneurial strategies are articulated by local urban governments, and by national governments in the case of some Asian cities. In Ahmedabad, however, the State government (that is, the regional government) plays a key role in this regard. This is because many urban projects and plans are formulated by State governments or require their sanction. As a result, State governments invariably play a significant role in the shaping of Indian cities. But this prompts questions about whether their involvement shapes entrepreneurial strategies in particular ways. In Ahmedabad, with regard to the particular entrepreneurial strategies of city imagineering and place marketing explored in this chapter, this has led to what I call a 'promotional coupling of city and region'. The reason for this promotional coupling is also to be found in the history and political economy of Gujarat and Ahmedabad's evolving place in this.

The region of Gujarat has been an important place of business and entrepreneurship for centuries, with Ahmedabad as well as other cities (especially along Gujarat's coastline) playing a crucial role in this regard. Ahmedabad's prominence heightened from the late 19th century onwards with its development as a major centre for textile production, indeed as 'Manchester of India' as it came to be known.[3] After Independence, when Gujarat was formed as a separate State in 1960, Ahmedabad became its capital. The city became a hub of educational and research institutions of national repute over the next couple of decades. Although the administrative capital moved in 1970 to Gandhinagar (a new urban centre built 30–40 kilometres away) and Ahmedabad's textile industry declined over the 1980s and 1990s, the city has continued to be Gujarat's commercial capital. It is the State's largest and India's seventh largest city today. While Ahmedabad is thus regionally and nationally important, it is crucial to recognize that Gujarat is one of India's most industrialized and urbanized States with an extremely diversified economy. Over the past decade, the State government has further pushed Gujarat's economy in this direction. It has aggressively sought to attract investment into various regions of Gujarat in a wide range of sectors such as chemicals and petrochemicals, agro-business, biotechnology, ports and shipbuilding, tourism, financial services, textiles, mining, and so forth. It is in this context that I argue that the present State government has been interested in Ahmedabad not only because it is an important city and for the city's own sake. Rather, Ahmedabad has served the State government in two ways: as a gateway of investment into Gujarat and as representative of the shape of affairs in Gujarat as a whole. In other words, Ahmedabad's significance lies not only in being an important city of the region, but also in what it can do for the region. These relationships between city and region form the basis for the State government's 'promotional coupling of city and region' and are important for understanding entrepreneurial urbanism in Ahmedabad.

As already mentioned, this chapter focuses on particular entrepreneurial strategies such as city imagineering and place marketing. In other cities, such strategies have included city branding, organizing urban mega-events (such as parades, festivals, and sporting events), and constructing flagship architectural and urban projects. Often integrating the economic and the cultural in various ways by using art, heritage, and other cultural markers as a tool for urban regeneration and imaging, these strategies reveal the relationship between the political economy of place and the cultural politics of place (Hall 2000; Yeoh 2005). Hall and Hubbard (1998) have, moreover, argued that these practices are seldom restricted to extolling existing virtues of the city. Rather, these seek to re-image and reinvent the city by consciously manipulating the image of a city, discursively and materially. They have shown how these practices have been deployed in many North

American and European cities—where economic decline had led to a 'crisis of representation'—so as to re-insert these cities in the restructured capitalist space-economy and secure a new economic role for them. In this chapter I show that in Ahmedabad a 'crisis of representation' arose in the context of dramatically different processes, namely, State-government-supported violence against religious minorities. Even though many of the images and narratives emerging from urban imagineering practices to address its 'crisis of representation' were similar to those in other cities, here they served not only to overcome this crisis but also to legitimize and reproduce the power of an illiberal political regime. This underscores the need to carefully analyse such images and narratives—and the manipulations they involve—in the broader social, political, and material context in which they are situated.

These practices also have profound implications for different groups of urban residents. Urban imagineering produces images of the city that are 'sanitized, commodified, and distorted in accordance with the perceived demands of the global marketplace' (Doel and Hubbard 2002: 360). As a result, scholars have argued that these practices usually contain within them silences about the spaces and experiences of marginalized groups and attempt to mask social, ethnic, and class polarizations (Short 1999; Yeoh 2005). Through their imagineering, they may also facilitate a material remaking of the city that serves elite interests and marginalizes subaltern voices. Discussing the uneven processes of globalization, Lee and Yeoh (2004) have drawn attention to the 'politics of forgetting' that this entails, with dominant groups monopolizing space by intentionally and strategically forgetting and marginalizing particular cities, spaces, and groups. I argue that such a politics of forgetting is crucial in urban imagineering as well and it is necessary to unpack this to understand the particular forms and vectors of exclusion that these practices produce. In Ahmedabad, this has involved a politics of erasure and denial that reinforces symbolic and material exclusions based on class and religion. It is in these ways that city imagineering and place marketing have profound implications for substantive citizenship, that is, the social, cultural, economic, and political rights that people have in practice as opposed to the legal rights they are entitled to on paper (Holston and Appadurai 1999). Scholars have also observed that city imagineering and place marketing also often play an important role in galvanizing local support and fostering civic pride. In some analyses, this is seen as serving as 'an instrument of false consciousness by the elite in the advancement of their own entrepreneurial interests' (Hall and Hubbard 1996: 162). While I refrain from making any such argument in the absence of research on the reception of such practices, I do explore the identities that these practices seek to craft and the terms on which urban residents come to be considered legitimate urban citizens.

THE VIBRANT GUJARAT EVENTS

The Gujarat government began to play a key role in purposefully re-imaging Ahmedabad in 2003 through its Vibrant Gujarat events. These events, which have been organized twice a year, were qualitatively different from the annual business summits that the government had organized in the preceding two years. Whereas the summits had created and publicized investment opportunities in the region and provided a forum for global investors to interact with the government and Gujarat-based companies, the Vibrant Gujarat events strategically promoted Gujarat by integrating the economic and the cultural, the region and the city. Business summits came to be coupled with the celebration of festivals like Navratri (usually celebrated in October) and Uttarayan, the kite-flying festival (usually celebrated in January), and exhibitions on both development and culture were organized as part of the events. The city also came to be mobilized as an integral part of these events, articulating a 'promotional coupling of city and region'. Before turning to the images and narratives constructed through the events, let us first consider the 'crisis of representation' from which they emerged.

Violence and the 'Crisis of Representation'

The Vibrant Gujarat events and its strategies of promotion, including the imagineering of Ahmedabad that this entailed, emerged to address a particular moment of crisis and anxiety in the region. In 2002, under the Bharatiya Janata Party (BJP) led Gujarat government, the region saw its most widespread and brutal communal violence. The violence led to the death of over 2,000 Muslims, the rape of Muslim women, and the damage or complete destruction of over 100,000 houses and 15,000 business establishments belonging largely to Muslims (CCT 2002: 27; HRW 2002: 4). Also destroyed were a great number of mosques and tombs, both in Ahmedabad and elsewhere, including a famous 500-year-old mosque, which was an Archeological Survey of India monument and which was destroyed with the help of cranes and bulldozers (HRW 2002; SAHMAT 2002). The violence followed the burning of a train compartment in the town of Godhra in Gujarat and the death of 54 *kar sevak*s (volunteers to the Hindutva cause) who were returning from Ayodhya. Investigations and court judgements about the Muslim mob that allegedly attacked the train and how the train compartment went up in flames have been politically charged and have not yet yielded any clear conclusions. According to Hindu nationalists, the communal violence that followed in different parts of Gujarat was a spontaneous reaction of Hindus to the Godhra incident. Independent investigations by human rights groups and the media have, however, pointed to the systematic planning and targeting of Muslims during the violence, the role of the state under Chief Minister Narendra Modi's leadership in supporting the violence, and subsequently the state's purposeful ineffectiveness in addressing the relief and rehabilitation needs of the victims of violence (CCT 2002; HRW 2002; *Tehelka* 2007).

As the violence unfolded across Gujarat, its business elites expressed concern that the riots had delivered a serious blow to Gujarat's economy and were affecting Gujarat's image as an investor-friendly destination. The Gujarat Chamber of Commerce and Industry made a presentation to the Prime Minister of India requesting help in restoring peace and normalcy on the grounds that it was crucial for the State's economy (GCCI 2002). Some groups of business elites outside Gujarat, such as the Confederation of Indian Industry (CII), expressed concern about the violence itself and criticized the Gujarat government. In response, many members of Gujarat's business elite met under the banner of the 'Resurgent Group of Gujarat' and threw its weight behind Modi, criticizing groups like CII for causing an embarrassment to the State globally (*Indian Express* 2003). While the nature of concerns amongst business elites thus varied, it was in this context of violence—and the 'crisis of representation' that this created around Gujarat as riot-prone, unsafe and as the BJP's 'Laboratory of Hindutva'—that the Vibrant Gujarat events came to be organized as an aggressive attempt by the Gujarat government to rebuild the State's image as a safe investment destination. Gujarat government's principal chief industrial advisor explained it thus: 'The business meet has been deliberately scheduled during the Navratri festival when every citizen of the state is out on the streets to participate in festivities. Let the people of the state speak for themselves and dispel the propaganda that the state is unsafe' (Principal Chief Industrial Advisor quoted in Ahmedabad.com [2003]).

Such statements from inside the government betrayed an anxiety around the images and narratives that had arisen during and after the 2002 violence and their implications in the context of a globalizing economy. It also revealed that the Vibrant Gujarat events were the State government's attempt to counter these images and narratives.

But the events not only constructed images and narratives of Gujarat as an economically and culturally vibrant region to rehabilitate its image, it also discursively and materially re-imaged Ahmedabad so as to rehabilitate its image from a communalized and riot-prone city to a vibrant and lively city making huge strides in development. While the 2002 violence had been widespread across many parts of Gujarat, Ahmedabad had been the site of many of the most brutal incidents against Muslims. In fact, as I have argued elsewhere, Ahmedabad has played an important role in the entrenchment of Hindutva politics (Desai 2010) and it would not be incorrect to say that Hindutva's future in Gujarat is closely tied to its future in Ahmedabad and other large cities of the region.[4] However, these links between city and region in Hindutva politics also contributed to post-2002 urban anxieties about the image of the city itself and about what this might convey about the region. Therefore, attempts to manage the crisis of representation created by Hindutva politics and its violence folded the city into new 'vibrant' narratives of the region through the promotional coupling of city and region. The rehabilitated image of Ahmedabad through cultural and development narratives at the events was meant to represent the shape of affairs in Gujarat as a whole and thus contribute to a rehabilitation of the region's image as well. Indeed, with every passing Vibrant Gujarat event, it seems that the State has attracted more and more investment. In 2009, Gujarat even succeeded in securing 10.3 per cent of the total foreign direct investment that came into India (*Indian Express* 2009). While this is certainly due to the State government's aggressive policies of liberalization, the courting of corporates as well as a reaching out to tourists and the city's residents has occurred around the Vibrant Gujarat events. Let me turn then to the events themselves.

Promotional Coupling of City and Region

From the beginning the Vibrant Gujarat events have been replete with narratives and imagery that have portrayed Gujarat as economically and culturally dynamic (see Figure 2.1). The objectives of the first Vibrant Gujarat event in 2003 were clearly outlined in economic terms, such as enhancing the rate of foreign direct investment into Gujarat, while the 'strategy' that was articulated was 'the Timing—the days of Navratri—the world's longest dance festival, where the State is more Vibrant than ever... so that the visiting business delegates can have enthralling experience of the culture and hospitalities of the state'. The 'approach' was 'to blend culture with commerce, trade with tradition, enterprise with entertainment'.[5]

FIGURE 2.1. ADVERTISING BANNER ON THE GUJARAT GOVERNMENT'S VIBRANT
GUJARAT WEBSITE, 2004

Source: http://www.vibrantgujarat.com, accessed on 9 December 2004.

In subsequent events, the ways in which the economic and the cultural were
brought together were more elaborate and attempted to mobilize the city
for this purpose. The events were organized on Ahmedabad's riverfront, the
site of the ambitious Sabarmati Riverfront Development project, and created an urban spectacle in this central area of the city.[6]

In January 2006, this involved cultural performances, a large space for
kite-flying, and numerous exhibitions which showcased Gujarat's culture and
development. A series of floats exhibited historical and religious sites in
Gujarat through images and 3D models. These exhibits were linked to the
State government's declaration of 2006 as 'Tourism Year'. Three exhibition
pavilions themed as 'Revolutionary Gujarat', 'Responsive Gujarat', and 'Re-
sourceful Gujarat' showcased Gujarat's strides in development and outlined
the investment opportunities it offered in a variety of sectors. In the spaces
between the pavilions numerous images of Ahmedabad were scattered. A
model of the riverfront project and seductive renderings of what Ahmedabad's
riverfront would look like once the project was completed were on display
(see Figure 2.2). Ahmedabad's skyline or its other redeveloped urban spaces
were used to promote the making of 'State-of-the-Art Cities' in Gujarat. In
one poster, Ahmedabad was represented through a collage of images inter-
spersed with words like 'vibrant', 'scintillating', 'multi-cultured', 'historical',
and 'lively' (see Figure 2.3).

Although the development exhibitions for the January 2007 Vibrant
Gujarat event were moved to another venue where they were coupled with
seminars and investor meets, the remaining activities were once again organized on the riverfront. Visitors to the event were able to walk—for the
first time in the city's recent history—along a long stretch of the riverside

FIGURE 2.2. A MODEL OF THE SABARMATI RIVERFRONT DEVELOPMENT PROJECT
AT THE JANUARY 2006 VIBRANT GUJARAT EVENT

Source: Photo by author.

promenade that was being created under the riverfront project (see Figure
2.4). In fact, since the event was organized entirely on land reclaimed
from the river for the riverfront project, one could stand on one of the

FIGURE 2.3. A poster at the January 2006 Vibrant Gujarat event representing Ahmedabad

Source: Photo by author.

city's bridges and imagine the future riverfront. As a taste of what would be possible once the project was complete, boat-rides on the river were also offered to visitors for the duration of the event. Although the fact that the riverfront project was still in its preliminary phase of construction limited the potential of the events to achieve a truly spectacular effect, the riverfront nonetheless became a space of urban spectacle and allowed for the representation and experience of Ahmedabad and Gujarat as sites of both culture and development.

Ahmedabad thus served a particular utility for promoting Gujarat—this lay in its significance in Gujarat but also its significance for Gujarat. As a gateway for pursuing investment and profit opportunities in Gujarat, Ahmedabad's re-imaging became an integral part of re-imaging and promoting Gujarat. Scholars have written about the ways in which cultural events such as parades, outdoor performances, festivals, and sporting events have become increasingly common as strategies for enhancing a city's competitiveness. In Ahmedabad, however, the state-sponsored Vibrant Gujarat events were strategies aimed at enhancing Gujarat's competitivenes in which

FIGURE 2.4. The January 2007 Vibrant Gujarat event organized on Ahmedabad's riverfront

Source: Photo by author.

Ahmedabad was itself re-imaged and mobilized towards this purpose. What implications did this rehabilitation of Gujarat and Ahmedabad's image have for urban citizenship?

The Politics of Erasure and Denial

The narratives at the Vibrant Gujarat events re-imaged the city and the region in a more positive light and shifted the discourse away from the blatant anti-Muslim rhetoric and violence of Hindutva politics—which had been in evidence not only during the 2002 violence but also during the subsequent State elections in which the BJP and Narendra Modi came back to power in Gujarat. However, there were unsettling continuities and exclusions at the events. For instance, at the January 2006 cultural exhibitions, the majority of historical and religious sites showcased were Hindu and Jain temples and places of pilgrimage. For a region whose cultural heritage includes a vast legacy of architecture built over its long history by rulers and communities belonging to other religious faiths, the almost complete absence of such sites as part of Gujarat's history and culture was clearly an act of symbolic erasure.[7] Seen in conjunction with the erasure of Islamic heritage from Ahmedabad's landscape through the destruction of mosques and tombs during the 2002 violence, this symbolic erasure takes on even deeper connotations.

At the earlier 2004 cultural exhibitions, the Gujarat government had indeed invited three 'minority' religious communities—two Gujarati Muslim sects (the Khojas and the Bohras) and the Parsis—to set up theme pavilions. However, the print media had observed that while the Gujarat government was attempting to woo religious minorities after the 2002 violence, it had rolled out the red carpet only for moneyed minority communities and various other Muslim sects had not been invited to showcase their culture (*Indian Express* 2004, *Times of India* 2004).

While such symbolic erasures characterized the representations of Gujarat, the representations of Ahmedabad's past and present (see Figure 2.3) seemed more pluralistic with a collage of images of all kinds of historical sites, modern buildings, people, and activities. However, this seemingly benign image of a multi-cultural, lively Ahmedabad also takes on a new dimension when seen in relation to the State government's support of the 2002 violence as well as other practices by the same political regime in Ahmedabad outside the space of these events. For instance, in the run up to Ahmedabad's 2005 municipal elections, the BJP's campaign—in which Narendra Modi took on a central role—not only promised that it would make Ahmedabad into the top-ranked city in India like it had made Gujarat the top-ranked State in India, but also coined slogans such as 'Bring an end to Congress' Mughal rule. Vote for the BJP'.[8] This slogan, which lashed out at the Congress Party leader who was mayor of Ahmedabad at the time, and who happened to be Muslim, sought to reignite communal passions, mistrust, and antagonisms between Hindus and Muslims in the city and by doing so obtain the 'Hindu vote' and wrest control of the city's municipal corporation from the Congress Party.[9] In this context, the narrative of Ahmedabad as multi-cultural—which was constructed at events organized by the same BJP- and Modi-led Gujarat government—appears almost schizophrenic.

However, rather than viewing this as schizophrenic, I argue that narratives of Ahmedabad as historical, vibrant, scintillating, multi-cultural, and lively articulated a strenuous politics of denial which has been crucial to the rehabilitation of Ahmedabad's image, and by extension Gujarat's image. That is, they contained within them an oppressive refusal to acknowledge the long-term implications of the 2002 State-government-supported violence wrought on Muslim bodies and material histories. They also denied the significance of the deeply divided urban geographies of religion in the city. Since the late 1960s, Ahmedabad's landscape has seen the gradual emergence of new forms of segregation that seek to create fixed and antagonistic Hindu and Muslim identities in space. These have unfolded not only through episodes of violence—in which the 2002 State-government-supported violence was the last straw—but also through the longer-term geographies of suspicion and fear that these episodes and the political environment of a pro-Hindutva State government produce. This has led to segregated religious enclaves, divisive urban borders, discrimination against Muslims in the housing market, and ghettoization of Muslims in areas with fewer services and amenities (Desai 2010; also see Breman 1999; Mahadevia 2007). Through the politics of denial the events have come to serve as a visible arena of entrepreneurial and benign state action. It has thus rehabilitated the city's and region's image as well as carved out a space of legitimacy for this illiberal political regime on the national and global stage even as this regime has continued to pursue and sanction the divisiveness of Hindutva politics in other arenas.

City imagineering has usually contained image manipulations and silences around the spaces and experiences of marginalized groups, producing sanitized and conflict-free images of the city. Indeed, with their emphasis on projects such as the Sabarmati Riverfront Development project and narratives such as 'State-of-the-Art' cities, the Vibrant Gujarat events have privileged particular class aspirations and have remained silent about the impacts of these on the urban poor. However, in light of the above discussion it should be clear that the manipulations and silences at the Vibrant Gujarat events have served insidious political purposes and have disturbing implications for urban citizenship beyond exclusions based on class. Through a politics of erasure and denial, these practices of place marketing and city imagineering silently reproduce urban exclusions along the axes of both class and religion.

Although Hindu nationalism and a militant Hindu identity did not blatantly enter into the vocabulary of the Vibrant Gujarat narratives, Hindutva politics was thus imbricated in these state-organized events. Elsewhere, Narendra Modi has also often articulated discourses of 'Gujarati *asmita*' (Gujarati pride) as a call to Gujaratis to take pride in their identity, culture, and entrepreneurialism in a globalizing and developing Gujarat (Suhrud 2008). In doing so, he has successfully deployed a discourse of Gujarati pride to reject 'propaganda' against Gujarat, and counter critiques of Hindutva politics in the region, the 2002 violence, and his government. The Vibrant Gujarat events—which are targeted not only at outside investors and tourists but also ordinary residents of Ahmedabad and Gujarat—came to be folded into these political discourses as both emanated from the same source: the BJP-led Gujarat government and its chief minister, Narendra Modi. In complex ways then, the Vibrant Gujarat events and the images and narratives constructed through them, when seen in the broader social and political context, emerged as participants in the folding of a Hindu identity, a proud Gujarati identity, and a class identity into each other. In Ahmedabad, these overlapping identities came to define who might be legitimate urban citizens. By no means does this imply that the subjectivities of Ahmedabad's inhabitants have been successfully reshaped through such attempts to align such identities with each other. Rather, my intention is to underline the ways in which such events and practices are mobilized as part of wider political practices that craft exclusionary citizenships.

THE BRAND AHMEDABAD EVENTS

In early 2005 the Government of India launched the Jawaharlal Nehru National Urban Renewal Mission (JNNURM), in which Ahmedabad was included as one of India's seven mega-cities. Mumbai, New Delhi, Kolkata, Chennai, Bangalore, and Hyderabad had been given the mega-city tag under the previous government's Mega City Scheme under which India's 'mega-cities' qualified for financial assistance from the central government for urban development projects. Efforts to persuade the government to declare Ahmedabad as a mega-city and include it in this scheme had failed at the time. Its inclusion in the mega-city list under JNNURM was therefore received with much enthusiasm by the municipal government, social and economic urban elites, and the local news media. Ahmedabad was seen to have finally joined the ranks of cities like Mumbai, Bangalore, and Hyderabad in national importance. This spurred Ahmedabad's elites to re-imagine Ahmedabad's future and cityscape as well as articulate their interests and desires in new ways. Here, I examine the attempts by two organizations, the Ahmedabad Management Association (AMA) and the Gujarat Institute of Housing and Estate Developers (GIHED), to brand and re-image Ahmedabad. Both directed their city branding and place marketing activities at outside investors and tourists as well as the city's residents.[10]

In mid-2005, the AMA—which is a professional managers' association, an educational institution and a well-reputed civic institution[11]— organized a public seminar which launched its 'Brand Ahmedabad' initiative. Over the next couple of years, this involved a series of activities to build Ahmedabad's image as a desirable destination for business and tourism and as a city offering a high quality of life. An AMA monthly newsletter described the launch of the initiative in the following words:

> The aftermath of Godhra incident, communal riots and unprecedented media backlash has portrayed our state and particularly Ahmedabad in such poor light for last couple of years, which we know is far from the truth. We were wondering how we could regain the lost image. 'Brand Ahmedabad' is our humble initiative to revive the image and popularity of our city. . . . We seek help of all Amdavadis and our progressive media to help us represent the true and fair image of Ahmedabad to the world at large.[12] (AMA 2005)

The AMA's city branding initiative was thus motivated by its concern with the image of Ahmedabad that had emerged in the aftermath of the 2002 violence and its desire to represent 'the true and fair image of Ahmedabad' to the world.

The keynote talk at the public seminar was given by a well-known figure from India's advertising world who had lived in Ahmedabad for many years. After explaining what branding is and how various countries and cities around the world, particularly Dubai, have been branded successfully, the speaker presented a series of arguments to explore how and why Ahmedabad needed to be branded. He began by contrasting what he called 'insider perceptions' to 'outsider perceptions' of Ahmedabad, arguing that insiders and outsiders held diametrically opposite views of Ahmedabad. Thus, while insiders perceived Ahmedabad as a city of successful businessmen and entrepreneurs, of excellent higher education, of affordable real estate and as providing excellent entertainment because of its large number of multiplex theatres, outsiders perceived Ahmedabad as having no social life and no professionalism. Furthermore, while insiders perceived the city as a 'safe city' and a 'city of peace and prosperity', outsiders perceived Ahmedabad as a 'violent city—always with religious tension'. Presenting a SWOT (Strengths, Weaknesses, Opportunities and Threats) analysis, he argued that Ahmedabad had the 'opportunity' to become the most desirable destination for business and tourism, but the 'threat' to realizing this was 'the continued wrong perception of Ahmedabad and Amdavadis'.[13] This is why Ahmedabad had to be branded and positioned to correct these perceptions.

The following year another public seminar was organized which revolved around Ahmedabad's quality of life. While certain issues like the city's traffic and air pollution were flagged up as requiring the municipal government's urgent attention, Ahmedabad was otherwise represented as eminently livable compared to other Indian metropolises which were discussed as overpopulated, with unaffordable real estate or with infrastructure

that had been unable to keep pace with urban growth. Factors such as affordable housing for its middle classes, good roads, reliable power supply, and
safety and security were evoked to drive home the point about Ahmedabad's
livability. These factors were subsequently highlighted by AMA delegations
in their visits to corporate houses, industry associations, and local media in
other Indian cities as well as other countries.

These narratives, in seeking to brand Ahmedabad and 'represent its
true and fair image', not only leveraged selective aspects of Ahmedabad
to resurrect its image, but in the first instance set up a binary of insider/
outsider perceptions that ignored that it had in fact been certain groups of
residents within Ahmedabad who had experienced the brutality of the 2002
violence. Whether all of Ahmedabad's residents experienced and perceived
the city in the same way and whether all residents felt the city was safe and
peaceful were not put up for debate or discussion. In the second instance,
the representation of Ahmedabad as a more livable city compared to cities
like Mumbai and Bangalore once again narrated the city through the experiences of its Hindu middle and upper-middle classes. This was possible
only through a politics of forgetting in which different marginalized groups
and their varying experiences in the city were strategically ignored and denied significance. Thus, the experiences of the city's working class as a result
of the closure of its large organized cotton textile industry over the 1980s
and 1990s (Breman 2004) and the experiences of many slum dwellers as a
result of increasing evictions and displacements (Our Inclusive Ahmedabad
2010) were smoothly elided in these narratives of the city's 'true and fair
image'. So were the experiences of many Muslim residents as a result of the
violence of Hindutva politics, increasing discrimination against them in the
housing market, and increasing ghettoization.

The re-imaging of Ahmedabad through these narratives also attempted to create and mobilize civic pride amongst Amdavadis through the public seminars. Through these narratives of representing Ahmedabad's 'true
and fair image' to counter the post-2002 images of Ahmedabad which were
'far from the truth', this city branding initiative subtly linked civic identity
to a class identity, a Gujarati identity, and a Hindu identity. This does not
imply that these practices articulated an urban citizenship that included
only middle- and upper-middle-class Gujarati Hindus from Ahmedabad.
As one speaker suggested, one could also be a non-Gujarati who, by virtue
of living in Ahmedabad/Gujarat for many years, had come to appreciate
and understand Ahmedabad and Gujarat from an 'insiders' perspective'. It
is important to keep in mind that I am not arguing that because of these
narratives, class, regional linguistic, and religious identities successfully

converged in the crafting of the civic identities of seminar attendees. However, these narratives certainly outlined the contours of what constitutes an 'insider' and thus who legitimately belongs to the city and can participate in articulating what the city's 'true and fair' image ought to be.

Other city branding and place marketing practices were articulated in Ahmedabad by GIHED. As Gujarat's real estate developers' association, GIHED has organized annual property shows in Ahmedabad since many years. These events provide a platform for developers to exhibit new residential, office, and commercial properties to potential buyers. In 2005, inspired by Ahmedabad's inclusion in the list of Indian mega-cities, GIHED organized its property show under the slogan 'Mega Vision for a Brand New Ahmedabad'. This marked GIHED's first attempt at articulating and promoting its visions and imaginaries for the city as a whole as opposed to simply exhibiting and marketing individual real estate properties. Colourful posters lined the entrance path leading to the main space reserved for the developers' individual stalls. The posters showed artist renderings and representations of highly anticipated urban projects in Ahmedabad, such as the Bus Rapid Transit System, the Metro Rail, and the Sabarmati Riverfront Development project. Other posters included artist renderings of high-rise buildings urging its viewers to 'rise for the High Rise Ahmedabad' and of flyovers that would allow people to 'fly-over the traffic'. These posters articulated bourgeois imaginaries for Ahmedabad's future and sought to impress them on the visitors to the property show, mainly middle- and upper-middle-class urban residents.

In 2007, GIHED organized its property show under another slogan: 'Brand Ahmedabad Target 2020'. Various personalities were brought in from Ahmedabad's cultural and business spheres to serve as ambassadors for the event and for the city's future (see Figure 2.5). Billboards on street-crossings and at bus-stops showed these ambassadors mouthing the following slogans to urge Ahmedabad's residents to partake in GIHED's visions of the city: 'The Future Is Here, See It'; 'The Future Is Here. Hear It'; 'The Future is Here. Speak for It'; and 'Lets Build the Ahmedabad of 2020' (see Figure 2.5). The 'future' that was being envisioned to brand the city clearly privileged elite residents of the city. For instance, the widely advertised laser show used laser beams projected on a screen to sketch out what Ahmedabad would look like in 2020. The graphics created through the laser beams were set to dramatic music and sketched out an urban fabric of tall multi-storey buildings with the audience feeling that they were rapidly travelling through its streets. At times, the perspective shifted to show a view across the city's river of a spectacular high-rise skyline—presumably its skyline in 2020.

FIGURE 2.5. Bus-stop in Ahmedabad advertising GIHED's annual
property show that was organized in January 2007 under the slogan
'Brand Ahmedabad Target 2020'

Source: Photo by author.

These property shows also pitched real estate properties to Non-resident
Indians (NRIs), particularly Non-resident Gujaratis (NRGs), encouraging
them to partake in the lifestyle that 'Brand Ahmedabad' had to offer. Not
only were these property shows targeted at the middle and upper-middle
classes of Ahmedabad and NRIs, thus articulating a politics of forgetting
and denial with regard to the city's less well-off residents, but they did the
same with regard to the city's Muslim middle and upper-middle classes who
could not easily buy any of the properties exhibited at the show due to
the housing discrimination they face in the city (*Ahmedabad Mirror* 2009).
While NRIs were thus invited to partake in the city and its amenities, particular class and religious groups amongst the city's own inhabitants were
increasingly denied these.

ALTERNATE URBAN IMAGINARIES

The Vibrant Gujarat events' promotional coupling of city and region and
attempts by elite groups to brand and promote Ahmedabad constructed

particular images and narratives of the city's present and future that privileged the experiences of particular class and religious groups of urban residents and their inhabitation of the city. They also folded into each other various identities, constructing an exclusionary urban citizenship along class and religious lines. Here, I briefly consider how elsewhere in the city, outside of these state and elite spaces of imagineering and marketing, subaltern residents articulated critiques of dominant narratives and crafted alternate urban imaginaries and alternate conceptions of urban citizenship.

While the mega-city declaration inspired elites in the city to brand Ahmedabad and promote its development along particular trajectories, marginalized groups imagined the mega-city through profoundly different narratives, which critiqued dominant representations. A community leader in one of the city's slums remarked to me that Ahmedabad was going to become a *mehenga* city (an expensive city) and not a mega-city. He laughed out loud, pleased with his play of words which reworked the elite celebratory narratives of the mega-city and instead directed attention to the vulnerabilities that these narratives evoked for him and many others living on the lower rungs of the socio-economic ladder. From the celebratory mega-city narratives and discursive re-imaging of the city in the newspapers and on the city's billboards in 2005, he anticipated that the mega-city status would lead to aggressive urban redevelopment, which would further marginalize urban inhabitants like him. Many of the initiatives being undertaken in Ahmedabad around this time to develop and regulate the city—such as the Sabarmati Riverfront Development project, the widening of roads, the required conversion of rickshaws to CNG (Compressed Natural Gas), the introduction of a rule that all drivers of two-wheelers in the city must wear a helmet—were signalling eviction, displacement and/or rising costs for the lower classes and the urban poor of the city.

Subaltern urban residents expressed their opposition to these initiatives not only through everyday conversation—such as by evoking the notion of the *mehenga* city—but also through everyday practices of subversion as well as overt acts of protests. For instance, the helmet rule specified norms vis-à-vis the helmets that drivers of two-wheelers had to wear. Helmets had to be sturdy enough to protect the driver from head injury in the event of an accident, and so the rule stipulated that the helmet must bear the ISI mark, which is the mark of approval by the Bureau of Indian Standards. However, there were numerous small protests against the rule since helmets with the ISI mark were expensive. One newspaper carried an image of a group of residents protesting by wearing stainless steel cooking pots on their head (3 September 2005). The market was also soon flooded with ISI stickers and one could now simply buy a cheaper helmet and an ISI sticker, both for less than one-fourth the price of an ISI-marked helmet. Because of these subversions, ultimately the state had to relent and drop the ISI requirement. Elsewhere, subversion was not easily possible and people turned to acts of mass protest to challenge the elite imaginaries that were driving the material remaking of the city.

Protests emerged against the Sabarmati Riverfront Development project and the impending displacement and marginalization of riverfront slum dwellers under the project. The Sabarmati Nagrik Adhikar Manch, a grassroots network of riverfront slum dwellers, also approached the High Court of Gujarat with a public interest litigation to demand their rights to information and to proper resettlement. Over 2005 and 2006, in mass protest rallies and in meetings to mobilize slum dwellers to attend these rallies, the leaders of this grassroots network contested the elite urban imaginaries that undergirded the project and its imagineering of the city. Their slogans—such as '*riverfront ka dekho plan, garib ka jhopda ameer ke naam*' and '*har jhopdawasi ki ek hi baat, jahan jhopda wahan makaan*'—pointed to the ways in which the riverfront would be gentrified under the project and articulated the demand that instead riverfront slum dwellers be given a house on the sites where they currently live. They moreover crafted radically different conceptions of civic identity and urban citizenship from those articulated by the state and elites. Contrary to the folding of a Hindu identity, Gujarati identity, and class identity into an exclusionary civic identity, this network of slum dwellers—which comprises Hindus, Muslims, and Christians—argued for housing rights and communal unity in the same breath, also at times invoking Muslim–Dalit solidarity based on their shared experiences of marginalization. In this way, it articulated an urban citizenship based on solidarities amongst marginalized socio-economic groups, traversing religious lines, and their shared claims to the city. In 2009, a loose collective of academics, activists, and citizens also emerged under the banner of 'Our Inclusive Ahmedabad' to organize a public hearing on livelihood and habitat displacements in the city. This marked a rare moment in Ahmedabad with certain groups of middle-class citizens showing solidarity with and support for the struggles of marginalized groups in the hope for a more inclusive city. Although the success of these efforts to materially challenge state and elite urban imaginaries has been limited, they reveal that alternate imaginaries are struggling to be heard.

CONCLUSION: CITY IMAGINEERING, PLACE MARKETING, AND EXCLUSIONARY URBAN CITIZENSHIPS

Discursive and material processes of city-making are key arenas through which substantive citizenship is realized and denied in practice (Holston and Appadurai 1999) and this chapter has explored the denials through an unpacking of city imagineering and place marketing strategies in Ahmedabad. Whereas in many States in India, State governments seem to have focused almost entirely on particular cities to the neglect of the larger region, in this chapter I have examined what I call a 'promotional coupling of city and region' wherein Ahmedabad has been re-imaged and mobilized by the Gujarat government towards the larger agenda of promoting Gujarat. I have also examined the role of urban elites in practices of city imagineering and place marketing and how they have sought to brand the city and create visions of a future Ahmedabad based on upper-middle-class aspirations. The images and narratives constructed through these practices have successfully countered the post-2002 'negative' images around Ahmedabad and Gujarat in mainstream discourses. This has done three things which have long-term implications for substantive citizenship. First, the city's and region's image has been rehabilitated, creating a discursive shift towards the city and region as vibrant and a space of development. This has allayed the fears of investors and aggressively re-inserted the city and region in the capitalist space-economy. Second, this rehabilitation of the city's and region's image has also served to rehabilitate the image of the political regime in Gujarat, and in doing so, it has insidiously legitimized and reproduced the power of this illiberal regime, which continues to pursue its Hindutva politics in other arenas and clearly ignores the deep spatial divides in Ahmedabad. Third, these practices, which have involved a politics of erasure and denial, have silently reproduced and reinforced class and religious divides and exclusions in the city rather than opening up a space to challenge them. Moreover, they also sought to craft particular civic identities that meshed class, religious, regional, and national identities in complex ways. In doing so, they shaped the terms by which urban residents come to be considered legitimate urban citizens. This profoundly shapes contours of inclusion and belonging to the city, the region, and the nation.

The urban citizenship articulated through entrepreneurial strategies in Ahmedabad is not only class-based then, but has an exclusionary regionalism and nationalism at its core. While scholars have argued that cities have increasingly challenged, diverged from, and replaced nations as the important space of citizenship (Holston and Appadurai 1999), the Ahmedabad case reveals that the city is also the space where powerful links are made between urban citizenship and exclusionary constructions of national and regional identities. This has profound implications for the city and citizenship: both in terms of belonging to a national, regional, and urban community as well as in terms of access to urban resources such as land, housing, and amenities. By examining entrepreneurial strategies, this chapter has moreover attempted to unpack some of the practices through which exclusionary citizenships have been articulated in Ahmedabad long after the shocking moments of blatant violence are over.

The notion of urban citizenship is of course useful not only to interrogate the ways in which substantive rights are denied to people in practice, but also to interrogate the practices through which ordinary urban citizens make claims on the city and the state. While this chapter interrogates and emphasizes the former, it has also briefly touched upon the latter. My intention here has been to flag up ordinary people's enactments of claims and solidarities to show that there are also processes involving alternate urban imaginaries of the future and expanded notions of urban citizenship at work in Ahmedabad. While their potential to create more inclusionary citizenships will certainly require in-depth analysis, they do hold a promise of more inclusive ways of re-imagining the city and urban citizenship in Ahmedabad.

NOTES

1. The term 'entrepreneurial urbanisms' has been used by Kevin Ward (2003) to talk about the processes involved in the entrepreneurial turn that cities have taken in recent decades. He connects this to earlier writings on 'urban entrepreneurialism' as a new mode of governance (Harvey 1989) and 'entrepreneurial cities' (Hall and Hubbard 1998). As Hall and Hubbard observe, there are significant differences in these processes across different urban and national contexts. However, entrepreneurialism has become 'a convenient catch-all term used to describe a number of distinctive changes in the working of the city' (Hall and Hubbard 1996: 169–70).

2. When I refer to the 'state' it refers to the state apparatus while 'State' has been capitalized when referring to a geographic-political entity such as the State of Gujarat or the State government.

3. See Raychaudhuri (2001) on how the textile industry emerged in Ahmedabad through indigenous and not British or European capital and enterprise.

4. This can be gleaned, for example, from the keen attention with which Narendra Modi, the BJP chief minister of Gujarat, has campaigned for the BJP in Ahmedabad's municipal elections since 2005. Elsewhere, chief ministers have rarely taken on a central role in municipal election campaigns.

5. The 'strategy' and the 'approach' were described on the Vibrant Gujarat website: http://www.vibrantgujarat.com, accessed on 9 December 2004.

6. The Vibrant Gujarat event was organized on the Sabarmati riverfront in January 2006 and January 2007. The Gujarat government had tried to organize the event on the riverfront in October 2005 and October 2006 as well. For the October 2005 event, the city's municipal corporation had worked overtime to complete the land reclamation (from the river) for the riverfront project so that the Gujarat government could hold the event on this stretch of riverfront land. However, because of approaching municipal elections in Gujarat the State Election Commission banned such government events within the city and the event had to be downsized and moved elsewhere (*Times of India* 2005). For

the October 2006 event, the river's flooding during the monsoons and damage to the constructed pathways along the river forced the government to move the event to Gandhinagar (*Times of India* 2006).

7. There were several floats, each representing a particular district of Gujarat, and each replete with more than several images and/or miniature models showcasing different cultural sites. It was immediately evident that there were dozens of Hindu and Jain temples and pilgrimage sites exhibited. Among the few architectural sites built by communities belonging to other religious faiths that were displayed were a neighbourhood of the Dawoodi Bohras (a Muslim sect) and a Muslim tomb, both in the district of Patan.

8. Translated from the BJP's election campaign ads in a local Gujarati newspaper—*Sandesh*, 13 October 2005.

9. The BJP indeed won the municipal elections in Ahmedabad and in a number of other cities in Gujarat.

10. I am concerned here solely with the city branding initiatives of these organizations. An analysis of these practices is not meant to make any argument about the political stance (vis-à-vis religious minorities) of these organizations as a whole, or indeed about the political stance of any particular individual who might have participated in these initiatives.

11. Ahmedabad Management Association was established in the 1950s to promote exchange of knowledge and experience in management. Today it has over 370 institutional and 2,000 professional manager members and other entrepreneurs and businessmen (http://www.amaindia.org, accessed on 12 December 2010). Notably, AMA does not focus only on corporate management and facilitating corporate ties between its members and businesses in India and abroad, but also promotes the importance of management in all spheres of life. It thus organizes lectures, seminars, courses, and training workshops on subjects as diverse as international trade, hospitality management, health management, improving teaching skills, managing growing children, and youth empowerment. This wide range of activities means that AMA is not only an association of professional managers, but also an educational institution as well as an influential civic institution in Ahmedabad.

12. 'Amdavadi' is the Gujarati for the residents of Ahmedabad (or Amdavad, as the city is called in Gujarati).

13. A SWOT Analysis is a strategy development tool used to evaluate the strengths, weaknesses, opportunities, and threats involved in a project or business venture.

BIBLIOGRAPHY

Ahmedabad.com. 2003. 'State to Cash in on "Vibrant Gujarat" to Attract Investors', 30 May. Available online at http://www.ahmedabad.com/news/2k3/may/30state.htm (accessed on 04 April 2004).

Ahmedabad Mirror. 2009. 'No Room for Muslims at GIHED Show', *Ahmedabad Mirror*, 14 September.

AMA News. 2005. 'From the President's Desk', *AMA News*, July.

Asian Age. 2003. 'State to Cash in on "Vibrant Gujarat" to Attract Investors', *Asian Age*, 30 May.

Breman, J. 1999. 'Ghettoization and Communal Politics: The Dynamics of Inclusion and Exclusion in the Hindutva Landscape', in J. Parry and R. Guha (eds), *Institutions and Inequalities: Essays in Honour of Andre Beteille*, pp. 259–83. New Delhi: Oxford University Press.

Breman, J. 2004. *The Making and Unmaking of an Industrial Working Class: Sliding Down the Labour Hierarchy in Ahmedabad, India*. Amsterdam: Amsterdam University Press.

Brenner, N. and N. Theodore. 2002. 'Cities and the Geographies of "Actually Existing Neoliberalism"', *Antipode*, 34(3): 349–79.

Bunnell, T. 2002. 'Cities for Nations? Examining the City–Nation–State Relation in Information Age Malaysia', *International Journal of Urban and Regional Research*, 26(2): 284–98.

Concerned Citizens Tribunal (CCT). 2002. *Crime against Humanity: An Inquiry into the Carnage in Gujarat Volume 1–2*. Report on the Gujarat violence by the Concerned Citizens Tribunal—Gujarat 2002, published by Anil Dharkar for Citizens for Justice and Peace, Mumbai.

Desai, V. and R. Imrie. 1998. 'The New Managerialism in Local Governance: North–South Dimensions', *Third World Quarterly*, 19(4): 635–50.

Desai, R. 2010. 'Producing and Contesting the Communalized City: Hindutva Politics, Urban Space and Citizenship in Ahmedabad, India', in N. AlSayyad and M. Massoumi (eds), *The Fundamentalist City*, pp. 99–124. London: Routledge.

Doel, M. and P. Hubbard. 2002. 'Taking World Cities Literally: Marketing the City in a Global Space of Flows', *City*, 6(3): 351–68.

Gujarat Chamber of Commerce and Industry (GCCI). 2002. 'Shri Kalyan J. Shah, President Gujarat Chamber of Commerce & Industry Represented the Impact of the Godhra Carnage on the Trade and Industry', 4 April 2002, available online at the GCCI website: http://www.gujaratchamber.org/memorandum-PM1.htm (accessed on 12 March 2006).

Human Rights Watch (HRW). 2002. *We Have No Orders to Save You: State Participation and Complicity in Communal Violence in Gujarat*. Report on the Gujarat violence.

Hall, T. and P. Hubbard. 1996. 'The Entrepreneurial City: New Urban Politics, New Urban Geographies?', *Progress in Human Geography*, 20(2): 153–74.

———. 1998. *The Entrepreneurial City: Geographies of Politics, Regime and Representation*. Chichester: Wiley.

Hall, P. 2000. 'Creative Cities and Economic Development', *Urban Studies*, 37(4): 639–49.

Harvey, D. 1989. 'From Managerialism to Entrepreneurialism: The Transformation in Urban Governance in Late Capitalism', *Geografiska Annaler*, 71(1): 3–17.

Holston, J. and A. Appadurai. 1999. 'Cities and Citizenship', in J. Holston (ed.), *Cities and Citizenship*, pp. 1–17. Durham and London: Duke University Press.

Indian Express. 2003. 'Gujarat Inc Throws Weight behind Modi, Takes on CII', *The Indian Express*, 21 February. Available online at http://www.indianexpress.com/oldStory/18783/ (accessed on 02 May 2010).

———. 2004. 'Bridging the Divide the Pavilion Way', *The Indian Express*, 14 January. Available online at http://cities.expressindia.com/fullstory.php?newsid=73669 (accessed on 04 April 2004).

———. 2009. 'Gujarat to Get Asia FDI Award, Not Modi', *Indian Express*, 3 September. Available online at http://www.indianexpress.com/news/gujarat-to-get-asia-fdi-award-not-modi/511656/ (accessed on 15 March 2011).

Lee, Y. and B. S. A. Yeoh. 2004. 'Introduction: Globalisation and the Politics of Forgetting', *Urban Studies*, 41(12): 2297–298.

Mahadevia, D. 2007. 'A City with Many Borders', in A. Shaw (ed.), *Indian Cities in Transition*, pp. 341–89. New Delhi: Orient Longman.

Our Inclusive Ahmedabad. 2010. 'Report of a Public Hearing on Habitat and Livelihood Displacements in Ahmedabad', Our Inclusive Ahmedabad (a Forum of Concerned Citizens of Ahmedabad), Ahmedabad.

Pow, C. P. 2002. 'Urban Entrepreneurialism, Global Business Elites and Urban Megadevelopment: A Case Study of Suntec City', *Asian Journal of Social Science*, 30(1): 53–72.

Raychaudhuri, S. 2001. 'Colonialism, Indigenous Elites and the Transformation of Cities in the Non-Western World: Ahmedabad (Western India), 1890–1947', *Modern Asian Studies*, 35(3): 677–726.

SAHMAT. 2002. *Ethnic Cleansing in Gujarat: A Preliminary Report.* Report on the Gujarat violence by the SAHMAT Fact Finding Team to Ahmedabad, 10–11 March.

Short, J. R. 1999. 'Urban Imagineers: Boosterism and the Representation of Cities', in A. E. G. Jonas and D. Wilson (eds), *The Urban Growth Machine: Critical Perspectives Two Decades Later*, pp. 37–54. Albany: State University of New York Press.

Suhrud, T. 2008. 'Modi and Gujarati Asmita', *Economic and Political Weekly*, 43(1): 11–12.

Tehelka Magazine. 2007. 'The Truth—Gujarat 2002', *Tehelka Magazine*, 4(43), 3 November.

Times of India. 2004. 'Modi Rolls Out Red Carpet for Moneyed Minorities', *Times of India*, Ahmedabad, 9 January.

———. 2005. 'SEC Code May Take Sheen Off Navratri Show', *Times of India*, Ahmedabad, 15 September.

——— 2006. 'Vibrant Navratri Shifted from Risky Sabarmati Banks', *Times of India*, 31 August.

Vale, L. J. and Jr. S. B. Warner (eds). 2001. *Imaging the City: Continuing Struggles and New Directions.* New Brunswick, NJ: Center for Urban Policy Research.

Ward, K. 2003. 'Entrepreneurial Urbanism, State Restructuring and Civilizing "New" East Manchester', *Area*, 35(2): 115–27.

Yeoh, B. S. A. 2005. 'The Global Cultural City? Spatial Imagineering and Politics in the (Multi)cultural Marketplaces of South-East Asia', *Urban Studies*, 42(5/6): 945–58.

Chapter 3

Democratic Urban Citizenship and Mega-project Development in Globalizing Mumbai*

Liza Weinstein

Over the past two decades, research on the globalization of urban development and the rise of global cities has shed new light on the conditions of local democracy and opportunities for democratic urban citizenship. Among its contributions, this research has revealed that pro-business local governments have promoted globally oriented development to the exclusion of more representative or inclusive politics, thus hindering opportunities for democratic participation (Brenner 2004; Fainstein 2001; Logan and Molotch 1987; Swyngedouw 1996). Meanwhile, a second strand of research has revealed that global cities may actually be creating the conditions for otherwise disenfranchised groups to enact citizenship claims and gain democratic voice (Boudreau 2000; Brodie 2000; Holston 2008; Isin 2000; Sassen 2002, 2006). Representing the second strand, Saskia Sassen (2006: 315) writes:

> If we consider that large cities concentrate both the leading sectors of global capital and a growing share of disadvantaged populations—immigrants, poor women, people of color generally, and, in the megacities of developing countries, masses of shanty dwellers—then cities have become a strategic terrain for a series of conflicts and contradictions.

By engaging directly in these conflicts, seemingly powerless actors gain a form of political presence, or what Holston (2008) has called 'insurgent citizenship'. Although, while these scholars have identified important democratic implications of these engagements, they may be treating the

---

* Another version of this chapter was published in 2009 (see Weinstein 2009).

conflicts and actors too generally and, in doing so, overstating the opportunities for democratic participation. On the other hand, those identifying the political disenfranchisement entailed in global city formation have emphasized the specificities of these conflicts, but have failed to account for the 'actually existing' democratic spaces remaining or emerging in globalizing cities.

This chapter seeks to explain the emergence of democratic citizenship produced through conflicts and engagements around globally oriented mega-project developments currently underway in Mumbai, India. In the process, it aims to carve out a middle ground between the generally polarized assessments of the democratic implications of global city formation. Based on an analysis of the ongoing Dharavi Redevelopment Project (DRP)—a US$2 billion housing and infrastructure mega-project designed to transform Mumbai's largest 'slum' settlement into a multi-use, mixed-income township, and attract global real estate investment to India's commercial capital—it argues that by participating in the project's planning process, some residents, workers, and activists have acquired political presence and a form of democratic citizenship. By examining the specific nature of the conflicts, it becomes clear, however, that the opportunity to engage has not been available to all disadvantaged populations equally. Consequently, this chapter argues that the form of democratic citizenship produced through the engagement of poor and working-class people in the struggles around globally oriented urban development is inherently uneven, open only to those groups with the political resources required for participation.

The first section reviews some of the recent scholarship on the relationship between global city formation and democratic urban citizenship. Highlighting the polarized nature of this literature, this section concludes that a detailed focus on the specific conflicts and actors involved in globally oriented development schemes may offer a more balanced perspective on the democratic implications of global city formation. The subsequent sections discuss the actors involved in the specific conflicts surrounding the DRP and the government's broader efforts to 'globalize' Mumbai. This narrative suggests that democratic inclusion may be emerging in spaces we may least expect it to. As the state government and DRP administrators have sought to create a hospitable arena for domestic and foreign investment—including a receptive, if not overtly supportive local community—they have worked to build support among certain groups in Dharavi, specifically those groups with the desire, resources, and opportunities to delay the project and generate negative publicity for already skittish investors. Seeking inclusion in key decisions about the project's planning process, these groups have garnered a form of urban citizenship not available to all of Dharavi's 'disad-vantaged populations'. The final section considers the implications of this case for understanding the uneven nature of democratic urban citizenship in Indian cities and cities throughout the world.

DEMOCRATIC CITIZENSHIP IN THE GLOBAL CITY

Concerns about the democratic consequences of the globalization of urban space arose along with the first identification of global or world cities in the late 1980s as strategic spaces created by the increasingly super-national character of financial and production systems (Friedmann 1986, Harvey 1985, Sassen 1991). In his now classic 'world city hypothesis', Friedmann (1986) hypothesized that the residents and workers in world cities are so-cially and economically polarized, clustered at the ends of the labour market spectrum. Sassen (1991) made a similar recognition, positing that the con-centration of producer services in global cities corresponds to the growth of employment among both the professionals who service the global economy and the poorly paid, often immigrant workers who service the professionals. But because these early accounts of global cities were made by economic so-ciologists and geographers, the consequences of global city formation were generally framed as economic and spatial disparities, rather than in terms of political inclusion and democratic representation. However, implicit in these analyses was the consideration of the unequal distribution of power, including political power, in global cities.

Meanwhile, much of the research conducted by political sociologists and urban political economists in this period on pro-business or neoliberal shifts in urban politics was fed into the growing study of governance in globalizing cities. One of the seminal pieces in this vein was Logan and Molotch's *Urban Fortunes.* Logan and Molotch (1987: 13) observed that 'the pursuit of exchange values so permeates the life of localities that cities become organized as enterprises devoted to the increase of aggregate levels of rent through the intensification of land use'. Although Logan and Mol-otch's identification of the 'growth machines' that coordinate the promo-tion of urban growth above all other objectives of local governance is rooted in the study of urban political regimes, they break from regime theory by emphasizing the new competitive frame that marks urban politics in an era of capital mobility and inter-urban competition.

Over the next decade, a group of scholars brought these insights to-gether with the study of global cities, identifying the so-called glocal or neo-liberal forms of governance as exclusionary or undemocratic. Such forms, it is suggested, include 'new elite coalitions on the one hand and the systematic exclusion or further disempowerment of politically and/or economically already weaker social groups on the other' (Brenner and Theodore 2002; Keil 2002; Swyngedouw 1996: 1499, Ward and Jonas 2004). Reflecting upon this literature, Purcell (2006: 1921) notes that 'there is a pervasive (if not thoroughly examined) sense that urban neo-liberalization threatens urban democracy. Partly as a result of this literature, there has been much interest recently in new ways to democratize the decisions that produce urban space'.

Another strand of research, however, presents a different assessment of the democratic opportunities available to the economically weaker residents of globalizing cities. Situating their inquiry more in notions of citizenship than in analyses of democratic forms of governance, this research nonetheless posits that the characteristics of global cities create the conditions for the enactment of democratic practices and the expansion of certain democratic rights (Boudreau 2000; Brodie 2000; Holston 2008; Isin 2000; Sassen 2002). These theorists suggest that as the sovereignty of the nation state is challenged by the shift of power and authority to the transnational or global scale, the nation becomes a less effective guarantor of citizenship rights. Consequently, the urban scale, and particularly the global city, emerges as a site for the potential enactment of citizenship claims. According to these scholars, global cities have emerged as both a site in which disadvantaged groups have come to renegotiate political rights and as an issue invoked in these negotiations (Holston 2008; Isin 2000; Sassen 2002).

This argument is grounded in studies of social movements and protest politics, as the right to challenge the actions of state and non-state actors in global cities is conceptualized as a fundamental expression of democratic citizenship (Boudreau 2000). These theorists consider the movements emerging in and in response to the conditions of global cities to be some of the most articulate expressions of citizenship in the era of globalization. As Isin (2000: 6) suggests,

> Being at the interstices of global networks of flows and commodities, services, capital, labor, images, and ideas, the global city, as both a milieu and object of struggle for recognition, engenders new political groups that claim either new types of rights or seek to expand modern civil political and social rights.

Furthermore, by engaging directly with the powerful actors operating in global cities, such groups acquire a form of political power. As Sassen

(2006: 217) writes, 'The fact that the disadvantaged in global cities gain "presence" in their engagement with power but also vis-à-vis each other does not necessarily bring power, but neither can it be flattened into some generic powerlessness.' Although careful not to claim that this engagement with power equates directly with political power, these theorists' assessments of the democratic opportunities within global cities are clearly more optimistic than the critics of neoliberal or 'glocal' governance.

While the first strand of research highlights the disproportionate power held by urban regimes and globally oriented growth machines to set political agendas and deny access to certain groups and their interests, the second strand emphasizes the contested nature of agenda-setting in global and globalizing cities. This latter group acknowledges that by participating in contestations, so-called disadvantaged groups help shape these agendas, even if in subtle or seemingly insignificant ways. This is an important recognition, providing a corrective to the often monolithic conception of power presented by the critics of neoliberal governance. However, closer examinations of specific contestations reveal that although participation has given some groups political presence and enabled these groups to attain a form of recognition akin to democratic citizenship, the urban poor and working classes do not have equal opportunities to engage in these conflicts. As the following case study of the DRP reveals, only certain groups within Dharavi have possessed the political resources required for access to the negotiations and conflicts entailed in global city formation. These are the groups that have held symbolic power and other means to capture the attention of the DRP's project administrators, thus creating space for themselves in the negotiations. These somewhat intangible political resources, not typically included in analyses of urban democracy and global city formation, have enabled these groups to make claims and seek recognition. Consistent with those theorizing the presence of global urban citizenship, I find that contestations over the transformation of Dharavi and the globalization of Mumbai have given some groups expanded opportunities to participate in democratic politics and make citizenship claims. However, breaking from these scholars, I find that the possession of even these less tangible political resources is uneven, thus barring some groups' access to the contestations.

REDEVELOPING DHARAVI

Until quite recently, the settlement of Dharavi was a marshy swamp on the northern edge of Bombay Island populated by members of the Koli fishing caste. The area began its transformation, first to an industrial settlement and later to a slum, in the 1870s with the establishment of the area's first leather tannery. Dharavi's population soon expanded with the migration of Muslim leather workers and low-caste Hindus from the southern state of Tamil Nadu. By the 1930s, leather workers were joined by Kumbhar potters from the Saurashtra district of Gujarat. Other groups settled and, over time, Dharavi became a hive of snack food manufacturing, scrap-dealing, recycling, machine repairing, and a slew of other industries, due to an abundance of cheap land, limited administrative oversight, and an influx of migrant workers. By the time the first survey of Dharavi was conducted in mid-1980s, the area was home to approximately 300,000 people and countless productive enterprises (Sharma 2000). Despite its productivity, Dharavi remained extremely poor; infrastructure was limited; housing and sanitation were unhygienic; and industrial activities were dangerous and highly polluting.

Given these conditions, most of the slum improvement and housing programmes undertaken in Mumbai (Bombay) over the past 40 years have, at least to some extent, focused on Dharavi. In 1985, the Indian Government's Prime Minister Grant Programme allocated more than 8 million dollars for the improvement of Dharavi's infrastructure and housing stock. Other housing programmes introduced in the 1980s and 1990s resulted in the replacement of thousands of Dharavi's single-storey hutments with mid-rise apartment blocks. Today, the 1-square-mile settlement houses countless industries and commercial enterprises and approximately 1 million residents, with roughly half living in mid-rise buildings and the other half in single-storey hutments.

Unlike earlier housing and infrastructure programmes, the DRP was not initiated by government to address Dharavi's poor living conditions and inadequate infrastructure. Rather, it was designed by a private architect and developer, Mukesh Mehta, as a for-profit development scheme. In the late 1990s, Mehta returned to Mumbai after decades of living and working as a property developer in the area around New York City. Recognizing the potential value of Dharavi's centrally located land, he soon devised a plan to use the state's existing slum policy to redevelop the entire square-mile settlement. His plan proposed the replacement of the remaining single-storey hutments with high and mid-rise buildings, thus freeing up hundreds of acres of land for market rate development. Consistent with the existing policy, the profits from these market rate developments could be used to subsidize the housing for the current slum residents. After years spent trying to launch the project independently, Mehta found his plan constrained by state regulations and the difficulty of securing financing and so he began seeking government backing for the project. In January 2004, the State of Maharashtra endorsed his plan and it was reborn as a state-sponsored project, part of the state's broader efforts to transform Mumbai into a global city. Mehta's role on the project shifted from that of a private developer to a consultant hired by the state to manage the project.[1]

The plan divides Dharavi into five sectors of roughly equal size, each of which will continue to house most of the current residents, and much of the commerce and industry currently located in that sector. Each household deemed eligible for 'rehabilitation'[2] will receive a 265-square-foot apartment in a mid-rise building in their current sector. Although the apartments will be given free of charge, the residents will have to pay municipal taxes and maintenance fees, which are expected to raise the housing expenses for most Dharavi residents. It is estimated that 90,000 new apartment units, divided throughout the five sectors, will be constructed under the plan.[3] These units will be financed by five private developers or developer consortia, in exchange for additional land and increased height allowances to construct market rate commercial properties. Given Mumbai's high land prices and the desirability of Dharavi's location, developers are expected to recoup their expenses and make considerable profit from the sale of the market rate constructions. These expectations were revealed when expression of interest (EOI) documents were invited in June 2007 and 78 development firms applied to bid on the project.

The broad features of the DRP, including the cross-subsidization financing formula, are simply a continuation of the current slum housing policy, in place since the early 1990s. The project's novelty lies in its scale, the support it has garnered from government and local elites, and its solicitation of participation by large domestic and international developers. The DRP is the first government-sponsored scheme allowing and encouraging bidding by foreign investors and global real estate developers. Although the project administrators claim that the most qualified developers will be selected for the project, there has been a clear preference throughout the planning process for international developers. The project administrators have taken steps to elicit interest abroad, making frequent presentations about the project around the world, particularly in the US, Canada, the UK, Dubai, and Singapore. When developer interest was invited in June 2007, the tender was published in newspapers in more than 20 countries, as well as throughout India. Of the 78 developers interested in bidding on the scheme, over a third were non-Indian firms (Deshmukh 2007).

Given these efforts to attract international investment and use the project to help facilitate Mumbai's transformation to a global city, it seems unlikely that the planning for the DRP would be an inclusive process. As I describe in the remaining sections, however, the political resources and symbolic power held by certain groups in Dharavi has compelled the state to engage more directly with them than might be expected. Considering the ability of these groups to mobilize the public opinion that would likely generate negative publicity and create further complications for cautious investors, the state has worked to disarm these opponents and prevent oppositions from arising. In doing so, it has engaged in an unprecedented way with these groups, facilitating a kind of democracy through cooptation. This form of democratic urban citizenship is not the product of high liberal ideals, but, as I argue, emerged in response to practical, and largely material, considerations.

DEMOCRATIZING DEVELOPMENT

When the Maharashtra government decided to endorse the DRP and carry out Mehta's plan as a government initiative, officials recognized that the project's planning should be presented as consensual and participatory. Mehta attributes the then housing secretary Suresh Joshi with helping him recognize the importance of local support in the project. In 2003, as the chief minister's cabinet debated endorsement of the project, Mehta and Joshi began reaching out to the city's housing advocacy organizations, most of whom had expressed suspicion towards Mehta's plan. As Mehta recalls:

> It was (Suresh) Joshi's idea to call all of these groups together. He said that we should call together these groups and make a presentation and give them a chance to voice their concerns. Then they could never say that they were not notified.[4]

Another consultant in Mehta's office concurs that they had taken a systematic approach in the early years to build support, or at least notify potential opponents about the project:

> [Joshi] was very methodical. What he did initially, before the cabinet had passed it…was he took literally every type of stakeholder, starting with the NGOs, the slum dwellers, senior politicians, MLAs [Members of the Legislative Assembly], corporators [city council members], the ward officers. I mean literally every single stakeholder and we made presentations to each one of them and had thorough discussions with them where they were allowed to raise (questions)—in fact, we told them in those meetings, we want you to ask the toughest, the nastiest questions possible and we're not worth our salt if we can't answer your questions.[5]

According to Mehta, few criticisms of the plan were voiced in those meetings. Mehta contends that these groups could not find anything wrong with the plan, but chose to maintain their opposition purely for political reasons. Responding to this claim, Priya Shah, the head of a prominent housing organization, once explained her reticence to me:

> Our visions are so different. There is no conversation to be had. We cannot arbitrate with him. We cannot enter into criticism with him. He wants us to talk about his grand plan, but there's nothing to talk about. We would rather publish criticism of the plan than talk to him about it.[6]

Shah claims to have recognized the disingenuous character of these meetings, seeing them as little more than public relations stunts. But it was also apparent that Mumbai's community of housing activists was somewhat unsettled by Mehta's and Joshi's openness. More comfortable with letter writing and protest politics to have their voices heard, they did not quite know how to respond to this apparent willingness to include them in the planning process.

But even whilst many of these groups remained suspicious of Mehta's intentions and refused to engage in direct negotiations with the project administrators, these meetings provided Mehta a certain degree of legitimacy. The project, which had up to this point been designed and promoted by a single entrepreneurial developer with the political support of only the housing secretary, could now be presented as a government supported initiative with broad support and the involvement of local NGOs, politicians, and community members. When government announced their official backing of the DRP at a cabinet meeting in January 2004, the project was presented as a collaborative effort, developed in consultation with all of Dharavi's major stakeholders.

In addition to these meetings, Mehta had also set up an office in Dharavi in the late 1990s and spent time discussing the plan with Dharavi residents. While local leaders within Dharavi dispute Mehta's claims that he was a visible presence in Dharavi in these early years, he maintains that he had become integrated in community institutions. When the project is criticized as a top-down scheme—as it has been throughout the planning process—Mehta retorts that this time in Dharavi, discussions with residents that took place both informally and in meetings with the heads of more than 50 cooperative housing societies shaped the plan considerably (Menon 2004).

Years later, while sitting in his car as I accompanied him to appointments with government officials and private sector partners, Mehta recalled how those early meetings had forced him to compromise on his original vision. He drew a map of the plan he had originally wanted to pursue. The map showed a cluster of high-rise buildings along Dharavi's perimeter, adjacent to the train tracks that form the southern and eastern edges of the settlement. The rehabilitated slum dwellers would be re-housed in 20-storey buildings along the perimeter and their homes would face out on a golf course. The market rate buildings would be clustered on the other side of the golf course, along Dharavi's northern and western edges, adjacent to the nearby office complex. Looking longingly at the map, he said that it was a good plan that should have made everyone happy. The residents would have had access to transportation, the commercial occupants would be near the Bandra Kurla Complex (BKC) and the city would have a golf course and park as a public amenity. But, as he explained:

> I had to give up this plan because of the iterative process that revealed that slum dwellers didn't want to move from the place in Dharavi where they are now. People objected to a golf course on principle. So I changed the plan and came up with the sectors.[7]

He conceded that this 'iterative process' ultimately improved the plan, but it was clear that he felt his original vision was superior.

Despite these consultations and a process that Mehta claims was open to considerable public scrutiny, project planning remained a private endeavour with limited democratic oversight. Mehta established MM Consultants, a private entity subcontracted to draft the plan and manage its implementation, and most planning activities were centralized in this office. Critics generally describe his Dharavi meetings as one-way interactions in which he would simply present the plan to audiences who had no opportunity to respond or critique it. According to some attendees, the plan he presented sounded like a fantasy. An attendee at one of these meetings quipped that Mehta had proclaimed that he would 'make Dharavi like America' (Bunshe 2004). Even as Dharavi residents attended these meetings, most remained suspicious of Mehta's promises and assurances that there would remain a place for them in a redeveloped Dharavi.

RESIDENT CONSENT AND OPPOSITION

These suspicions were confirmed at an infamous meeting in mid-2004.[8] The state had recently announced its endorsement of the scheme and many residents were concerned about the security of their housing tenure and whether they would continue to have access to employment. Rumours had been circulating about the scheme for years and many saw the meeting as an opportunity to clarify the actual elements of the project and voice their concerns. As the attendees entered the meeting, they were asked to sign what most believed was an attendance sheet, but later learned was a statement of written consent for the project. When, after the meeting, it was learned that hundreds of Dharavi residents had unknowingly given their consent to a scheme that many of them actually opposed, a vocal public opposition to Mehta and his scheme emerged.

Speaking about the incident years later, Mehta still angrily blames the officials in the Slum Rehabilitation Authority (SRA) who he claims were attempting to sideline the project and deliberately mislead meeting attendees. He claims that government bureaucrats, concerned about retaining their 'turf', had intentionally tried to sabotage his credibility among Dharavi residents. Officials in the SRA, meanwhile, refer to the incident as an unfortunate miscommunication. Regardless of whether the attendees were deliberately misled and by whom, most observers, including Mehta, recognized that the incident undermined his credibility and had the potential to disrupt the project. This was revealed when activists quickly mobilized to oppose the scheme. In response to the public outcry, the signatures were eventually discarded and no further attempts were made to collectively acquire resident consent.

In addition to highlighting the contested nature of the project, this event was the first in a series of disputes about the 'resident consent clause' of the Slum Rehabilitation Scheme (SRS) in the case of the DRP. At the time of this meeting in mid-2004, the policy governing the project stipulated that the scheme would require the written consent of at least 60 per cent of Dharavi's residents in order to proceed.[9] As SRA officials explain its rationale, the consent clause was a measure to prevent unscrupulous builders from coercing residents to participate in the scheme. Most believe that the consent clause has done little to prevent such abuses, as residents now claim to be coerced to give their official consent. But while the effectiveness of the consent requirement has been questioned, residents and housing advocates have viewed the clause as the only democratic check on the SRS. With authority held by builders and the SRA, the only input residents have had in the scheme is the granting of their consent.

After the meeting, opposition to the DRP began to mount. Although the emergence of an opposition movement in mid-2004 can only partially be attributed to this incident, it is frequently cited by project opponents as evidence of Mehta's dubious character. Shekhar Varde, a Mumbai-based housing activist and former politician, once explained to me that the incident simply affirmed what many had understood about the scheme for years: that Mehta was attempting to trick Dharavi residents and steal the land out from under them. The incident proved to be a political opportunity effectively seized by the project's most vocal opponents.

One of the groups that assumed leadership at the time was the People's Responsible Organization for United Dharavi (PROUD). Typically shying away from contentious politics, PROUD has its roots in church-based community organizing, mobilizing residents to make demands for improved civic infrastructure and the protection of their housing security. At times, however, PROUD has taken a more confrontational stance. In the early 1980s, when municipal authorities notified roughly 80 Dharavi families that their homes would be imminently demolished, PROUD's leadership mobilized in response and managed to prevent the demolition (Chatterji 2005). Seeking again to protect the housing security of Dharavi residents, the advocacy organization took a strong stance in mid-2004 in opposition to the DRP.

Among those working with PROUD at the time was Ramesh Khandare, a Dharavi resident who had been an active member of the local branch of the Communist Party. Using his community newspaper to disseminate information about the project, Khandare became one of the project's most visible opponents. On 4 July 2004, Khandare and hundreds of critics of the scheme, including representatives from all of Maharashtra's major political parties, staged a protest march in Dharavi and formed the Dharavi Bachao Samiti (Menon 2004). Under Khandare's leadership, other protests were held over the next several months. Speaking to a newspaper reporter at an event in August 2004, a prominent housing activist explained that because Dharavi was built by its residents, they should be involved in its redevelopment. Mehta, he explained, had not involved them in the plan (Menon 2004).

These project opponents did not have a clear set of demands, but simply opposed the way the project had been handled. All opponents were clear to assert that they too wanted Dharavi 'to be developed'. They wanted residents to have better quality housing, access to sanitation facilities, and less dangerous work spaces, but they were sceptical that the DRP would bring these benefits to the area's current residents. A leader with Dharavi Bachao Samiti whose family has lived in Dharavi for four generations, expressed the general concern held by most of the opponents:

In Dharavi, the poor people are suffering. But government doesn't want to solve that. The actual motivation is to take the highly valuable land. They don't want to help the people.[10]

Organized now as an opposition movement, the activists felt they could better ensure that the benefits of redevelopment remained in Dharavi.

COOPTING THE OPPOSITION

When I arrived in Mumbai to begin fieldwork in September 2005, the opposition movement that had seemed strong a year before had all but disappeared. Khandare had stopped publishing his community newspaper and the city's housing activists had moved on to other concerns. I soon came to realize that two factors explained the movement's dormancy: project delays and the relatively successful cooptation of project opponents. Because there had been no significant activity on the project since the state endorsed it in January 2004, many residents and opponents had grown sceptical that it would ever be implemented. When I asked project critics about the movement, some responded by asking why they should actively oppose a scheme that will exist only on paper.

The movement's dormancy was also an outcome of a tactical change adopted by Mehta and the SRA. Recognizing that participatory rhetoric had been insufficient to secure community support and prevent a visible and politically harmful opposition movement from arising, the state began a series of more substantive negotiations with certain groups identified to have more symbolic authority and the opportunity to mobilize.

In late 2004, Mehta recognized the need to respond to the protestors and to work to build support within Dharavi. He began meeting with representatives from PROUD and requested meetings with the scheme's most vocal opponents. Although Ramesh Khandare and Priya Shah still refused to meet him, PROUD's leadership was more than willing to discuss ways in which they could be involved in the planning process. The willingness of PROUD to negotiate with Mehta created a split in the opposition movement. A project opponent once explained to me, 'PROUD started out nicely; now they are not functioning properly.' He noted that because 'they are good friends with Mukesh Mehta', he decided to join Dharavi Bachao Samiti instead and work with them to undermine the scheme.[11] Other vocal opponents disassociated themselves from PROUD and many accused them of taking money from Mehta in exchange for their support.

Ashwin Paul, a community organizer who remained active with PROUD, adamantly refutes this charge, insisting that he and others simply recognized that Mehta's plan could be beneficial to Dharavi's residents. Furthermore, if they worked with Mehta, they could help ensure that the residents benefitted from the scheme. As Paul explained:

This will be PROUD's role, to hold them to these promises. PROUᴅ have to keep people aware of the promises and keep demanding that the builders and SRA keeps them. PROUD can mobilize the people to pressurize them.[12]

With Mehta apparently willing to invite PROUD into the planning process, Paul recognized that they could play an important role.

These more convivial relations were revealed at a meeting I attended early on in my field work.[13] At a town-hall-style meeting held in the up-stairs auditorium of Dharavi's Saint Anthony's Church, I noticed Ashwin Paul sharing the lectern with Mehta, along with representatives from other Dharavi-based organizations. As Mehta presented his plan to the roughly 70 Dharavi residents gathered for the meeting, Paul and the other repre-sentatives sat quietly, offering their silent endorsement of the project. Even after the audience turned more antagonistic and began arguing with Mehta about his plans for implementation, his efforts seemed more legitimate be-cause of this apparent community support. Other meetings like this were held over the coming months, following roughly the same format of Mehta making a PowerPoint presentation that detailed the plan's most attractive features, and then opening the floor to questions. Mehta openly welcomed criticism in these meetings, requesting that his critics make their opposition public. With less vocal opposition and the legitimating presence of commu-nity groups, discussions about the DRP took on a more consensual tone.

In addition to these public displays, Mehta and SRA officials also began holding a series of more targeted negotiations with the leaders of particular communities in Dharavi. Recognizing the need to establish firmer ties within Dharavi, the SRA had hired Mrs Shinde as the Chief Community Development Officer for the project. Charged with managing community relations, she had become a visible presence in Dharavi and was referred to affectionately by many of my informants. Speaking in her office one day, Shinde explained the importance of what she referred to as Dharavi's 'sensitive populations', those with symbolic claims to housing or productive space in Dharavi.[14] She explained the importance of addressing these groups' demands because of the symbolic recognition they had both in Dharavi and throughout the city.

Two of the most important sensitive populations Shinde identified were the Kolis and the Khumbars. As Dharavi's original inhabitants, the Kolis have a politically important position in the city. Also, as long-time Dharavi residents with recognized leases on their land dating back to the late 18th century, the Kolis have made significant investments in Dharavi and have constructed some of the nicest homes in the area (Rajyashree 1986). The prospect that these homes could be demolished and replaced with 269-square-foot apartments has invoked ire both in and outside of the community. Dharavi's Kolis are also a politically active group, frequently running for and holding office on Shiv Sena party tickets.[15] This political presence has provided them a particular bargaining position in the planning for the DRP, as Shinde explained. Mehta also echoed this sentiment, explaining that among all of Dharavi's communities, 'they are the most important and government recognizes it, because they are the original "sons of the soil"'.[16] Given this position, however, and the robust legal claims on their land, they have been the most difficult community to negotiate with. While acknowledging the importance of the Kolis, both Mehta and Shinde explained that they are putting off substantive negotiations until the other features of the plan are settled.

The Kumbhars, on the other hand, have a more disputed position in Dharavi's legal and symbolic landscape. Residents of Dharavi since the 1930s, the Kumbhar potters had resettled in Dharavi after the pollution from their kilns caused problems in other, more desirable parts of the city (Lynch 1979). Upon resettlement, the Kumbhars were given a lease to their land in Dharavi, which they claim protects them from resettlement under the DRP. Government officials, however, contend that the Kumbhars' lease expired decades ago and that, unlike the Kolis, they have no legal claims to their land. Yet, as one of Dharavi's oldest settlements, Mehta and Mrs Shinde recognize that Kumbharwada, in many people's minds, is Dharavi.[17] Furthermore, because they have resided in Dharavi since before its emergence as a slum, neither do the Kumbhars consider themselves slum dwellers, nor are they considered so by most Mumbai residents. Instead, they are generally thought of as members of a traditional Hindu labouring caste, giving them a heightened status in Dharavi.

Another group recognized as a critical constituency in Dharavi is the area's industrialists, whose engagement was actively elicited in the early planning process. This group is ethnically and occupationally diverse, comprising Tamil leather workers and snack food manufacturers, north Indian Muslim scrap dealers and soap makers, and Maharashtrian garment manufacturers. Many of these groups have lived in Dharavi for generations, working in shops built by their fathers or grandfathers. These groups give Dharavi its industrial character and their productivity is publicly commended. Aside from their symbolic position, Dharavi's industrialists are also politically influential. As one of the settlement's wealthier groups, the industrialists, especially the scrap dealers, are recognized to be regular contributors to the election coffers of local politicians. As a result, these groups have been invited to play a significant role in drafting the DRP's industrial policy, including what activities will be allowed to remain in Dharavi and how much space manufacturers will receive under the plan.

Sitting in a small air-conditioned office amidst Dharavi's scrap piles and recycling plants, Ahmed Khan, a wealthy scrap dealer and head of Dharavi's largest industrial cooperative, expressed his satisfaction with the DRP's planning process. Khan had been living in Dharavi for almost 40 years, having relocated with his family from the northern state of Uttar Pradesh after several bad seasons in agriculture. With the support of relatives working in Mumbai's scrap business, he set up one of Dharavi's first plastic processing plants. His business grew over time and he now employs more than 75 workers, all of whom live in Dharavi. Given this history and his contributions to the area's productivity, he explained his importance to the redevelopment efforts:

> Dharavi is both a residential and a commercial space and it must remain as both. Finding space for the residents is less of a problem than for us. They will build tall. Government will make a profit and this will be good for everyone. But we are Dharavi. We have seen this area when it was in bad condition. We want to see it when it is in good condition…. If they don't meet our demands, we won't support the project…and they need our support.[18]

In order to garner this support, Mehta and Mrs Shinde had held several meetings over the preceding months with Khan and other industrialists to discuss the plan's industrial policy. He seemed genuinely satisfied with the negotiations, asserting that 'the industrialists have had a say in the decisions about the plan' and elaborating that they were 'consulted about the whole industrial policy'.[19] While he recognized that compromises would be reached, he expressed confidence that the industrialists would be well accommodated under the plan.

While these efforts were being made to win over the industrialists, as well as the Khumbars and Kolis, Shinde and Mehta continued holding public forums and worked to elicit the support of the city's prominent housing activists. Shinde's office also printed pamphlets in the six major languages spoken in Dharavi and distributed details of the plan throughout the area. While the information dissemination, public forums, and private negotiations did not represent a major shift from the earlier, more rhetorical approach to democratic participation, what seemed to change most was the urgency with which Mehta and SRA officials undertook these activities.

Despite these efforts and the growing appearance of local support, government officials remained concerned that they would not be able to secure resident consent required by the SRS. Although the consent requirement had been reduced to 60 per cent, it was becoming apparent that even that level would be difficult to secure. Consequently, efforts were being made to eliminate the consent rule altogether in the case of the DRP. In the months leading up to its elimination, however, government officials denied that such efforts were being made. On mentioning some opposition to the scheme that I had observed in Dharavi, a high ranking official in the SRA contradicted me, explaining that there was almost universal resident support for the project. 'Although 70 percent consent is required,' he explained (even though the consent had already been reduced to 60 per cent by this time), 'the SRA is attempting to secure resident support at 85 per cent.'[20] He explained that this higher consent standard would be easy to garner given the support for the project and the efforts being made by Mehta and Shinde to expand this support in the community. But in November 2006, the state government adopted the housing policy that codified elements of the DRP. Included in the policy was the clarification that because the DRP, unlike other SRS projects, was an official 'government' scheme, it would not be necessary to elicit official resident consent for the scheme. While this clarification was presented as a minor detail, its consequences for the planning process were significant.

Sitting in a conference room at Mehta's office soon after the consent requirement was eliminated, I asked how the change would affect his efforts to secure local support. With consent being no longer required, I asked him if he still needed to engage the Kolis, the Kumbhars, and the industrialists in the planning process? He admitted the importance of eliminating the consent clause, acknowledging that it had been a barrier to implementation, but he mused that these groups still had power. 'India is an anarchy, not a democracy. If people have vested interests, they can stop something.'[21] When I pressed him to explain how these groups could stop the project, he explained that they could undermine his efforts and create delays. The energy he was expending at this point in the process, trying to bring these groups on board, he explained, would pay off down the road with a smoother implementation.

He suggested the importance of a smooth implementation, in part, because of the project's efforts to secure the participation of the somewhat elusive international developers. With a regulatory context perceived to be cumbersome, overly bureaucratic, and corrupt, international development firms have generally found it financially unviable to invest in Mumbai's

land markets (Nijman 2000; *Times of India* 2005). In addition to these barriers, there has also been a history of project delays and projects abandoned
because of local opposition and direct agitation.[22] But as Mehta explained:

> This project will show that if it's done in a systematic manner, and the gov-
> ernment is involved, they can hold your hand through the process. So if you
> want to buy an open track of land and invest a hundred million dollars or
> you want to do it in clumps, both can be done without fear of the ten differ-
> ent issues that could possibly arise on a project.[23]

His efforts to build local support for the scheme and draft a policy
able to withstand legal challenges represented efforts to dispel these perceptions and make Mumbai a more attractive site for investment.

THE PROJECT AND ITS OPPONENTS GO GLOBAL

The fruits of Mehta's labour were revealed in June 2007 when developer
interest was invited on the scheme and 78 firms submitted applications to
bid. On 1 June 2007, an advertisement, published in newspapers in 20 cities around the world, 'invite[d] international developers to transform Dharavi, one of the largest slum pockets in the world, into an integrated town-
ship of Mumbai with all modern amenities and complete infrastructure'.
The advertisement promised that the scheme would be both a profitable
opportunity and a chance to participate 'in a noble cause with a plentitude
of rewards'. Seventy-eight firms, organized into 26 developer consortia,
submitted EOI forms to the Government of Maharashtra by the time the
invitation period closed at the end of August 2007. Of the 26 consortia,
almost all included at least one foreign investment or development firm,
including firms from the US, Dubai, the UK, China, and South Korea. In
January 2008, the 26 consortia were whittled down to 19 by a government
committee evaluating the financial and technical viability of the consortia
(*Indian Express* 2008a).[24] Meanwhile, the bidding has been delayed by investor concerns arising from the current global financial conditions.

Responding immediately to the invitation of investor interest in the
summer of 2007, Dharavi Bachao Samiti and other project opponents re-
vitalized the opposition movement that had been dormant for two and a
half years. A series of direct actions were held and local opponents made
appeals to transnational activists to help pressure the State of Maharashtra
and Government of India to intervene in the development process. Meanwhile, fearing that such actions might frighten skittish investors, the state

responded quickly, exhibiting an unprecedented willingness to address the demands of activists and resident groups.

In late May 2007, as the Maharashtra government was preparing the invitation of EOIs, housing activists announced their plans to undertake acts of civil disobedience. A prominent housing activist explained to a newspaper reporter that if the global tender issued by the state government was found to be unacceptable, then the residents would take to the streets, blocking roads and railway lines, in protest (*DNA* 2007). Although they did not create blockades when the tender was issued on 1 June 2007, thousands of protesters, including members of the Dharavi Bachao Samiti and representatives of all of the state's major political parties (except the ruling Congress Party) came out two weeks later to protest the DRP. Some protesters shaved their heads and most wore orange hats and t-shirts in solidarity (*Hindu* 2007). Despite the strong stance taken by the protesters, project opponents continued to insist that they did not oppose the merits of the scheme, but simply wanted to be included more directly in the planning process. Other demands were more specific, such as the demand that the size of housing units be increased (from 225 square feet per unit to 400 square feet per unit), that more Dharavi residents be deemed eligible for the scheme (from those who could prove residency in Dharavi since 1995 to those who could prove residency since 2000), and that a detailed survey of Dharavi residents be initiated before the scheme is implemented (Tare 2008).

In addition to staging protests and submitting their demands to the state government, Mumbai-based activists solicited the support of prominent activists and scholars from outside India including Professors Arjun Appadurai, Partha Chatterjee, and Saskia Sassen, former under-secretary-general of the United Nations, Shashi Tharoor, and the former president of Ireland, Mary Robinson. In the letter addressed to the Indian prime minister and the chief minister of Maharashtra, the signatories expressed their 'profound sense of disquiet' and requested that the project be looked at afresh and the support of the larger community be secured before the government proceeded with the scheme (*Hindu* 2008).

Over the next several months, the Government of Maharashtra responded by addressing certain demands of the transnationally linked activists. In March 2008, the state commissioned a detailed census of Dharavi to be carried out by the Pune-based research firm Mashaal (*Indian Express* 2008b). The chief minister announced the following month that the size of housing units constructed under the scheme would be increased from the original 225 square feet to a compromised 269 square feet (Ghadyahlpatil 2008). Also, in April 2008, the Indian Supreme Court found in favour of a legal claim and extended eligibility to residents who had resided in Dharavi since 2000 (Menon 2008). Although they continued to press for the unmet demands—including larger housing units and the reinstatement of the consent clause—the Maharashtra government exhibited an unprecedented willingness to accommodate the activists. As the government now prepares to select the project's five developers, it has continued to assure them that investing in the DRP will be smooth and profitable. In the process, the state has been compelled to construct a relatively inclusive space within which activists and certain groups within Dharavi have been engaged in the project's planning process.

DISCUSSION: FRAGMENTED URBAN CITIZENSHIP

With a focus on a globally oriented mega-project currently underway in Mumbai, this chapter reveals that the ongoing globalization of the South Asian city may be facilitating the creation of a more inclusive space in which certain groups have gained access to the highly contested field of global urban politics. Even while the DRP's administrators may not have been driven by liberal democratic values, they have come to recognize the pragmatic and material utility of creating a more inclusive space for certain disadvantaged populations. According to this narrative, although Mukesh Mehta and certain government officials initially viewed inclusion as little more than a rhetorical device, a mobilized opposition soon made them aware that rhetoric was insufficient and that the more meaningful engagement of project opponents would be necessary for the project's realization. As a result, Mehta and SRA officials undertook activities designed to garner more substantive support from within Dharavi. Among these activities, they co-opted a respected Dharavi-based organization; held town-hall-style meetings in which they publicly confronted and debated project critics; disseminated propaganda to convince residents of the project's benefits; and negotiated directly with groups deemed influential and symbolically important. Although these activities did not prevent opposition from arising once the global tender was issued in June 2007, officials had learned that a quick response was most advantageous and they worked to address many of the activists' demands and quieted the mobilization.

While this case supports the observation made by Sassen, Isin, and others that the formation of global cities may be facilitating the creation of new democratic spaces and new forms of urban citizenship, it also reveals that only certain groups possess the symbolic power and political resources required to gain access to these spaces. In Dharavi, these groups have included the so-called sensitive populations or those with the legal and symbolic power to mobilize public opinion and facilitate a broader opposition movement. As in the case of the Kolis, Kumbhars, and even the industrialists, their historic claims on space and religiously conferred occupational positions provided them disproportionate influence and the means to capture the attention of the DRP's project administrators. While caste position and historical claims on space are not typically considered political resources that can help groups gain political access and citizenship rights, the possession of these resources has proved useful for these groups to gain access to the negotiations surrounding the DRP. Although the same resources are not likely to prove as advantageous in other instances of globally oriented urban development, this case reveals the importance of symbolic power. It also reveals that when groups are not in possession of such resources, they are less able to command the attention of project administrators and broader publics, and can be barred access from the negotiations and contestations that give shape to the globalizing city.

In this chapter, I have argued for the need to consider the fragmentations and barriers that may mark the forms of democratic urban citizenship created by globalization and global city formation. While scholars of global urban citizenship have demonstrated that the right to challenge the actions of the growth machines that drive urban political agendas in globalizing cities represents a fundamental expression of democratic citizenship, their theorizations have not adequately revealed the barriers that prevent some groups from challenging these actions. Consequently, when considering how disadvantaged populations may gain presence in global and globalizing cities by engaging directly with power, it is important to identify the specific means by which groups are able to engage with power. While in this case, the opportunity to shape public opinion and mobilize domestic and transnational activists has given certain Dharavi-based groups the opportunity to engage with power, the means in other cases are likely to be distinct but similarly important to recognize.

NOTES

1. Mehta's consultancy fee is 1 per cent of total project expenditures, which are estimated at US$2 billion, making Mehta's share approximately US$20 million.
2. 'Rehabilitation' refers to the onsite resettlement of slum-dwellers into mid-rise buildings. Eligibility is based upon whether residents can prove continuous occupancy in their current dwelling since 1 January 2000. It is difficult to assess the number of residents currently ineligible, but a conservative estimate places this population at about 200,000 people or a quarter of Dharavi's current population.

3. This estimate is based on early projections provided by Mashaal, the research firm hired to conduct a census of Dharavi in advance of the DRP. This number will likely be revised once their census is completed and the estimates are made available.

4. Discussion on 14 November 2006.

5. Discussion on 19 June 2006.

6. Discussion on 14 November 2006.

7. Discussion on 18 August 2006.

8. This meeting occurred before I began my fieldwork and I was not present for it. It was described to me, however, by several informants throughout my research period. Some of the accounts I was given have conflicting details and I have not been able to corroborate their accounts. Consequently, my description of the meeting remains vague.

9. The consent clause is discussed in the Development Control Rules of Greater Mumbai, DCR 33(10), the policy governing all projects entailing the rehabilitation (or re-housing) of slum dwellers in mid-rise buildings. Although the policy requires resident consent at the 70 per cent level, the SRA quietly reduced the consent requirement to 60 per cent for the DRP in 2004. Few activists or housing advocates and practically no Dharavi residents were aware of the rule change until years later. Public officials with whom I spoke in 2005 and 2006 were cagey about the consent clause, sometimes explicitly citing the 70 per cent figure, although it had been reduced to 60 per cent months earlier.

10. Discussion on 20 September 2006.

11. Discussion on 20 September 2006.

12. Discussion on 27 June 2006.

13. Meeting held on 8 May 2006.

14. Discussion on 17 October 2006.

15. The Shiv Sena is one of the dominant political parties in Maharashtra, representing the right of the political spectrum. At the state level, the Shiv Sena is currently part of the political opposition. In Mumbai, however, the Shiv Sena holds the largest number of seats in the municipal corporation. Koliwada's political importance is partially due to the Kolis' support for the Shiv Sena, while the remaining districts in Dharavi are considered Congress strongholds.

16. Discussion on 14 November 2006.

17. The association of Dharavi with Kumbharwada can be discerned, for example, in the newspaper articles highlighting the impacts of the plan on Dharavi residents, focusing disproportionately on the implications for the Kumbhars.

18. Discussion on 7 September 2006.

19. Discussion on 7 September 2006.

20. Discussion on 14 February 2006.

21. Discussion on 14 November 2006.

22. In a high-profile example, the scandalized energy firm Enron had attempted to construct a power plant 80 miles south of Mumbai, but was met with considerable protests in the mid-1990s. Although these mobilizations were not the only political problem facing the project, they provided the state justification to stall on implementation. The power plant was still not completed in 2001 when Enron collapsed under the weight of scandal (Mehta 2000).

23. Discussion on 19 June 2006.

24. After the casualties of the global financial crisis of 2008–09, however, four consortia were forced to withdraw from consideration, including one consortium that had included the now defunct financial firm Lehman Brothers (Tembhekar 2009).

BIBLIOGRAPHY

Bombay First. 2003. *Vision Mumbai: Recommendations for Transforming Mumbai into a World Class City*. Mumbai: Bombay First.

Boudreau, J. A. 2000. *Mega-city Saga: Democracy and Citizenship in This Global Age*. Montreal: Black Rose Books.

Brenner, N. 2004. *New State Spaces, Urban Governance, and the Rescaling of Statehood*. New York: Oxford University Press.

Brenner and N. Theodore. 2002. 'Cities and the Geographies of "Actually Existing Neoliberalism"', *Antipode*, 34(3): 356–86.

Brodie, J. 2000. 'Imagining Democratic Urban Citizenship', in E. Isin (ed.), *Democracy, Citizenship, and the Global City*, pp. 110–28. New York: Routledge.

Bunshe, D. 2004. 'Developing Doubts', *Frontline*, 05–18 January. Available at http://www.flonnet.com/fl2112/stories/20040618002704400.htm. Last accessed on 11 July 2011.

Chatterji, R. 2005. 'Plans, Habitation and Slum Redevelopment: The Production of Community in Dharavi, Mumbai', *Contributions to Indian Sociology*, 39(2): 197–218.

Deshmukh, S. 2007. '78 firms in Race for Dharavi Makeover', *DNA*, Mumbai, 31 August.

DNA. 2007. 'Dharavi Slum Dwellers Threaten Agitation', *DNA*, Mumbai, 29 May.

Fainstein, S. 2001. *The City Builders: Property Development in New York City and London, 1980–2000*. Lawrence: University of Kansas Press.

Friedmann, J. 1986. 'The World City Hypothesis', *Development and Change*, 17(1): 69–84.

Ghadyalpatil, A. 2008. 'Govt's Bid to Hike Flat Size Halts Dharavi Makeover', *Economic Times*, Mumbai, 1 May.

Harvey, D. 1985. *The Urbanization of Capital: Studies in the History and Theory of Capitalist Urbanization*. Baltimore: Johns Hopkins Press.

Hindu. 2007. 'Dharavi Protesters Shave Their Heads', *Hindu*, Mumbai, 24 July.

———. 2008. 'Residents of Dharavi Oppose Redevelopment Plan', *Hindu*, Mumbai, 19 June.

Holston, J. 2008. *Insurgent Citizenship: Disjunctions of Democracy and Modernity in Brazil*. Princeton: Princeton University Press.

Indian Express. 2008a. 'Dharavi Makeover: 19 Consortia in the Running', *Indian Express*, Mumbai, 10 January.

———. 2008b. 'Govt Urges MLAs to Help Baseline Dharavi Survey', *Indian Express*, Mumbai, 26 March.

Isin, E. 2000. 'Introduction: Democracy, Citizenship, and the City', in E. Isin (ed.), *Democracy, Citizenship, and the Global City*, pp. 1–21. New York: Routledge.

Keil, R. 2002. '"Common-Sense" Neoliberalism: Progressive Conservative Urbanism in Toronto, Canada', *Antipode*, 34(3): 578–601.

Logan, J. and H. Molotch. 1987. *Urban Fortunes: The Political Economy of Place*. Berkeley: University of California Press.

Lynch, O. 1979. 'Potters, Plotters, and Prodders: Marx and Meaning or Meaning versus Marx', *Urban Anthropology*, 8(1). 1–27.

Mehta, A. 2000. *Power Play: A Study of the Enron Project*. Mumbai: Orient Longman.

Menon, M. 2004. 'Dharavi Residents Wary of New Project', *Hindu*, Mumbai, 8 August.

————. 2008. 'Supreme Court Order Cheers Dharavi Residents', *Hindu*, Mumbai, 6 April.

Nijman, J. 2000. 'Mumbai's Real Estate Market in the 1990s: De-regulation, Global Money, and Casino Capitalism', *Economic and Political Weekly*, 35(7): 572–82.

Purcell, M. 2006. 'Urban Democracy and the Local Trap', *Urban Studies*, 43(11): 1921–941.

Rajyashree, K. S. 1986. *An Ethnolinguistic Survey of Dharavi*. Mysore: Central Institute of Indian Languages.

Sassen, S. 1991. *The Global City: New York, London, Tokyo*. Princeton: Princeton University Press.

————. 2002. 'The Repositioning of Citizenship: Emergent Subjects and Spaces for Politics', *Berkeley Journal of Sociology*, 46: 4–25.

————. 2006. *Territory, Authority, Rights: From Medieval to Global Assemblages*. Princeton, NJ: Princeton University Press.

Sharma, K. 2000. *Rediscovering Dharavi: Stories from Asia's Largest Slum*. New Delhi: Penguin Books.

State of Maharashtra. 2004. *Transforming Mumbai into a World-class City*. Mumbai: Chief Minister's Taskforce.

Swyngedouw, E. 1996. 'Reconstructing Citizenship, the Re-scaling of the State and the New Authoritarianism: Closing the Belgian Mines', *Urban Studies*, 33(8): 1499–521.

Tare, K. 2008. 'Parties Rally behind Sena on Dharavi', *DNA*, Mumbai, 13 March.

Tembhekar, C. 2009. '4 Firms Drop Out of Dharavi Plan', *Times of India*, Mumbai, 13 March.

Times of India. 2005. 'Set the Stage', *Times of India*, Mumbai, 19 March.

Ward, Kevin and A. E. Jonas. 2004. 'Competitive City-regionalism as a Politics of Space: A Critical Reinterpretation of the New Regionalism', *Environment and Planning A*, 36(12): 2119–139.

Weinstein, L. 2009. 'Democracy in the Globalizing Indian City: Engagements of Political Society and the State in Globalizing Mumbai', *Politics & Society*, 37(3): 397–427.

Chapter 4

The Politics of Persuasion

Gendered Slum Citizenship in Neoliberal Mumbai

Sapana Doshi

As Mumbai's elites embark on projects of redevelopment, thousands of informal 'slum' residents are facing eviction on a massive scale. While bourgeois visions of urban transformation have progressed at the expense of the majority of the urban poor, slum clearances have not been advanced in a simply authoritarian fashion. Land and housing struggles have generated new and often contradictory articulations of citizenship, where slum dwellers themselves have negotiated and facilitated elite-biased redevelopment interventions. This essay ethnographically examines the citizenship discourses and mobilization processes of slum dwellers displaced by a state-led, World Bank-funded infrastructure expansion project, the Mumbai Urban Transport Project (MUTP). With the assistance of a non-governmental organization (NGO), slum-based leaders and project-affected residents collectively mobilized to facilitate the clearance and resettlement of their own neighbourhoods. Gendered discourses and women slum dwellers' participation played an especially important role in enabling cooperation under tense political circumstances. I argue that an examination of the gendered discourses of citizenship and the micro-political processes and material outcomes of this resettlement project reveals the inequalities and limitations of participatory movements.

While recent scholarship has explored examples of citizen mobilization in working class neighbourhoods of post-colonial cities, several key silences suggest the usefulness of critical geographical perspectives. First is the minimal attention given to social differentiation within slum spaces and among slum dwellers. While concepts such as 'insurgent citizenship' (Holston 2008), 'political society' (Chatterjee 2004), and 'deep democracy' (Appadurai 2002) offer important insights into urban social movements, they tend to theorize movements of the urban poor in terms of singular groupings based on class or housing conditions. Even when acknowledging diversity and the influential participation of groups such as women, they underplay the significant role that difference plays in consolidations of power and rule in projects of neoliberal urban transformation. As this ethnographic study shows, spatially produced, overlapping, and hierarchical axes of difference—including gender, ethnicity, and class—fundamentally shape slum dwellers' political subjectivities and governance practices. Such attention to difference is not meant to simply highlight a complex multitude of subject positionalities. Rather, I argue that strategic, spatialized 'couplings of power and difference' (Hall [1992] in Gilmore [2002]) reveal the connections between citizenship practices and broader political economic agendas.

This leads to the second major silence in much of the Third World urban citizenship literature: an analysis of whether and how movements enable or challenge globalized, market-oriented projects of urban transformation. As Nikolas Rose (2000) has argued, modern 'citizenship games'—the rules that define the conduct of citizens—correspond to advanced liberal rationalities of governing societies and political economies. Citizens and private groups take on increased responsibilities as public social welfare resources are curtailed and scepticism about state capacity abounds. As this essay shows, for instance, understandings of citizenship come not only through direct interaction with the state but also through the mediation of NGOs. The actions and discourses of displaced slums dwellers and their representative entities have followed, but also inflected neoliberal rationalities of community and individual responsibility. However, the meaning and actions associated with citizenship have not been constituted through plays of neoliberal logics alone; they are contingent on the political specificities of time and space. It may be useful to think of slum-based mobilizations as 'citizenship formations' (Marston and Mitchell 2004), wherein understandings of self and community and related forms of actions derive from specific histories of local land struggle.

This essay argues that differentiated spatial productions of citizenship and community forged under conditions of large-scale displacement have, in many instances, facilitated slum dwellers' cooperation with elite-biased and market-oriented redevelopment projects. The MUTP case shows how participatory gendered citizenship has harnessed new configurations of community solidarity, while it has also advanced and elided deepening inequalities among the displaced along lines of both class and gender. By exploring the gendered tropes and material processes of cooperative community mobilization, this essay seeks to understand the rocky politico-ethical trajectory of neoliberal urbanization. A brief contextualization of the emergence of

⸌liberal slum redevelopment as a paradigm and practice will situate the subsequent ethnographic case study.

MAKING REDEVELOPMENT SPACE: NEOLIBERALISM IN SLUM POLICY AND POLITICS

While real estate development and evictions are not new to Mumbai, neoliberal practices shaping slum redevelopment have yielded significant changes in city politics. We may characterize these developments as neoliberal because of three key features. First, economic liberalization and deeper integration with global markets at the urban and national scale in the 1990s dramatically augmented real estate values, concentrations of wealth, and political pressures to enclose public spaces through slum clearances. Second, the distribution of compensation for eviction harnessed the profit motives of local real estate developers through new market-oriented policies. While state agencies regulated such projects, funding no longer came from public coffers. Third, local municipal government structures and party patronage politics have ceased to serve as the slum dwellers' sole channel of access to the state. Non-governmental organizations have increasingly begun to mediate relations between the state and the urban poor. Thus, neoliberal redevelopment has not only expanded opportunities for urban accumulation but also dramatically reworked the relationship between the state and slum dwellers. Research on 'actually existing neoliberalisms' in the European and North American context addresses similar patterns of urban and city-region governance, but the critical political and cultural dimensions that shape development trajectories are less well explored (Brenner and Theodore 2002; Leitner, Peck, and Sheppard 2007). The Mumbai case demonstrates that the privatization of governance alters urban spaces, populations, and eviction politics in significant ways. The emergence and specificities of new slum redevelopment policies will illustrate these points further.

In 1995, the regionalist and Hindu nationalist Shiv Sena–BJP coalition of parties entered into power in the state of Maharashtra riding on an ambitious campaign promise to the Mumbai electorate: to provide free formal flats to 4 million slum dwellers in the city. Upon its victory, the coalition established the Slum Redevelopment Authority (SRA), which introduced three major changes to slum policy. First, resettlement housing would be guaranteed for all slum and pavement dwellers displaced by redevelopment projects who could prove residency in Mumbai prior to 1 January 1995. Slum dwellers who failed to furnish proof of residency prior to this 'cut-off date' were to be quite literally cut-off from compensation upon demolition.[1] Second, resettlement compensation would be financed entirely by the market; SRA would offer incentives to private developers to build tenements for slum dwellers free of cost in exchange for coveted transfers of development rights (TDR) to build taller buildings throughout the city. Finally, all other public housing and slum improvement schemes were to be phased out and replaced entirely by SRA.

Though it is outside of the scope of this paper to thoroughly discuss the development ramifications of the SRA's neoliberal mandates, a few key outcomes are worth emphasizing. The SRA policy not only expanded the role of the private sector in low-income housing construction but also dramatically multiplied the availability of space for market-rate development because displacement compensation itself became lucrative for developers by creating a vigorous market for transferable development rights. The freed slum land in combination with transferable development rights to build more densely in high-value neighbourhoods was a boon to real estate and infrastructure developers involved in state-sanctioned slum redevelopment projects. Though benefits to developers far outpaced benefits to other parties, SRA's high-density development model has been showcased for other Indian cities as a win-win strategy for 'tax-paying citizens', the state, and slum dwellers (Mukhija 2003).

The SRA consolidated a number of interconnected processes including the rising role of NGOs, the rapid expansion of real estate and infrastructure development, the changing role of the state as a facilitator of the market, anti-migrant and anti-Muslim xenophobia, and increasing elite desires for a slum-free city. While SRA compensates qualified slum dwellers displaced by redevelopment projects, thousands of 'unqualified' slum dwellers are excluded from legal entitlement to compensation. Such eligibility exclusions combined with the pressures of rapid high-end development and state-sponsored demolition sweeps have severely squeezed affordable housing supplies.

Displaced slum dwellers who have qualified for compensation have increasingly relied on NGOs and community leaders to implement resettlement processes and assure fair compensation and protection from the bullying of private developers and state agencies. The MUTP is one example of an NGO-mediated participatory resettlement project in which a non-confrontational form of gendered participation contributed to cooperation in evicted communities. Through harnessing a particular form of gendered citizenship, participatory resettlement politically enabled, to a limit, the relatively smooth implementation of mass slum clearance.

ICIPATORY RESETTLEMENT AND THE MUMBAI URBAN
ANSPORT PROJECT

With over 20,000 project-affected households, MUTP is among the world's largest World Bank-funded urban resettlement projects and has been deemed a model for peaceful and participatory slum clearance and resettlement for more than a decade. The project consisted of railroad infrastructure expansion, road construction, and residential and commercial resettlement and rehabilitation ('R&R') financed jointly by the World Bank and the Government of India at a cost of over US$1 billion. Although the loan was made to the central government, the Bank managed and administered both the infrastructural and resettlement and rehabilitation components directly with a local parastatal entity linked to the State of Maharashtra: the Mumbai Metropolitan Region Development Authority (MMRDA).

Given the fact that past government slum clearance and redevelopment projects entailed very limited, haphazard, and patronage-driven resettlement, the World Bank insisted on universal compensation of all 'project-affected people' (PAP) regardless of tenure status. Bank resettlement policies reflected earlier experiences with public outcry over involuntary displacement in its development projects such as the Narmada Dam. Accordingly, Bank loan conditionalities required the local state implementing agency, the MMRDA, to expand its categories of qualification for compensation and revise its procedures for slum clearance. Thus, the MUTP resettlement policy reflected a compromise between State of Maharashtra slum redevelopment norms and World Bank loan conditionalities. The State of Maharashtra expanded its categories of compensation to include more (though not all) of the displaced according to World Bank mandates. However, resettlement units would still be financed mostly through the market-oriented SRA model, relying almost entirely on profit motives of participating private developers. For slum dwellers located in environmentally sensitive areas or along roads, railways, and other transport infrastructure, resettlement would be off-site in mass-constructed low-cost units on the urban fringes of the city.[2] Under MUTP, transfers of development rights, in addition to access to the 10 per cent of project funds allocated by the Bank for resettlement, resulted in high profits for participating local developers. However, the impact on evictees was more mixed.

The most publicized aspect of the MUTP was its unique participatory resettlement model. The massive scale of resettlement and the political nature of the project required working with a great number of slum communities along railway tracks and in the path of proposed road projects.

Thus, MUTP was negotiated to incorporate a partnership model wherein MMRDA contracted a local NGO, Society for the Promotion of Area Resource Centres (SPARC), to undertake community-level resettlement tasks including baseline socio-economic surveys, slum maps, and the formation of building cooperative societies. Society for the Promotion of Area Resource Centres was chosen for its good relationship with the state and its working relationships with two slum-based organizations, the National Slum Dwellers Federation and Mahila Milan (a coalition of women slum dwellers), collectively called the Alliance. Over the last 20 years, the Alliance has gained recognition and influence through developing a non-partisan and non-confrontational manner of negotiating with the state and slum dwellers (especially women). The following section provides a brief history of SPARC's gendered form of neighbourhood-based community organization and its work with the state.

THE 'POLITICS OF PATIENCE' AND THE ORIGINS OF GENDERED NON-CONFRONTATIONAL CITIZENSHIP

> What is the quality of woman? Woman is money. Woman is information. Woman is communication.... For me these are the basic ingredients of development.... [In] India you name woman as Laxmi. Who is the Laxmi? [In] any common house, how to change your son's behavior? Bring a Laxmi, he will change.... The daughter-in-law comes to the house and he will change. Otherwise he won't change. (A. Jockin, interview with author, 15 December 2007)

A. Jockin, quoted above, is one of the most famous slum community leaders in the world, the male head of the National Slum Dwellers Federation in India, and a key leader of the SPARC Alliance. In describing the role of the women slum dwellers of Mahila Milan in the Alliance, Jockin is echoing a well-known women-in-development mantra. From the World Bank to local NGOs, mainstream development agents extol the virtues of Third World women's participation as key to creating a positive change at the grassroots level. However, well-known critiques from critical development studies (Hart 2001; Mohan and Stokke 2000), urban studies (Miraftab 2004; Roy 2002), and transnational feminist theory (Mohanty 2003) have deconstructed the empowerment thesis of women's participation in development. Others have exposed the 'tyrannical' potential of local communities (Cooke and Kothari 2001; Hickey and Mohan 2004), which often reinforce structural inequalities. In many of these views, participation serves as a neoliberal political strategy for transferring the burden of a shrinking welfare state onto NGOs, communities, and, ultimately, the bodies of working-class women.

Yet, the quote above illustrates a less explored aspect of women in development: the participating woman's moral authority to transform the way development is done. Jockin invokes commonly held Hindu cultural representations of women in the family and extends them to society and development more broadly. A woman's role in the household is likened to that of the goddess of wealth and prosperity, Laxmi. She represents an auspicious contribution to the family and thus has moral authority to change the behaviour of the men around her. Jockin playfully explained that women are the essence of developmental information and communication because it is the housewife who spends her time observing and gossiping about the status and social dynamics of everyone in the family and neighbourhood. Upon asking Jockin to explain women's association with money in light of the fact that men still often control family wealth, his response is again playfully provocative: though the man of the house may control the money, it is the woman who understands where to use it and can indirectly control how the man spends it. 'Men have no idea what to do with their money and must always ask the wife.... [The woman] is in control,' he explained. In this rendering, the daughter-in-law's power—unlike that of the Goddess—comes from her auspiciousness, social role, and culturally ascribed moral authority, which are not necessarily associated with direct power over family wealth.

As we continued our conversation, Jockin advanced the claim that the participation of women in development projects extends beyond the family into the spaces of relations with the state as well as community social dynamics. The role of women in Alliance activities has consisted of ritualized practices of savings, community mobilization, information collection, and engaging with agents of the state in a non-confrontational manner. Arjun Appadurai (2002) has described these women-centred practices as 'the moral core of the politics of patience'. He argues that this is a politics that privileges a gradual path to the social and economic advancement of the poorest by avoiding threatening of the state and its base of power while also preventing co-optation and patronage by political parties. The Alliance leadership has also stressed the importance of a slow and steady mode of negotiation as the principle means of empowerment through increasing the visibility and legitimacy of slum dwellers in urban development policy.

The Alliance's community participation approach and engagement with the state began in the early 1980s with its initial work with women 'pavement dwellers' living on the precarious sidewalks of southeast

Mumbai—the women who originally formed Mahila Milan. Pavement dwellers have historically been among the poorest and most marginalized groups in the city, suffering repeated demolition of their homes. Society for the Promotion of Area Resource Centres assembled and disseminated information collected by the women of Mahila Milan in a landmark written work titled 'We the Invisible', which documented data on work and living conditions of pavement dwellers in the Byculla area of Mumbai, who were repeatedly evicted by city authorities. The document was distributed to evicting authorities to dispel myths of criminality in official state discourse and to cast light on pavement dwellers' lives as very poor day workers with no other choice but to live on the streets.

The SPARC leaders contrasted their pragmatic strategy with other more confrontational forms of protests. They argued against the confrontational, 'rights-based' strategy dominated in their view by middle-class advocates who often do not understand the needs of the poor. The SPARC prologue to Mitlin and Patel's (2005) paper asserted:

> Well-meaning middle class [leaders]…did not consult the pavement dwellers whose cause they espoused. Had they bothered to do so, they would have been told that pavements were the last places where these people wanted to live in—places without water, sanitation, and electricity, and exposed to inclement weather and the hazards of traffic. The people wanted to be resettled in proper housing with secure tenure.

Another SPARC publication, 'From Demolitions to Dialogue' (year unavailable),[3] connected the cooperative strategy directly to the women of Mahila Milan. Referring to the anti-eviction actions of NGOs and community-based organizations in the mid-1980s, the document recounted that 'women [pavement dwellers]…had a different perspective and did not want confrontation'.

These quotes exhibit two important discursive elements. First, rights talk and confrontation were positioned squarely as 'middle-class' tactics foreign to the poor.[4] However, as the subsequent discussion of the MUTP resettlement demonstrates, the eschewal of rights talk did not mean that the ideals of modern citizenship were absent in community organizing in SPARC-led and other mobilizations. Second, cooperative negotiation was relegated to the domain of women as a naturalized response to the experience of eviction. The SPARC Alliance discourse consistently claimed that poor women were more inclined to cooperating and finding solutions than fighting for an abstract set of rights. This discourse thus elided the possibility of a diversity of political strategies among the poor, with cooperation

(margin annotations: SPARC on rights (contra))

and protest mapping respectively onto dichotomies of 'poor' versus 'middle class' and 'women' versus 'men'. Non-confrontation was systematically cultivated as a pragmatic strategy at all levels of the SPARC Alliance. Non-confrontation thus became a principle facet of the 'politics of patience' which emerged and evolved over years of multi-sited struggles to promote the visibility of pavement and slum dwellers and the precariousness of their housing conditions.

The SPARC Alliance leaders regularly recount one almost legendary event as both the origin and quintessential example of the non-confrontational approach. It consisted of the novel and subversive approach taken by women pavement dwellers of Mahila Milan during an impending demolition drive of their homes. Instead of confronting the police and bulldozers, the women decided to kindly offer tea and biscuits to the men in order to negotiate a less destructive solution. They asked the men to wait while they 'helped them' by disassembling their homes themselves thereby saving their precious and few belongings. Another legendary story is of slum-based Muslim women leaders offering *rakhi*s as a symbolic appeal to their powerful 'brothers' in state agencies to protect them from homelessness.[5] Evictees and volunteers interpreted such strategies in diverse ways. For instance, one Mahila Milan member I interviewed claimed that 'no one in the government is really afraid of a bunch of women', but there was still a certain moral obligation; 'When a woman asks "brother please help me", he has to fulfil her request.'

Perhaps even more profound is the manner in which the non-confrontational mode of negotiation both implicitly and explicitly linked into a pro-development position. In public discourse for instance, Mahila Milan and the SPARC Alliance leaders repeatedly claim that the communities are not interested in fighting development and that slum dwellers just want a decent place to live in the city. It is in this manner that I argue that pro-development cooperation was grounded in the SPARC Alliance's non-confrontational strategy of negotiation. Mahila Milan activities and organizational tropes have maintained the non-confrontational ethos that has facilitated cooperation with redevelopment programmes of state bureaucracies, elected officials, real estate developers, transnational development organizations, and the World Bank. Collaboration with other city groups has expanded this participatory model.

In the late1980s, SPARC and Mahila Milan entered into partnership with the National Slum Dwellers Federation (NSDF), led by the world-renowned A. Jockin. The coming together of these groups occupies a legendary status in SPARC presentations and documents. In public speeches and meetings, Jockin has often described the merging of NSDF and SPARC as a marriage between a predominantly male slum dwellers' federation and the female-headed NGO, resulting in the auspicious birth of a 'girl child'— the emergence and proliferation of the Mahila Milan federation of women slum dwellers. The three groups are now collectively known as the SPARC Alliance in many local and international development circles. The SPARC Alliance leaders have often described the union of these groups as a transformative process where slum dwellers' participation has been channeled for community empowerment and habitat improvement. In an interview with the author, Jockin explained that the work of the NSDF was completely limited before it joined forces with SPARC and substantively included women through Mahila Milan.[6] The NSDF, in his view, had hit a wall where protest and confrontation against the government was achieving very limited results. Women were able to penetrate state bureaucracies because officials could not engage them in the same way as male slum-based leaders. 'I observed how quiet and articulate they were,' he recalled, adding that 'the male-dominated bureaucracy reacted differently to women'. He explained that bureaucrats could not just buy the women off with bribes and drinks but were forced to answer their questions. Furthermore, they were less threatened by women's requests than by the sometimes militant strategy of the men of NSDF.

The SPARC Alliance's strength has not been limited to its 'civil society' roots with women and men slum dwellers. It also may be argued that the global recognition of the Alliance has bolstered its privileged position with respect to the state. The SPARC Alliance's linkage with mainstream development institutions through the transnational Slum and Shack Dwellers International (SDI), the Cities Alliance, and the World Bank has arguably strengthened its sway over government officials (Appadurai 2002) even if its relations with other Mumbai-based NGOs and community groups were sometimes strained. The combination of state and grassroots connection indicates the critical intermediary role that the Alliance has played in slum governance practices. Both women's participation and linkages to the state yielded a supportive base for later large-scale redevelopment efforts such as the MUTP.

Community strategies of negotiation have also been significantly strengthened by the influential involvement of former bureaucrats of the Indian Administrative Services (IAS) in the Alliance's NGO arm. For instance, the MUTP resettlement model was formulated in conjunction with SPARC's key bureaucratic contacts in the IAS. Also, the popular support of SPARC through its affiliation with slum-based organizations such as NSDF and Mahila Milan has fortified its relationships with political parties and bureaucratic agencies. The extent of SPARC's good relationship with the state was evident in the fact that it was the only representative of slum dwellers invited to attend the SRA negotiations during the Shiv Sena government in 1995. In an interview, Sheela Patel, the Executive Director of SPARC, recalled that many of the city's NGO leaders were critical of her organization's involvement with the violent and exclusionary nativist and Hindu-nationalist politics of the Shiv Sena, the party that had instigated some of the bloodiest ethno-religious riots in the city in 1994.[7] She explained that she was compelled to participate by Jockin of the NSDF, who 'pushed SPARC to go beyond its middle-class role' and represent the interests of the urban poor.

Society for the Promotion of Area Resource Centres's role in the state-sponsored committee served to promote greater inclusion in slum rehabilitation policy, such as securing resettlement eligibility for 25,000 pavement dwellers and insisting that women's names be listed in resettlement unit titles. As a trade-off, however, the same negotiations also instated eligibility exclusions that subsequently resulted in mass demolitions of several hundred thousand informal structures without resettlement compensation in 2005. Furthermore, local developers maintained a strong foothold in the SRA policy, benefiting from lucrative development rights through their participation. The pro-development stance of SPARC involved not confronting the developers' lobby but instead advocating for compromise solutions. In my concluding sections, I will address some of the contentious politics and uneven geographies of eviction resulting from these compromise solutions.

Aside from these relations with the state and local and transnational agents of development, the SPARC Alliance practices of grassroots organization and gendered participation constituted a significant source of political strength and claim to legitimacy for the NGO. These mobilizational practices were adopted and expanded under the MUTP participatory resettlement, yielding a significantly different set of outcomes, however. With MUTP, the politics of patience and redevelopmental cooperation spatialized and morphed to produce not only new gendered citizenship formations but also influential reworkings of notions of community.

FROM PATIENCE TO PERSUASION: MUTP AND THE PRODUCTION OF COMMUNITY IN TRANSITION

With the launching of MUTP in the late 1990s, the rapid removal of slums and peaceful relocation of slum dwellers emerged as the principal governmental objective for the various state and non-governmental agents involved. Accordingly, the SPARC Alliance model of gendered participation was directed into different political arenas as new practical and political problems emerged out of the processes of mass relocation. Problems converged on how such a large and dispersed population of slum dwellers would be engaged to facilitate their own relocation within the prevailing paradigms of development and compensation established by the state and World Bank. This required more extensive ethico-political and practical work with displaced slum dwellers as a collectivity.

Accordingly, slum-based participation was also reoriented. If previous gendered 'citizenship games' engaged directly with state agents (with NGO assistance), the MUTP resettlement steered the actions and meanings of citizenship towards a more immediate collectivized identity: that of the community. The women of Mahila Milan involved in MUTP focused their attention squarely on mobilizing 'communities' to address the practical and political problems of efficient slum resettlement. In the process, I argue, the quiet 'politics of patience' transformed into a practice of facilitating cooperation within the community. I call this the politics of persuasion. Understanding this shift requires an examination of a key facet of the MUTP, the participatory resettlement model, and its inevitably uneven implementation.

The participatory resettlement model of SPARC showcased three principal elements: (*a*) a voluntary and conflict-free relocation of slum dwellers; (*b*) the participation of slum dwellers, especially women, in information collection and input on design and location of resettlement units; and (*c*) resettlement resulting in improved quality of life. The model was based on the experience of previous participatory activities in which SPARC Alliance leaders mobilized neighbourhood leaders and residents to help the NGO staff in the process of household surveying and slum mapping (Burra 1999; Patel et al. 2002).

The adoption of the model had very mixed outcomes in different locations and times, especially between the initial and later phases of the MUTP project. Despite difficulties and delays, slum-based leaders and re-settled residents involved in earlier and smaller scale phases of the project expressed a fair level of satisfaction with the processes and outcomes. Slum dwellers were informed and organized into committees well before state demolition squads arrived, and resettlement proceeded without a great degree of conflict. In many instances, women helped to facilitate relocation through participating in slum mapping and surveying, processes that helped to promote trust in the resettling neighbourhoods. Though stays in transit camps were long and arduous, many of the displaced slum dwellers were relocated close to their former neighbourhoods (Sharma 2003). Mahila Milan women also helped garner sustained cooperation by addressing neighbourhood social and environmental concerns during long and difficult stays in transit camps. Later, they facilitated maintenance activities within the cooperative building society (Burra 1999).

Though the participatory model continued to represent the MUTP experience in international and local development circles, few of the subsequent rounds of demolition and resettlement followed its main steps. The demands of the state implementing agency (MMRDA) and anti-slum sentiments of middle-class residents of the city led to rapid court-ordered demolitions in 2000 that strained the participatory process. As the scale and pace of the project expanded into other parts of the city, subsequent evictions were characterized by sudden demolition, involuntary and distant relocation, and long waits in harsh transit camp environments.

Interview data collected among more recently resettled residents revealed several inconsistencies with the participatory model. During the 2001 court-ordered Harbous Line Railways eviction, for instance, the NGO arm of the SPARC Alliance was only notified to administer resettlement after demolitions took place. Evicted slum dwellers began staging riots and railway line blockades. One woman, Asha, who later joined Mahila Milan, likened the demolition to an explosively violent scene from *Bombay*, a highly political Bollywood film about Hindu–Muslim communal riots in the city during the early 1990s: 'People were charging the police with sticks and setting fires on the train tracks.' Though the Alliance sanctioned the blockade (Patel et al. 2002), Asha recounted, Mahila Milan leaders nonetheless later explained that such tactics were 'wrong'. 'Before, we did not know how to behave, always fighting. Now we are improved,' Asha explained. Several other resettled residents relayed their experience of camping out on the cleared railways slum site for up to eight months before moving into the transit camp site. In other cases, slum dwellers were brought into contact with the Alliance less than two weeks before the demolition to quickly facilitate movement into transit camps.

At the time of eviction, many of the evicted slum dwellers attempted to appeal to ward politicians who had served as their main channel of connection to the state. In prior years, such officials offered protection from demolition and basic services in exchange for electoral support. Now, however, ward politicians, with virtually no access to the workings of large-scale projects, directed slum dwellers to their new connection to the state, the SPARC Alliance. This non-governmental entity thus became the organizing structure of resettlement governance and linkage to state power when slum dwellers no longer had recourse for negotiating with municipal government.

The circulating image of the participatory model thus did not match the experience of the large majority of subsequent MUTP evictions. Nonetheless, the ideal of non-confrontation and community organization and leadership played a critical role. Under the pressures of rapid slum removal and resettlement on the cheap, Mahila Milan leaders from earlier rounds of resettlement were recruited to train women leaders among the newly evicted to participate in various relocation and rehabilitation activities. In the process, participants helped to redeploy and adapt the 'politics of patience' towards the politics of persuasion and cooperation in addressing the problems of resettlement. For instance, as I demonstrate below, Mahila Milan women helped to harness community solidarity and morale by articulating gendered idioms of entitlement through patience. The ethos of non-confrontation did not emerge in the realm of discourse alone. Formative spatial experiences helped to mould new moral paradigms of citizenship and community.

In particular, the transit camp offers an especially revealing site for examining how the 'politics of patience' spatialized and advanced community solidarity and cooperation. The transit camp was an important space of community organizing because the majority of the resettled railway line dwellers spent a significant length of time there even if they had little or no prior history of working with the SPARC Alliance. Project-evicted families lived in transit camp accommodations for as long as five to seven years between slum demolition and resettlement. Uniformly, people look back on their time in the camps as one of extreme hardship, inhuman conditions, and deep suffering—among the worst periods of their lives. Many of these high-density camps lacked water and sanitation and were prone to monsoon flooding. Residents complained of increased incidences of illness and death due to the lack of clean water, pests, and toxic fumes from a nearby chemical plant and adjacent garbage dumps.

In this space of transition and hardship, women volunteers had regular contact with families. Original Mahila Milan leaders trained other women in the transit camps to form savings schemes as a means of not only improving economic security but also as a way to maintain close ties with community members. They made visits to the camps to follow up on the activities and help new members to address problems. New Mahila Milan leaders and other evictees were also invited to assembly meetings with NSDF leaders including A. Jockin. The majority of the attendees were women who recalled how NSDF and Mahila Milan leaders would relay the Alliance philosophy of participation, non-confrontation, and progress to the participants. They explained the virtues of community cooperation, joint savings and the need for slum dwellers to improve their housing and sanitation situation. One resident recalled that at community meetings, Alliance leaders 'explained to us that the railways was not the right place for us to live, that it was government land and that we needed to progress and move into a better, permanent place'. Another interviewee recounted that when residents confronted the Alliance with complaints of resettlement difficulties, leaders would explain the value of the life improvements they would achieve in their lives. Jockin would often scold residents for the complaints, explaining that improvements to life through resettlement—including environmental sanitation, infrastructure, and the sense of legitimacy of living in formal housing—would require cooperation and patience. 'He kept telling us that before we were living in filth and that he was trying to get us to understand how to come out of it and live a better life,' a resident recalled.

New Mahila Milan members and leaders became involved in a variety of activities in the transit camps. Members explained to me that there were four committees in which women residents could participate. These committees were formed under the guidance of other Mahila Milan and NSDF leaders during the period of stay in the transit camps and continue to exist in the resettlement colonies today. One was a 'finance committee' which organized the communal savings programme. Activities included daily collections of savings contributions throughout the camp or colony and making decisions regarding loan distributions. Another was the 'BMC committee', which dealt with issues of environmental management (garbage collection, water service, and so on).[8] The third committee was the 'police panchayat', which dealt with issues of conflict management in slums and resettlement colonies in liaison with the local police. Finally, the 'management committee' assisted with various administrative issues in the compound. In the transit camps, and later in the resettlement colonies, the activities of these committees were geared towards what many members described as community and individual progress for a better life. Progress consisted of moving away from the unhygienic and precarious ways that slum dwellers were used to living. These values were reinforced in large meetings where Alliance leaders would motivate newer members to change their lives and the lives of those around them.

Such everyday and special occasion interactions reinforced the Mahila Milan members' efforts to address the challenges of resettlement and advance the Alliance philosophy of community progress and cooperation in interactions with other residents. Building community awareness and solidarity was not easy under the dire conditions of transit camp life, as several members admitted. One Mahila Milan leader recalled facing distressed and enraged mobs of residents complaining of living conditions in transit camps as being far worse than what they suffered in the slums and fearing that the resettlement flats would never materialize.

In addressing such outbreaks and other problems, women volunteers repeatedly used one word to express the work they would do: *samjhana*. As they described it, *samjhana* consisted of patiently 'persuading' others to cooperate during trying times, 'explaining' the processes of resettlement or 'making them understand' the situation at hand. *Samjhana* also connoted a slow and painstaking process of dealing with diverse strong personalities. In various South Asian cultural narratives, women are positioned as the more flexible gender, naturally more understanding and tolerant of difficult situations. It is precisely a woman's non-complaining, suffering, and self-sacrificing nature that makes her virtuous. Women and men leaders involved in the MUTP resettlement activities regularly referred to this gendered stereotype. In being more understanding, patient, and self-sacrificing for the good of the community, Mahila Milan leaders and members expressed that they had what they deemed to be a natural proclivity and duty to impart understanding and patience to the community at large. In this way, Mahila Milan women worked with the SPARC leadership towards softening the sting of eviction and transit camp conditions that may otherwise have been interpreted as a raw deal.

The collective memory of transit camp experience also had a distinctly gendered character reminiscent of idioms of long and 'silent' suffering of dutiful wives and mothers celebrated in diverse cultural narratives throughout Indian society. One male leader even used the analogy of a wife covering her mouth to silence her own screams while being beaten by her husband to describe how slum dwellers endured the treatment of the government during the transit camp days. In this manner, entitlement, patience, and suffering were articulated in the lived experiences of the transit camps. The gendered discourses and participation helped to stem dissent and garner cooperation under highly adverse circumstances.

As it promoted solidarity, patience, and suffering, such gendered tropes of community and citizenship also established several exclusionary divisions. One hierarchical sentiment fostered in the transit camp experience was a sense of entitlement based on seniority. For example, in discussions with resettlement colony residents in 2007 who gained access to flats after years of transit camp suffering, I observed a marked disdain for newly resettled residents. Because resettlement structures were built en masse, there were extra buildings built to resettle new rounds of evicted residents affected by the MUTP and other state-sponsored slum clearance projects. Some newly evicted slum dwellers were resettled directly into the apartment buildings without being required to stay in a transit camp beforehand. One irate Mahila Milan volunteer exclaimed, 'They did not suffer the way we did for so many years in the transit camp. We should get the best apartments and they have no right to complain.'

Similarly, when asked about their thoughts on recent mass uncompensated demolition drives of more recently settled slums (in Mumbai, but unrelated to MUTP), residents' opinions diverged. Some sympathized with the evictees while others felt the demolitions were justified. Among the latter group, one resettlement colony resident exclaimed, 'I understand what government thinks. It cannot keep giving housing to everyone. We have been here suffering for years. We deserve this room. Why should the new people have such an easy time?' These observations point to divisions embedded in the articulation of patience and entitlement within and beyond the MUTP project. Such divisions have contributed to instabilities in and resistances to slum redevelopments, an issue that I will address in later sections.

The community-mindedness of Alliance activities and discourse was not mutually exclusive with the strategic use of participation for self-advancement. For some members, participation in Mahila Milan opened the space for negotiating better resettlement from the Alliance leadership. It was common for the most seasoned and powerful leaders—women and men—to receive first choice of flats and even extra rooms. But less powerful members also found a space for negotiation. For example, one Mahila Milan member, Uma, recounted her long battle to correct a misallocation of flats that left her married daughter without her rightful room.[9] She would spend several hours per day over many weeks at the transit camp office, grandchildren in tow, trying to persuade SPARC Alliance staff to resolve her issue. Uma observed that not everyone had the time or capacity to confront a faulty or unfair flat allocation, like her daughters who worked all day as domestic workers. She also expressed adamantly the need to 'speak loudly' or face the possibility of getting marginalized in the resettlement process. This remark indicated that gendered participation was not always docile. However, as Uma explained, those who are 'not used to' persistent or rowdy complaining would not be able to confront the administrators to address such mistakes. She laughed as she recounted that she taught her daughters to be rude and even curse like men when necessary. The effects of gendered participation thus were not singular. Women instrumentalized their participation in Mahila Milan for various ends. The following sections will elucidate further the meaning and experience of gendered participation and the resettlement process, especially as they fostered inequalities and difference among residents.

ENTREPRENEURS, HOUSEWIVES, LABOURERS: GENDERED HIERARCHIES OF SLUM CITIZENSHIP

If community participation enabled cooperation with resettlement, it also reworked gender roles in contradictory ways, simultaneously empowering participants but also sharpening inequalities among evictees. However, public discourses on the positive gender impacts of resettlement have generally elided such disparities among women and across resettlement populations. For instance, an independent impact evaluation report commissioned by the World Bank highlighted environmental infrastructure as the greatest benefit accrued to project-affected families, especially for women (Tata Institute for Social Sciences 2007). For over 10 years, SPARC Alliance members and leaders have similarly confirmed the gendered advantages to piped water and toilet facilities (Bapat and Agarwal 2003). While the independent impact evaluation also reported increased work commute times and costs due to the distance of resettlement sites, locational concerns were understood to primarily impact men. However, my ethnographic findings demonstrate a more complex story revealing highly uneven experiences among resettled women. To this end, I argue that the gendered readings of resettlement impacts emerged from an incomplete understanding of women as 'housewives' affected primarily by social reproduction concerns. Both the impact survey and Alliance discourses were silent on the experiences of women engaged in wage labour and other income-generating activities.

The 'housewifization' of women is not new or unique to the discourses of participation and resettlement. Since the 1980s, transnational feminist critiques have chided male-centred development projects for dangerously omitting or underestimating women's work in both productive and reproductive labour (Mies 1998). Yet, the MUTP case demonstrates the discursive repercussions of the domestication of women's roles in the Alliance's participatory resettlement model. Women's empowerment itself was conflated with participation in and access to the reproductive dimensions of housing, namely environmental services and shelter. This partial analytical lens in both developmental impact assessments and Alliance discourse has not only tended towards a homogenized understanding of resettled women's experience, but has also read the cooperative participatory process as an outgrowth of positive impacts. Indeed, as Jockin often exclaims, slum dwellers do not want to live in slums and are happy to move to resettlement flats. Furthermore, the naturalization of women's volunteer community work—as an extension of household social reproductive roles—has privileged the involvement of women with more leisure time and resources. Women with greater household labour responsibilities or those engaged in wage labour and place-specific piecemeal production work simply could not afford to take up positions within the Alliance. Herein lies the key to what appears in fact to be a deepening of inequalities resulting from the resettlement processes. Ethnographic data elucidates these widening disparities among residents as they are experienced along axes of gender and class difference.

Through the hierarchical channels of participation, a small number of Mahila Milan's key leaders have been able to redirect this domesticated positioning, launching lucrative new business ventures in slum-based construction contracting. In a citywide gathering of Mahila Milan leaders, I spoke with a broad range of women involved in the MUTP and other projects. Leena, an important Mahila Milan leader, explained the difference her involvement in the early rounds of MUTP resettlement had made in her life. Leena was clearly a seasoned interviewee who has represented the SPARC Alliance in many cities and international development venues. Using the terminology of micro-enterprise development, she described how her business grew from a small food-stuffs shop earning less than US$20 per month to contracts totalling more than US$300,000. Through her work with SPARC, Leena has won several state contracts to build slum public toilets and small-scale resettlement buildings all over the country. 'Women know a little bit about construction because of working at home and making household repairs; I also learned about construction supplies from my brother-in-law,' she explained. Juggling business-related cell phone calls and interactions with other members, Leena recalled that it was Jockin and the SPARC Alliance who guided her into success. She continues to engage in Mahila Milan's volunteer activities locally as well as in SPARC transnational NGO exchange events.

The Mahila Milan gathering also revealed unequal relations among members of Mahila Milan. As I spoke with Leena, I observed that the other members greeted each other by name but greeted her and two other women as 'madam', signalling a recognized difference in class among the members. Indeed, the dream of success through participation, saving, and work was not realized uniformly. There were marked class hierarchies in the coalition of women forming Mahila Milan despite the Alliance's egalitarian discourse of community participation. Yet, the implications of such hierarchies go beyond the simple enriching of a few Mahila Milan women over many others. Mahila Milan leaders regularly privilege their roles as housewives, community volunteers, and entrepreneurs working for the SPARC Alliance. Rarely did discussions concerning wage-labouring women emerge in official meeting spaces. Indeed, there was little room in the structure and discourse of participation to address such concerns. Discussions with women in the MUTP resettlement colonies revealed some of these implications.

I spent a morning with Rani, a former member of Mahila Milan, accompanying her on her daily commute from the Mankhurd resettlement site to work as a domestic servant in the central Matunga area of the city where she used to live. Normally Rani is awake before 5 a.m., preparing the day's food and getting the children ready for school before leaving for work at 7 a.m. But for this day Rani asked her employer if she could arrive a bit later so that she could show me around. We walked down five flights of stairs to the main exit and into the dusty main throughway of the resettlement colony. Passing through block after block of resettlement buildings, then through a neighbouring slum and down a ditch, we finally arrived at the railway tracks. Along with dozens of other residents on their way to work we walked for 10 more minutes along the tracks to reach the train station. The platform was packed and Rani explained to me that the station could not handle the thousands of people being resettled in the Mankhurd area. She warned me that we may not be able to get on to the first train because of the crowd and that I should not be afraid to push my way in. After more than an hour and half on foot and train, we passed the area where her house once stood. She showed me around explaining that it used to take her only 20 minutes to walk to work. When she lived in the slum she was able to come home to cook and care for her children in between her cleaning jobs. Now her parents pick her children up from school and take care of them until she gets home in the evening. She explained that she was grateful to have a resettlement flat but lamented the effects of the distant resettlement location.

Rani had originally become involved in the Alliance's community-based resettlement activities to seek the best resettlement deal after residents came to the conclusion that there was no alternative but to move. Rani explained that she began to participate just prior to the scheduled demolition to ensure that resettlement was done properly and was located closer to their original homes. The key male leader of the slum neighbourhood had worked closely with Jockin, and they were told that the move to Lallubhai Compound in the eastern suburb of Mankhurd would be temporary; Rani had maintained hope for relocation closer to her former Matunga neighbourhood in central Mumbai. She was soon forced to quit Mahila Milan activities because of the strain of the increased workload and commute. Rani's building-neighbours had all moved together to the Mankhurd Lallubhai resettlement site (Figure 4.1) from their slum neighbourhood.

FIGURE 4.1. LALLUBHAI COMPOUND RESETTLEMENT COLONY

Source: Courtesy of Jaideep Gupte.

Several building-women recounted that they were also either commuting to their former neighbourhoods for work or had lost their jobs because they could not afford to commute and simultaneously meet their household and child-rearing responsibilities. Their experiences appear to match survey data showing that real household incomes have decreased along with an increase in the cost of living due to transportation and maintenance fees (Tata Institute for Social Sciences 2007). As one resident put it, 'What good are toilets when one can no longer eat?'

One Mahila Milan resettlement site leader, Farzana, has attempted to address the issue of lost wages for women by creating a work cooperative. When I arrived to interview her one day, a group of women were seated in a line on her small apartment floor waiting for payment for work that they had done in a SPARC food production project. Farzana had to explain to them that they would not receive the full day's wage that they had been promised for the work. As they left, she lamented to me the lack of support she received from top SPARC Alliance leaders and the Mahila Milan including Leena and Jockin. She has tried to get paid work for women in SPARC Alliance projects, but their labour is often sorely remunerated. She argued that the success of SPARC and NSDF resulted from the power of women who could 'get work done'. She has tried to get financing from Jockin for some of these activities but has not pushed her demands because she is worried about being construed as a demanding troublemaker. She argued that as the leaders of the SPARC Alliance expanded their work, they were failing to pay attention to the base of women that have long strengthened the movement. Besides the top leaders of Mahila Milan who work in the area of construction contracting, she confirmed, most women are mobilized for voluntary activities and presentation to international visitors. 'They speak of women's empowerment, but perhaps do not want too much of it,' she said.

The foregoing examples reveal the contradictions of women's participation; a small number of women have advanced socially and economically through participating in resettlement and other SPARC Alliance activities while others remain in volunteer and labouring positions. Nevertheless, many active members who continue to work as volunteers cited the honour they received through their membership. They claimed to enjoy the social aspects, the sense of growth and accomplishment of being involved in the SPARC Alliance, and learning from Jockin. It is important to note that, with a few exceptions, these women claimed to have less need to work in wage labour due to the earnings of other family members. Inequalities across Mahila Milan members and other residents in the resettlement colonies have thus widened through the process of resettlement. The disparate meanings of participation for resettled women and men often map on to these inequalities. Such contradictions of market-based resettlement in subsequent evictions reveal some of the political limits of the Alliance's participatory model.

RESISTING RESETTLEMENT: CITIZENSHIP AND THE LIMITS OF REDEVELOPMENTAL PERSUASION

The ethos of non-confrontational citizenship was challenged when MUTP entered its third phase of expansion into new road construction. When Farzana, a Mahila Milan volunteer from a railway-affected slum, was sent by SPARC Alliance leaders to facilitate the process of slum clearance for an MUTP road project, she was in for a shock. After she visited her first few homes, residents began to threaten her and forced her out of the area. Farzana recalled discovering that her job was not a simple administrative one but one that required 'convincing' a volatile and unwilling group of people to relocate. In 2005, the MUTP resettlement project came under serious international scrutiny due to allegations of faulty displacement and compensation practices. Protests and petitions by evicted slum dwellers led the World Bank to temporarily suspend the release of its funds pending an independent investigation of MUTP. Evicted residents and shop owners found support in the National Alliance for People's Movements (NAPM), a coalition of anti-displacement movements led by the world-renowned Medha Patkar of the Narmada Valley anti-dam movement. The movement propelled MUTP into national and international spotlights.

This newer coalition of movements presented a formidable challenge to projects of urban transformation, which, it argued, marginalized its working-class residents. Charges were made against the Bank and MMRDA for endorsing slum redevelopment projects that unfairly favoured global business and local real estate interests. They demanded resettlement close to their neighbourhoods arguing that distant, offsite relocation for slum dwellers was unfair and negatively affected their livelihoods. Couching their demands in terms of citizenship-based rights to the city rather than simply the right to participate, evicted slum dwellers questioned the very roots of democracy and inclusion in the nation. Though it is outside of the scope of this essay to fully address the political processes and ramifications of this movement, briefly highlighting this divergent political response indicates how spatio-temporal conditions can yield very different citizenship formations.

My future work will compare these distinct ethico-political spaces of slum citizenship.

CONCLUSION

In this essay, I have ethnographically examined the ethico-political processes of neoliberal slum redevelopment in one resettlement programme. I have shown that while the local state relied entirely on the profit motive of private developers for financing low-cost resettlement on the urban fringes, it also harnessed community groups and an NGO to facilitate slum clearance through participatory mechanisms. Participatory resettlement processes were contradictory in that they simultaneously enabled a space of citizenship and negotiation for evictees but also produced and reinforced other inequalities and relations of power. Gendered participation of women's groups employing non-confrontational discourses of patience and community solidarity helped to politically enable community consent to rapid slum clearance under difficult conditions.

What does this form of political participation mean for the experience of modern urban democracy in cities like Mumbai? Partha Chatterjee has argued that the politics of the urban poor cannot be understood in terms of citizenship at all. He argues that because of their illegal status, slum dwellers cannot claim legitimate rights as citizens, and are instead positioned as populations managed by governmental technologies of welfare (Chatterjee 2004). In one way, the SPARC Alliance discourse against rights-based activism seems to corroborate such a formulation. However, upon deeper ethnographic examination of the MUTP participatory resettlement processes, we can see that gendered participation harnessed the essential feature of citizenship according to T. H. Marshall's (1998) much-cited classic formulation: responsible membership in the modern community. In the MUTP case, we can see that the political engagement of evictees was deeply shaped by neoliberal and gendered cultural ideals of individual and community responsibilities as well as aspirations for modernization through formalization of housing status. Furthermore, these tropes of citizenship also entailed participation and consent to the larger modern project of global city redevelopment.

As the contradictions and inequalities of market-oriented resettlement and neoliberal citizenship have surfaced in other sites in Mumbai, more confrontational articulations of rights-based citizenship have also emerged. In this manner, this ethnography reveals that the politics of the evicted cannot be understood homogenously. Rather, it is precisely the spatialized production of difference along multiple axes that has formed the basis of hegemony and consent to neoliberal redevelopment. However, as new projects unfurl for transport infrastructure such as airports and metro-rail, or large-scale commercial and residential redevelopment such as the famed Dharavi project, the question of how citizens stake claim to urban space remains critical. The idioms, practices, and fault lines of citizenship will play a crucial role in whether and how the urban poor will be able to partake of an essential substantive component of democracy: freedom from poverty.

NOTES

1. Exceptional extensions to the cut-off date policy were made for the MUTP in order to meet the 'universal resettlement' conditionalities established by the World Bank. However, significant restrictions remained which continued to exclude informal renters and other unrecognized residents from resettlement compensation.

2. The SRA policy stipulates onsite rehabilitation only for dwellers of slums located on open plots. In these cases, developers would resettle slum dwellers into higher rise units and use the remaining space for market-rate housing. Onsite rehabilitation has been generally more favoured among slum dwellers who are eligible to receive such units and have had protections from developer pressures and corruptions. The majority of the resettlement since 1995 has taken place offsite for infrastructure projects and river basin clearances (statistics from MMRDA). For more on the SRA, see Burra (2005) and Nijman (2008).

3. Available at http://www.ucl.ac.uk/dpu-projects/drivers_urb_change/urb_governance/pdf_capa_building/SPARC_Mahila%20Milan_learning_to_talk.pdf (accessed on 7 July 2011).

4. Ample historical and present day evidence of slum-based mobilizations for services and housing security demonstrates that middle-class leaders have not been the only promoters of the 'rights-based approach'. Lower income neighbourhood groups and leaders have also extensively deployed more confrontational, protest-based strategies (see Seabrook [1987] for examples).

5. *Rakhi*s are colourful symbolic threads that blood-related or adoptive 'sisters' tie on the wrists of their 'brothers' as a blessing in exchange for material gifts and promises of protection. This bond between sisters and brothers holds immense symbolic value in South Asia, originating as a culturally sanctified promise made by male heirs of family property to ensure the well-being of female siblings who cannot inherit property. The *rakhi* thus partially acts as a moral regulator of unequal and gendered property and inheritance customs.

6. Interview with A. Jockin, 15 December 2007.

7. Interview with Sheela Patel, 18 December 2007.

8. This committee was named after the Brihanmumbai Municipal Corporation (BMC) since the municipal government is generally the principal provider of environmental services. However, in the transit camps, residents devised their own systems of getting water from private sources and organizing communal clean-ups of camps.

9. The names of all resettled residents and participants have been changed to protect their anonymity.

BIBLIOGRAPHY

Appadurai, A. 2002. 'Deep Democracy: Urban Governmentality and the Horizon of Politics', *Public Culture,* 14(1): 23–43.

Bapat, M. and I. Agarwal. 2003. 'Our Needs, Our Priorities: Women and Men from the Slums in Mumbai and Pune Talk about Their Needs for Water and Sanitation', *Environment and Urbanization,* 15(2): 71–86.

Brenner, N. and N. Theodore. 2002. 'Cities and the Geographies of "Actually Existing Neoliberalism"', *Antipode,* 34(3): 349–79.

Burra, S. 1999. *Resettlement and Rehabilitation of the Urban Poor: The Story of Kanjur Marg.* Mumbai: Society for the Promotion of Area Resource Centres.

———. 2005. 'Towards a Pro-poor Framework for Slum Upgrading in Mumbai, India', *Environment and Urbanization,* 17(1): 67–88.

Chatterjee, P. 2004. *The Politics of the Governed: Reflections on Popular Politics in Most of the World.* New York: Columbia University Press.

Cooke, B. and U. Kothari (eds). 2001. *Participation: The New Tyranny?* New York: Zed Books.

Gilmore, R. W. 2002. 'Fatal Couplings of Power and Difference: Notes on Racism and Geography', *The Professional Geographer,* 54(1): 15–24.

Hart, G. 2001. 'Development Critiques in the 1990s: Culs de sac and Promising Paths', *Progress in Human Geography,* 25(4): 649–58.

Hickey, S. and G. Mohan (eds). 2004. *Participation: From Tyranny to Transformation?* New York: Zed Books.

Holston, J. 2008. *Insurgent Citizenship: Disjunctions of Democracy and Modernity in Brazil.* Princeton: Princeton University Press.

Leitner, H., J. Peck, and E. S. Sheppard. 2007. *Contesting Neoliberalism: Urban Frontiers.* New York: Guilford Press.

Marshall, T. 1998. 'Citizenship and Social Class', in G. Shafir (ed.), *The Citizenship Debates: A Reader,* pp. 93–112. Minneapolis: University of Minnesota Press.

Marston, S. and K. Mitchell. 2004. 'Citizens and the State: Citizenship Formations in Space and Time', in C. Barnett and M. Low (eds), *Spaces of Democracy: Geographical Perspectives on Citizenship, Participation and Representation,* pp. 93–112. London: SAGE.

Mies, M. 1998. *Patriarchy and Accumulation on a World Scale: Women in the International Division of Labour.* London: Zed Books.

Mitlin, D., and Patel, S. 2005. *Re-Interpreting the Rights-Based Approach: A Grassroots Perspective on Rights and Development,* Global Poverty Research Group, Economic and Social Research Council.

Miraftab, F. 2004. 'Making Neo-liberal Governance: The Disempowering Work of Empowerment', *International Planning Studies,* 9(4): 239–59.

Mohan, G. and K. Stokke. 2000. 'Participatory Development and Empowerment: The Dangers of Localism', *Third World Quarterly,* 21(2): 247–68.

Mohanty, C. 2003. *Feminism Without Borders.* Durham: Duke University Press.

Mukhija, V. 2003. *Squatters as Developers? Slum Redevelopment in Mumbai.* Aldershot, U.K.; Burlington, VT: Ashgate.

Nijman, J. 2008. 'Against the Odds: Slum Rehabilitation in Neoliberal Mumbai', *Cities,* 25(2): 73–85.

Patel, S., C. d'Cruz, and S. Burra. 2002. 'Beyond Evictions in a Global City: People-managed Resettlement in Mumbai', *Environment and Urbanization,* 14(1): 159–72.

Rose, N. 2000. 'Governing Cities, Governing Citizens', in E. F. Isin (ed.), *Democracy, Citizenship and the Global City,* pp. 95–109. London and New York: Routledge.

Roy, A. 2002. 'Marketized, Feminized, Medieval? Emerging Modes of Urban Governance', in J. Tulchin (ed.), *Democratic Governance and Urban Sustainability,* pp. 29–44. Washington D.C.: Woodrow Wilson Center.

Seabrook, J. 1987. *Life and Labour in a Bombay Slum.* London; New York: Quartet Books.

Sharma, R. 2003. *An Impact Assessment of the Initial Phase of R&R Implementation for the MUTP.* Mumbai: Tata Institute for Social Sciences.

Tata Institute of Social Sciences. 2007. *Impact Assessment and Evaluation of Phase II of the Mumbai Urban Transport Project.* Mumbai: Tata Institute of Social Sciences.

Chapter 5

Reengineering Citizenship

Municipal Reforms and the Politics of 'e-Grievance Redressal' in Karnataka's Cities

Malini Ranganathan

> *The emerging new paradigm worldwide for government organizations is that of an 'enterprising government,' a government which responds to what citizens want in a more market-oriented way, provides good quality services and products, and listens more closely to citizens. The reform steps include: public–private partnership, empowering citizens and clients, minimizing rules, measuring outcomes, redefining clients and customers, decentralizing authority, and employing competition/market-oriented government.*

—Sheila Dixit, Chief Minister of Delhi[*]

In line with prevailing global and national rhetoric advocating a lean, business-like, and customer-responsive government, in 2005, the Government of Karnataka (GoK) launched Nirmala Nagara (clean city), a municipal reform programme for 57 cities in the State.[1] The centrepiece of the programme—now being scaled up throughout the State via a World Bank loan—involves the application of information and communication technology in government services, or 'e-governance'. The e-Governments Foundation—a corporate philanthropic trust with influential donors from the high-technology sector and strong allies in the government, including Dixit herself, who had earlier outsourced Delhi's e-governance systems to the foundation—was recruited to design and implement all software modules under the programme. In this chapter, I focus on computerized complaint management, or what I refer to as 'e-grievance redressal', a highly publicized

---

[*] Dixit (2006).

aspect of Nirmala Nagara that sought to systematize and digitize how citizen grievances about core municipal services are recorded and responded to.[2] I explore what the development of e-grievance redressal, as an illustration of Dixit's 'enterprising government', reveals about the changing meanings of and implications for citizenship in contemporary urban India.

Programmes such as Nirmala Nagara and, at a larger scale, the Jawaharlal Nehru National Urban Renewal Mission (JNNURM) launched across India's largest cities in 2005, reflect the deepening neoliberalization of urban governance, or the embrace of market principles, private sector participation, and private sector-like behaviour by public agencies as prescribed by the 'New Public Management'.[3] While neoliberalization represents a transformation of state-making and rule (Sparke 2006), critical analysis also reveals that it is an unstable political–economic project that is contingent upon geographical and historical particularities. Programmes of neoliberal reform are often associated with micro-governing and subjectifying practices such as benchmarking, audits, credit ratings, and other market-based techniques that intend to instill conscientious economic behaviour in subjects. Following scholars situated in a Foucaultian tradition, these are rationalities and governmental techniques or 'governmentalities' that aim to direct the conduct not only of citizens, but also 'on the part of those who would govern' (Rose 1999: 52). Scholars of governmentality suggest that neoliberal rationalities are reconfiguring citizenship as consumer sovereignty and entrepreneurial ability (see, for instance, Dean 1999; Ong 2006; Rose 1999), while advancing 'an impoverished practice of political citizenship' (Swyngedouw 2005: 1993). Accordingly, the establishment of rights and responsibilities dictated by market forces has taken precedence in policy arenas over rights exerted through deliberative democracy and political participation.

Much of this scholarship draws implicitly or explicitly on T. H. Marshall's (1998[1950]) classic formulation of modern citizenship based on a three-step evolution from civil citizenship providing the basic conditions for capitalist development such as the right to sell one's labour; to political citizenship associated with the development of the public sphere, voting, and other political rights; to social citizenship ensuring entitlements to social justice, such as unemployment and health insurance. As Sparke (2006) notes, while the Marshallian definition continues to be limited to certain Western contexts, it nonetheless provides a starting point for interpreting how citizenship is being reformulated through neoliberal practices. Thus, for Sparke (2006: 155), not only have social and political forms of citizenship been 'increasingly restricted and economically recoded', but civil citizenship—especially in terms of labour and mobility—is also being rescaled from the national to the transnational scale.

Rose (1999), Hindess (1997), and Jayasurya (2002) further elaborate that following the erosion of the welfare state in advanced liberal democracies, social citizenship is now assuming contractualized forms. That is, neoliberal governments no longer consider citizens passive recipients of welfare and entitlements, but call on them to play a more proactive role in the services they obtain through established contracts between the individual 'customer' and 'service provider'. Importantly for Rose, 'whereas social rule was characterized by discretionary authority, advanced liberal rule is characterized by the *politics of the contract*, which '[shifts] the power relations inscribed in relations of expertise…especially…when they are accompanied by new methods of regulation and control such as audit and evaluation' (Rose 1999: 165, emphasis mine). For instance, in some cases, customers may become more empowered by the information provided in a contract to insist on service quality standards and new sanctions if they are not met. Similarly, higher levels of government can use the data generated by specific service contracts to surveil and discipline lower levels of government.

This chapter engages directly with debates on the implications of neoliberalism for citizenship—which is assumed here to mean a bundle of rights, obligations, and negotiated claims that frame the relationship between citizens and the state. I am motivated by the fact that despite the rich theoretical work on neoliberal governmentality, few studies delve into the nitty-gritty of how that power constitutes subjects, is reproduced, and is resisted, and even fewer engage non-Western contexts. E-grievance redressal provides a compelling case to fill this gap because, as a technology of neoliberal government that fits squarely within the New Public Management, it represents a particular coding of citizenship rights along contractual lines. As I show below, e-grievance redressal pre-selects the types of complaints citizens can file and the means through which they must be filed, and establishes norms for responding to complaints that municipal governments must adhere to, or face disciplinary sanctions by senior administrators. Yet, its development in a distinctly Indian urban context—one in which welfare is typically negotiated through what Kaviraj (2000: 150) calls 'unified pressure groups' or what Chatterjee (2004: 74) suggests is through collective appeals to 'ties of moral solidarity' made in political society—presents some interesting challenges to Euro-centric readings of citizenship. Through an analysis of Karnataka's e-grievance redressal experience in Bommanahalli and Bytarayanapura located on the outskirts of Bangalore, I aim to shed light on (*a*) the assemblage of neoliberal power supporting the emergence of municipal reforms and related technologies of governance; and (*b*) implications of e-grievance redressal for substantive aspects of citizenship (Holston and Appadurai 1999; McFarlane 2004)—that is, the social rights (in this case, basic municipal infrastructure) that people possess in practice.

I make four main arguments. First, despite policy pronouncements for urban decenrralization, there has been a tendency towards greater centralization in decision-making in Karnataka, particularly around international loans and urban reforms. This, in turn, has facilitated the entry of corporate actors into policy-making, and the adoption of private sector-like techniques in governance. Second, the urban policy-making environment in Karnataka, involving partnerships between international donors, corporate actors, financial intermediaries, and bureaucrats, is generating a considerable amount of expert knowledge around urban services. Higher levels of government increasingly wield this expertise to subordinate local government and local political actors. This power equation is further facilitated through e-grievance contractual arrangements in which the data generated (number of complaints received, time taken to redress them, and so on) is used to hold staff accountable and make budgetary decisions—what Rose (1999) refers to as 'the politics of the contract'. Third, while e-grievance redressal does not necessarily serve as an improvement over previous ad-hoc systems of filing and responding to complaints, which, as I will show, continue to prevail, the data generated provides the semblance of efficiency and rigour. This serves as the basis for expanding reforms and continuing to leverage international loans. Finally, the system of e-grievance redressal presents a clear attempt to reengineer the act of complaining by privileging individual complaints over the 'messiness' of group complaints often made on the basis of moral solidarity. However, because poor women and groups that live in informal settlements make many such complaints—complaints that are not recorded in the e-grievance system—there are critical gender and socio-economic biases that have not been accounted for. The stakes of these findings are high given that e-grievance redressal is being rapidly scaled up throughout India's cities.

The rest of the chapter is divided as follows. In the next section, I explain the governance context in Karnataka that is amenable to the entry of corporate philanthropy into policy-making. In the section following this, I analyse the e-grievance system in depth and discuss its implications for citizenship. I conclude by revisiting certain key theoretical debates on citizenship within the context of urban reforms.

NEOLIBERAL GOVERNANCE IN KARNATAKA'S CITIES

Problem Framing: Municipalities Need Discipline

Over 30 per cent of Karnataka's 50 million people live in urban areas that fall under four major classifications depending on population size: 'corporations' with over a million people, followed by smaller 'city municipal councils', 'town municipal councils', and 'town panchayats', or village entities. Most of the State's population lives in municipalities and towns with fewer than one million people (KUIDFC 2004).

Following the implementation of the 74th Constitutional Amendment in 1992 for urban decentralization, local governments are responsible for the delivery of all services to its inhabitants in municipalities: streetlights, sanitation, solid waste management, stormwater drains, drinking water, and roads. Maintenance contracts are typically outsourced to a variety of private contractors overseen by elected councillors and engineers. Responsibility for day-to-day city management and budgetary allocation lies with the administrative and elected arms of the local government.[4]

In practice, however, the level of service delivery in most municipalities in Karnataka continues to be inadequate in comparison to demand. Private providers are sometimes required to fill gaps in service provision (for example, private water tankers) and citizens themselves pool their resources to fund new infrastructure (for instance, a neighbourhood borewell or streetlights for inner settlement roads). Thus, access to urban services varies according to income level, the tenure status of the settlement (authorized vs. unauthorized; more on this later), and prevailing environmental conditions (for instance, the depth of the groundwater table).

The reasons for poor urban service provision are complex and are connected both to broader political economic shifts, such as diminished fiscal devolutions from the centre since the 1990s owing to new political mandates for 'fiscal rectitude', as well as rapid growth in population and local mismanagement of municipal funds. However, the narrow manner in which senior administrators frame municipal problems—focusing almost exclusively on technical and managerial deficiencies—has, in turn, dictated the types of 'solutions' proposed.

Administrators hold municipalities to be weak, their management and accounting practices 'backward', and, quite bluntly, mere 'garbage' as one administrator put it to me—alluding to both the physical presence of trash lining the streets, as well as the perceived ineptness of municipal administration. As a response to the perceived problems of municipal government, the Directorate of Municipal Administration (DMA), whose director is an officer of the Indian Administrative Service (IAS), was created to oversee municipal management in every municipality in the State and to 'exercise disciplinary control over the staff of municipalities' (GoK n.d.).[5] By several accounts, DMA's role is one of a disciplinarian. One researcher intimately familiar with municipal budgeting in Karnataka described the DMA's director as a 'headmaster' that dictates to councillors in meetings, who, in turn, say and participate very little.[6] This is because, frequently, the resolutions pertaining to reforms are written in a technical language incomprehensible to elected representatives. There is thus a widening gulf between the administrative and political classes in local government reinforced through the implementation of reforms that are designed in institutional environments far removed from political participation. To add to its disciplinary role, the DMA periodically reviews the performance of municipalities and ranks them in order of worst to best performing via a scorecard system of output-based indicators. Such an assessment is then used to design 'corrective measures' (KUIDFC 2004: 58), or a variety of financial and managerial reforms. The 'politics of the contract', then, in which new relations of expertise are established between customer and provider, has also been established between different levels of government. In this case, senior bureaucrats are mandating the generation of new types of performance indicators for local government employees that are lower down on the hierarchy.

The Nirmala Nagara reforms programme is one among several that the DMA supervises. Although the programme involves a range of scattered, small-scale investments in infrastructure (for example, public latrines, rainwater harvesting, solid waste management, and so on), the main thrust was to develop and implement municipal e-governance systems in partnership with the e-Governments Foundation. The rationale behind e-governance maintains that because 'record keeping functions are poorly carried out and are a manual drudgery',[7] local governments are in need of 'process reengineering' (CMAK 2006: 3), and, further, that 'greater accountability and citizen participation', until now severely wanting, must be made 'the pivot' of urban governance (see note 7).

Several functions of city governments were computerized to this end: property tax collection, financial accounting based on a shift to double-entry corporate standards, the municipal employees' payroll, inventories for tracking contractors, public works, and assets, birth and death registration, and public grievances (covering a wide variety of complaints from municipal services to day-to-day administration). In addition to these technology applications, the e-Governments Foundation launched websites for all participating cities with content in both Kannada and English.

According to the foundation, Nirmala Nagara is the largest project for municipal e-governance in the world both in terms of the number of participating cities and range of software applications. The programme is financed through a combination of the Asian Development Bank's (ADB) second urban infrastructure loan to Karnataka and the foundation's own resources.[8]

Centralized Governance, Privatized Governance

The particular reforms and e-governance strategies selected under Nirmala Nagara are not unique to this programme: since the late 1990s, there has been a move, both at the central level and at the level of individual States in India, towards property tax reform and computerization of municipal functions in order to increase transparency, accountability, and efficiency—the language that universally frames notions of good governance. In Karnataka's case, several reforms were experimented with the Bangalore Agenda Task Force (BATF), a public–private partnership that the then pro-technology-industry chief minister S. M. Krishna himself created in 1999, and which lasted until he lost elections in 2004. The partnership, bringing together bureaucrats, civic organizations, and leaders of the business community who were determined to take the city's ailing infrastructure into their own hands, initiated participatory budgeting, public opinion polling of service providers, and corporate-style accounting of municipal finances—in total over 50 reform and infrastructure initiatives in Bangalore over a five-year period (see A. Ghosh [2005], Kamath [2006], and Nair [2005] for a detailed account of these measures). Kamath (2006) contends that they were designed in the pursuit of furthering the city's economic competitiveness in the global economy, but with much less regard to Bangalore's growing poverty. This is in line with Harvey's (1989) thesis that city governments are assuming an 'entrepreneurial' role in their bid to outcompete other cities for global capital. Although the partnership itself was considered controversial, there is little doubt that the BATF set a precedent for the type of techno-managerial reforms mimicking private sector principles witnessed in Nirmala Nagara (A. Ghosh 2005), as well as the involvement of corporate actors in urban policy-making spheres and the generation of governance expertise in Karnataka.

Along with the entry of private actors in governance, there has also been a trend in the State government towards vesting decision-making authority in corporatized and centrally operated public entities. Along with the DMA, the Karnataka Urban Infrastructure Development Finance Corporation (KUIDFC) also serves a key disciplinary role in municipal reforms. First set up as a conduit for ADB's loans to the State in the mid-1990s, KUIDFC is a state intermediary that negotiates and brokers loans, provides oversight for reforms, and assists municipalities in borrowing from the market. Its staff consists of approximately 20 full-time corporate executives, all of whom hail from management, finance, engineering, or accounting backgrounds. Its managerial culture and accounting practices are that of a corporate entity, but its close working relationship with the higher echelons of the urban bureaucracy also means that it is able to enforce loan covenants and reforms without much opposition.

The establishment of institutions such as DMA and KUIDFC is consistent with the notion that neoliberalism involves both the promulgation of market-based principles and some degree of authoritarian control (Harvey 2005). Over nearly two decades since the start of liberalization in 1991, cities in India have become strategic sites for both the downsizing of the state in areas such as social services, and its expansion into arenas such as land acquisition for special economic zones and the facilitation of market-based finance for cities. These trends indicate the simultaneous 'roll-back' of the neoliberal state in some arenas and its 'roll-out' in others (Brenner and Theodore 2002; Harvey 2005; Larner 2003; Peck and Tickell 2002), and as J. Ghosh (1998: 180) says of the Indian context: 'The centralized, centralizing and increasingly authoritarian state is in fact a necessary requirement for…liberalizing structural adjustment.' The important point to keep in mind here is that as a project of state rule, neoliberalism can often represent a hybrid between older political legacies and institutional formations (in this case, Karnataka's predilection for centralized, state-centric rule) and newer market-based models (Peck et al. 2009).

The KUIDFC is a parastatal organization that sits within the interstices of the state system, and, while not accountable to local government (it has no representation on local councils), it mediates between local government and consultants, donors, financiers, and other proponents of reforms. One of its specific roles has been to scale up Nirmala Nagara reforms in the rest of Karnataka through the World Bank-funded Karnataka Municipal Reforms Project, while continuing to work in close connection with the e-Governments Foundation.

The e-Governments Foundation is a not-for-profit trust co-founded by prominent technology and business entrepreneurs. Its clients include all the cities of Karnataka, the Municipal Corporation of Delhi, and the erstwhile Bangalore City Corporation. It coordinates over 500 volunteers around the world and has developed nine different software applications, including 'e-Gov Property' and 'e-Gov Financials'—both to increase local government revenue. The foundation describes itself as a 'new breed IT Social Startup whose mission is to provide an e-Governance Software System for use in city municipalities all across India—*for free*'.⁹

'New economy' corporate philanthropists—that is, those emerging from the high-technology sectors—have established a strong presence in Indian States that concentrate the country's software and biotechnology sectors, such as Karnataka (Sidel 2001). The main icons associated with philanthropic public interest organizing in Karnataka are Azim Premji (of Wipro Technologies), who founded the Akshara Foundation dedicated to issues of education, Nandan Nilekani (of Infosys), who co-founded the e-Governments Foundation, and Rohini Nilekani, his wife, who founded the Arghyam Foundation, involved in the water sector.

Although the e-Governments Foundation describes its activities as restricted to software, it has also played a powerful role in shaping policy discourse. The role of corporate actors in urban policy-making is a phenomenon well studied in Euro-American contexts, particularly among regulation theorists who stress the institutional and social relations responsible for capitalist restructuring (Jessop 2002). In the United States, in particular, ideas of 'growth coalitions'—strategic partnerships between business actors and urban governments to propel economic development and real estate growth—have held considerable sway (Logan and Molotch 1987). In Karnataka, despite policy announcements in support of decentralization, the reverse has been true; that is, there has been an increasing tendency towards centralization of decision-making and the creation of politically insulated government bodies (such as KUIDFC) that have supported private sector entry into policy-making. Moreover, high-ranking government officers and corporate actors influencing policy through philanthropic trusts share particular cultural understandings of 'good' governance, and the techno-managerial approaches associated with them. For instance, while not one councillor I interviewed in Bommanahalli recalled hearing about the e-Governments Foundation or the e-grievance redressal system, the DMA shares a close working relationship with the foundation. Its senior bureaucrats, moreover, are highly conversant with the now universal technical, financial, and managerial approaches of municipal reforms.

In Vithal's (1997) analysis of evolving trends in Indian bureaucracy, he suggests that academic specialization in neo-classical economics within the IAS starting from the 1980s is valued since it provides a gateway to jobs in the economic ministries, and greater opportunity for interface with international financial bodies such as the International Monetary Fund and the World Bank. For Vithal (1997: 215), there is thus 'a certain intellectual seepage' occurring between international development agencies, corporate actors, and senior bureaucrats, such that 'the players on either side of the international divide find themselves having more in common than the national officials and those who they are supposed to represent' (Vithal 1997: 215).

In sum, despite the constitutional amendment for decentralization, decision-making has been increasingly centralized in Karnataka, particularly around international loans for urban reforms. This institutional environment has enabled the entry of corporate actors into policy-making, and the embrace of private sector-like techniques in governance because of shared cultural understandings of governance among a select group of elite actors.

REENGINEERING THE COMPLAINT INTERFACE: THE CASE OF THE NIRMALA NAGARA E-GOVERNANCE REFORMS

In every town in which the computerized grievance redressal system was implemented, a helpline was set up to collect and respond to complaints in a centralized manner staffed by a local NGO (GoK 2006).[11] When residents face a problem, such as disruption in water supply, they have four options for reporting this grievance: (*a*) personally visiting the helpline front desk; (*b*) reporting the complaint over telephone; (*c*) submitting a written or faxed complaint to the helpline desk; or (*d*) lodging the complaint through the city's website. That is, even though the system is referred to as 'computerized' grievance redressal, it is accessible to users through avenues other than the internet. Non-internet routes for complaining were incorporated because of the low penetration rate of computers and the internet in India, which is a well-known fact.

The mechanics of the system are as follows: residents can choose from a set of 90 pre-coded complaints organized under 10 main categories, such as Engineering, Health, Community affairs and General administration (or if the complaint is made via telephone, the helpline personnel categorizes the complaint on behalf of the complainant). Under 'Engineering', by far the category with the most registered complaints in every participating city, citizens can register complaints about broken streetlights, blocked underground drainage, interruptions in water supply, and poor roads, among other types of infrastructural complaints. Under 'Health', citizens can complain about the lack of garbage removal and overflowing stormwater drains. Perhaps the most intriguing category is 'Community affairs': here, citizens can register a complaint with regard to, or against, 'slums'; further details on how exactly this complaint is to be interpreted are not provided.

After a complaint is registered (and, as I found, often in-person visits and phone calls are recorded in a log book first and are then inputted into the database), the complainant is provided with a tracking number that she/ he can use to follow up, and the complaint is routed (either through phone call, cell phone text messaging, or email) to the concerned engineer or city official. In turn, the concerned official must resolve the problem within a stipulated timeframe and input the status of the problem (that is, 'pending' or 'resolved') directly into the database or through the helpline.

There is much that is rationally appealing about the system, especially within the framework of customer satisfaction: it is intended to build accountability of local governments because it provides real-time information about problems experienced and whether they are addressed. As a contract between the 'customer' and 'service provider', it also sets a time limit within which grievances must be resolved, thus creating the threat (or at least the impression of a threat) of disciplinary sanctions on engineers with unresolved complaints. Finally, customized reports aided by GIS software can be generated showing the spatial distribution of complaints and the breakdown of complaints according to a category over a given time period.

These are potentially powerful types of data: the aggregation of citizen dissatisfaction with a local government's performance, for instance, can serve as a compelling basis on which to allocate budgets or request loans, deploy labour, and make hiring and firing decisions. Indeed, as Wallack and Nadhamuni (2008: 9–10) found through their survey of 74 commissioners, deputy commissioners, and chief officers across 38 cities in Karnataka three years following the implementation of the e-grievance redressal system, the data generated 'is used for work planning and short-term allocation of resources as well as for monitoring departments' performance'. Further, a report published by the Urban Development Department of Karnataka states that the data generated through e-grievance redressal 'enables performance measurement of municipal staff' (GoK 2006: 3) and introduced 'transparency and accountability of municipal staff'. This invokes Rose's (1999) 'politics of the contract': the information generated through the establishment of a contract (in this case, e-grievance redressal) enables increased monitoring by senior administrators and officials of frontline engineers and municipal employees. The higher number of unresolved complaints frontline engineers have, or the longer their average record in resolving complaints, the greater the potential disciplinary sanctions on them.

This may be a desirable outcome if the data is representative of the types and distribution of problems experienced in a particular municipality, and, more importantly, if the system does not bias against particular groups of people. In order to verify whether this was the case, I generated reports for the cities of Bommanahalli, Byatarayanapura, and Mahadevapura over the period of August 2005 (when the system was first launched) to June 2007 (that is, 22 months). I corroborated these results with 40 focus group discussions conducted with resident welfare associations (RWAs), civic welfare federations, and slum-based organizations across Bommanahalli and Byatarayanapura; 25 household surveys; 54 semi-structured interviews with lower- and mid-level bureaucrats, frontline engineers, ex-councillors, and members of the legislative assembly (MLAs); and 24 phone surveys with individuals who had visited the help-desk in June 2007. In addition, I drew upon the recent fieldwork results of a project titled 'Urban Local Government, Infrastructure Planning and the Urban Poor' reported in Kamath et al. (2008). The project, funded by Citizens Voluntary Initiative for the City (CIVIC) Bangalore, was conducted by an independent research organization (Collaborative for the Advancement of Studies in Urbanism through Mixed Media or CASUMM) with which I collaborated closely in 2007. This secondary data was based on 138 interviews conducted with residents, associations, politicians, and officials in Mahadevapura (a city municipal council), Kengeri (a town *panchayat)*, and Bellandur (an urban village). I was interested in what data is being recorded in the system and what is being left out.

The results of the e-governance reports for Bommanahalli in the 'Engineering' category are provided in Figure 5.1. According to the e-grievances data, problems with streetlights comprise the most significant in Bommanahalli (45 per cent of all reported complaints over two years, n = 2,862), followed by underground drainage (UGD) and water supply problems. I generated a similar report for the category 'Health' [n = 569] and found that problems related to garbage collection comprised 96 per cent of complaints made in this category. Other categories had a negligible number of complaints listed over the time period. Thus, streetlights, underground drainage, water supply, and garbage would appear to be the most common grievances from the data generated in descending order of priority. Within the category of water supply, leaking pipes were reported as the most common grievance in Bommanahalli. Similar results were obtained for other municipalities: over the same time period in Mahadevapura [n = 1,969], 66 per cent of all complaints in the 'Engineering' category were related to malfunctioning streetlights.

The picture provided by this data is not altogether incorrect when compared to anecdotal reports and the qualitative data I collected; undeniably, the lack of proper lighting, garbage removal, adequate sanitation and

FIGURE 5.1. GRIEVANCE DATA FOR BOMMANAHALLI,
AUGUST 2005–JUNE 2007 [N = 2,862]

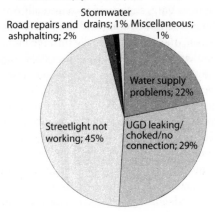

Source: Compiled from data obtained from Bommanahalli City.

drainage, and reliable water supply are problems experienced throughout Bangalore's outskirts. My qualitative results, however, do not support the conclusion that malfunctioning streetlights is the most important grievance.[12] More importantly, I discovered that the categorization and prioritization of grievances in this manner masks key differences related to formal and informal planning. It also neglects those arenas in which collective struggle, particularly by poorer women, is the norm. In fact, reporting of the latter is completely absent in the e-grievance data, suggesting a gender and implicit socio-economic bias that has serious implications for equitable infrastructure provisioning. In the following section I discuss these findings as garnered through ethnographic research.

Collective Complaining as a Form of Negotiating Substantive Citizenship

In many small municipalities—particularly those located on the outskirts of Bangalore—the majority of residential settlements are considered 'unauthorized', the planning term used in India for areas that have not been approved by, or do not conform to the norms specified by, the planning agency of the city. In Karnataka, these areas, known as 'revenue layouts', are formed through the subdivision of agricultural land by a private developer who then sells individual plots to buyers, often to the lower middle classes—what I have elsewhere called the 'peripheralized middle class' (Ranganathan 2010). Because these plots are not legally converted from agricultural use to residential use, and have not secured the appropriate planning permits, infrastructure is not provided upfront but is negotiated incrementally over time through the help of neighbourhood associations, and deals made with politicians, contractors, 'watermen' (those who physically turn the municipal water supply on and off), and city officials. As Chatterjee (2004) suggests, most subaltern groups negotiate access to public services and make claims on the state not through the terrain of established law or administrative procedure, but through a variety of political negotiations in the realm of 'political society'. This is in contrast to a small fraction of the population that can be considered 'civil society' and who claim rights on legal grounds.

Negotiations are particularly critical in the case of drinking water in which residents use a multiplicity of arrangements for obtaining access. While wealthier households and those settlements deemed 'authorized' can obtain formalized individual piped water connections from the utility and sink their own borewells as a supplementary source, lower-middle class and poor households depend on municipal borewells, often sunk at a much shallower depth than private borewells. The schedule of operation of public borewells is contingent on such factors as electricity supply, the dependability of maintenance contractors, relations with the water engineers, and the presence and depth of competing borewells in the vicinity. What follows then is a series of complaints, informal negotiations, and bribes to engineers and 'watermen' for water to be released. A single visit to the helpdesk of the municipality will rarely suffice.

Complexities owing to differences between authorized and unauthorized settlements and formal and informal planning modes are not captured in aggregate e-grievance data. I summarize the differences between what the e-grievance redressal system captures and the nature of existing modes of complaining amongst the lower socio-economic classes in Table 5.1.

Another potentially more serious omission is that the e-grievance system captures a much greater proportion of complaints filed by individuals than those voiced collectively. The following example is illustrative. While interviewing the Assistant Executive Engineer for Bommanahalli in 2007, I was interrupted by 20 or more distressed residents, mostly from lower-middle-class backgrounds, and mostly women, who stormed his office. They represented residents in one low-lying ward in Bommanahalli, Garvebhavipalya, which often gets flooded after a bad downpour. In this ward, several borewells sunk by the local government have gone dry, and in several others, the electric motor is worn so badly that the pump no longer draws water. The women complained to the engineer about the flooding in their homes

TABLE 5.1. DIFFERENCES IN COMPLAINT SYSTEMS

	Existing Systems	**e-Grievance Redressal**
Who complains	Groups of people	The individual (sometimes on behalf of a neighbourhood or group of houses/apartment complex)
How they complain	Petitions, storming office, to councillor, direct telephone calls	Visiting help-desk, calling
What they complain about	Top three complaints: drinking water, poor roads, clogged open drains/sanitary outlets. Other frequent complaints: flooding of homes, inter-family abuse, ration cards (especially in slums).	Categorized according to 'engineering'/'health'. Under community affairs, 'slums' are an unspecified category; streetlights comprise 50% of data
Whom they complain to	Community activist, councillor, engineer on spot visit, assistant executive engineer, MLA	Help-desk personnel
How complaints are redressed	Councillor puts pressure on contractors, extra money paid off	By directing complaints to specific engineering personnel
How data is tracked/monitored	Highly decentralized; very little systematic monitoring or collation of data	Highly centralized; through GIS maps, graphs, tables; can be broken down by ward, type of complaint
What data is used for	Future visits by engineers to troubled areas	Budgetary priorities and for scaling up reforms

Source: Interviews and focus groups in neighbourhoods carried out in Bommana-halli and Byataranyapura between 2007 and 2009.

and about the fact that there had been no drinking water for days. Public borewells had broken down and the local government had not sent supplemental tankers (in times of emergency, the municipal government ensures tanker delivery). The engineer ordered them to speak softly ('*nidhanavaagi heeli*') and proceeded to listen to them patiently, almost with the demeanour of a stern parent. A few minutes prior to this incident, when questioned about the e-grievance system, the engineer had told me: 'Mostly we get oral complaints from poor people because the poor would not be having access to email. We get around 20–25 oral complaints per day.' The mob appeared in his office as if to demonstrate the veracity of his statement.

In front of the women, the engineer picked up his cell phone and di-aled the contractor in charge of borewell maintenance. A few minutes later, he hung up in frustration telling me that 'the contractor is absconding, as usual!' What the engineer meant is that the contractor had failed to honour his responsibilities of regular maintenance check-ups and that he was now refusing to answer calls. He then turned to the women, reassured them that their woes would be attended to in four days, accepted their written com-plaint and laid it on top of a pile of complaints that had already come in that day and had not been fed into the system, and dismissed them. Before returning to his cell phone, he said to me: 'These people exaggerate when they say it has taken "one month" to repair. It has been less than that!'

I later spoke to the women and discovered that some number of them came to the municipal office at least once a week. Several felt that it was better to speak directly with an official—even if it meant being more con-frontational—than speaking with help-desk personnel because they felt that there was a greater chance of their complaint being attended to and that they could appeal to the engineer's 'sense of duty' directly to attend to their problems. Importantly, they noted that complaining in groups—either in spontaneously formed neighbourhood groups or through associations—is more effective than complaining alone. As one resident in Bommanahalli said:

> I am behind the officials all the time. Sometimes, I make fifty calls per day. I'll call and ask 'Why isn't the water coming?' If people are not responding, I'll take a crowd of people with me there.… It is not possible to solve all problems in all areas. But we should join together and the 'we' feeling should be there, not just the 'I' feeling. Nothing will get done with the 'I' feeling. (Interview with Bommanahalli resident, 27 August 2007)

What I witnessed that day was by no means rare: on nearly every subsequent visit I made to the municipal office, groups of women had col-lected to protest malfunctioning public borewells, floods, and problems with overflowing sanitary outlets. As Karen Coelho (2005) finds in her ethnography of water reform in Chennai, the poor exploit group-oriented strategies because of their recognized leverage in demanding a reaction out of frontline functionaries. For Coelho, 'the "complaint" as the key operational measure of the service represents a form of *individuation*—a technology of administrative control as well as, in its demands for order and specification, a way of perceiving' (Coelho 2005: 186, emphasis mine). Reforms that aim to structure and codify complaints as problems of individual consumers fundamentally mask or, worse still, undermine certain types of collective struggles. In my research, I found that several women also communicated problems directly to engineers in the field when they came for spot inspection visits. These informal reports usually do not get recorded in the e-grievance system.

In addition to spontaneous gatherings of people, several associations are formed to lobby for neighbourhood improvements. Some associations are trade union affiliated, such as the Bommanahalli Nagarika Hitaraksha-na Vedike (Civic Welfare Association), organized by the Democratic Youth Federation of India (DYFI), a cadre-based group of the Communist Party of India (Marxist). Others are caste-based, such as the Dalit Sangharsha Samithi and the Karnataka Janandolana Samithi—two grassroots political organizations fighting for greater Dalit rights, largely based in slums (whose concerns are not at all reflected in the e-grievance database). And others, such as middle-class resident welfare associations, are ubiquitous in most urban areas and focus on problems specific to their localities.

The example of DYFI is instructive of the type of 'claims to moral solidarity' that Chatterjee suggests is common in political society. The organization is mostly active in Hongasandra and Garvebhavipalya, two lower-middle-class wards in Bommanahalli. As a politically affiliated organization, and one with an agenda of expanding membership in Bommanahalli, for the past several years, DYFI has mobilized both working-class and middle-class residents in revenue layouts around compensation for rain and flood damage, ration cards, and urban services—sometimes in confrontational ways. For example, in April 2007, DYFI stopped traffic on the Hosur Road to protest the lack of water supply in Bommanahalli and the over-supply of water to elite areas and technology parks (*Hindu* 2007). In my interviews, DYFI members cited at least one other incident in the past few years in which they had blocked traffic as a form of protest against the municipal government's failure to provide services.

The group has also been successful at negotiating service improvements through less confrontational means. In one meeting I attended between DYFI and the joint commissioner for Bommanahalli, the leader invited the administrator to visit areas of Bommanahalli that were suffering acute water shortage. The site visits that I attended the following day involved detailed inspections of Bommanahalli's ailing infrastructure during which engineers patiently recorded the grievances of all citizens who approached them. When I followed up with DYFI after the visit, I learned that municipal workers had unclogged drains and cleared garbage, and that tankers were now plying the streets more regularly to provide drinking water. Such successes are not often observed, but this example demonstrates that historically in India, 'demands or complaints were taken more seriously if they were made on behalf of communities rather than individuals' (Kaviraj 2000: 150). One Bommanahalli resident and DYFI member described the achievements of the organization as follows:

> When we first came here [in 1996], there was no proper electricity or water, no telephone connection, and nobody used to even pass by here. Not even the postman and courier would come to this area. It was only after the big flood in 2005 that the municipal office opened their eyes and saw that we were living here. DYFI came and helped us at that time. We worked together as a group. Before that, I didn't even know who my next-door neighbour was. Because of DYFI, we've got things done in this neighbourhood like roads and water supply. (Member of DYFI and resident of Garvebhavipalya, May 2007)

Note that many of DYFI's constituents live in unauthorized revenue layouts. They do not make their claims, therefore, on the terrain of legal or established procedures, but rather on the basis of collective appeals to the right to basic services by virtue of their living there.

The e-grievance redressal system, however, does not capture these types of initiatives and interactions between citizens and local government officials, much less does its data reflect the types of complaints frequently made by groups. As Wallack and Nadhamuni (2008: 12) acknowledge about the e-grievance redressal system:

> Several cities mentioned parallel processes for managing public grievances.... Some department officials, for example, received complaints directly from citizens or specifically went out to worksites to check for potential complaints. Others mentioned using phone calls or direct communication to route complaints to the appropriate departments in emergencies. Modifying the system to motivate more complete usage is a high priority: the performance reports generated for citizens and city managers will be inaccurate and potentially biased if these parallel flows of information are not being captured in the public grievance redressal module.

What Wallack and Nadhamuni (2008) fail to recognize, however, is the systematic exclusion of particular types of complaints made by particular people—that is, the gender and socio-economic biases of the system. As Coelho notes of the institutionalized complaint management in Chennai's

Metrowater Board, 'the instrument of the complaint, structured as a problem of the individual customer that is amenable to being solved, denies or renders invisible the field of struggle implicit in the collective character of access to water and sanitation in the city' (Coelho 2005: 185). By codifying certain ways of complaining and not others, and by shaping the conduct of complaining through a process of individuation, these systems screen out a significant proportion of grievances.

Since municipal staff are being held 'accountable' to the data reported in the e-grievance redressal system and are being rewarded or penalized based on the data obtained by authorities higher up in the chain of command (for example, administrators in the DMA), the finding that group complaints are rendered invisible by the e-grievance system has a number of very serious implications.

First, if municipal engineers prioritize the complaints received through e-grievance redressal (since this is the basis upon which their performance is judged), then the complaints received through alternative routes (for instance, women complaining in groups) are not as likely to be taken seriously. Second, if budgetary allocations and work plans are decided on the basis of e-grievance data, then it is likely that particular types of infrastructure that are reported through individual complaints will get more financial support than those reported through collective complaints. Thus, I argue that the contractualization of social citizenship through e-grievance redressal undermines the ability of certain groups to gain access to substantive social rights (in the sense of basic urban infrastructure). Jayasurya (2002) comes to a similar conclusion when he finds that the very liberal notion of individual choice and freedom embedded in the 'new contractualism' in the UK produces a decidedly illiberal set of outcomes, including the further marginalization and neglect of deprived groups. In the case of India, however, the reason is because certain ways of accessing the state—that is, collective complaints and appeals made on the basis of moral solidarity in political society—are simply not amenable to contractualization. The 'politics of the contract' in which new power relations are being established through the data generated in e-grievance redressal is ensuring that lower levels of government are subordinated to higher levels, thus causing the latter to be less likely to respond to collective complaints not made through the system. It is foreseeable that collective, spontaneous, and ad-hoc complaining may be increasingly marginalized in favour of complaints recorded in the database. This is not to say that all types of associational activities will be undermined by institutionalized complaint systems: indeed, all evidence points to thriving associational life in Indian cities, particularly among the middle class.

At the same time, questions of which groups are gaining better access to the state and how e-grievance and other institutionalized forms of complaint management further reinforce these inequities should not be dismissed.

CONCLUSION: REVISITING CITIZENSHIP DEBATES IN THE CONTEXT OF MUNICIPAL REFORMS

This chapter attempts to contribute to the existing literature on citizenship in urban spaces by combining the study of the analytics of neoliberal government with the study of collective struggle and practices of claiming substantive rights in Karnataka's municipalities. It takes the case of the Nirmala Nagara reforms involving the implementation of e-grievance redressal in 57 of Karnataka's municipalities, now being scaled up in the State through the World Bank-assisted Karnataka Municipal Reform Project. The system individuates the act of complaining, codifies the possible range of complaints about the municipal government, and establishes norms for resolving them—in essence, it establishes new contractual norms between the 'customer' and the 'service provider'.

An analysis of the institutional environment in Karnataka reveals the ongoing entry of corporate actors, now through charitable trusts such as the e-Governments Foundation, in urban policy-making further facilitated through the centralization of decision-making authority. The language and assumptions of the New Public Management enables the establishment of shared norms between corporate actors and senior members of the bureaucracy and a widening gulf between the administrative and political classes. Institutions created to mediate between local government, financiers, consultants, and international development agencies—but which are not accountable to the electorate—further encourage the involvement of the private sector without public knowledge or scrutiny. The 'politics of the contract' indeed signals a shift in the relations of expertise (cf. Rose 1999). In this case, expertise about local government performance is increasingly being held by higher levels of government to discipline municipal staff. This power equation, in turn, ensures that frontline engineers increasingly heed the data and performance statistics that are being generated through the e-grievance redressal system, rather than responding to collective complaints not being captured by the system.

An ethnographic approach reveals fields of struggle beyond institutionalized complaint management that are especially prevalent in unauthorized layouts and slums in smaller municipalities. In these areas, basic infrastructure is typically negotiated over time through the help of associations, side-payments made to contractors, and negotiations with local bureaucrats and frontline engineers. Groups of women, in particular, commonly make complaints to municipal workers about flood damage and water supply in person—complaints that are rarely recorded in the e-grievance database. Further, the example of the DYFI demonstrates that associations and 'unified pressure groups' (Kaviraj 2000) continue to be the most common way of routing complaints to and about city authorities. Thus, by omitting complaints filed by groups of poorer women, and certain types of associations, the data generated by the e-grievance system is inherently gender and socio-economically biased.

As frontline engineers are increasingly held accountable to their seniors based on the performance data generated through the e-grievance system, and elected representatives are increasingly shut out of decision-making processes related to reforms, the implications for substantive citizenship are profound. As Swyngedouw (2005) and Chandhoke (2003) have observed in different contexts, the practice of political citizenship, in the sense of collective consciousness and representative democracy, is seriously hindered when citizens are reduced to consumers of services. Although the challenges and failures of representative democracy are well known, the risk of exclusion inherent in the market-driven alternatives may be even more severe.

NOTES

1. To avoid confusion, 'State' has been capitalized whenever referring to a geographic entity within the country, such as the 'State of Karnataka' and used in lower case when referring to government, as in 'the state apparatus'.
2. The formal term used in project documentation is 'public grievance and redressal module' or PGRM which has been shortened here to 'e-grievance redressal' in order to avoid the excessive use of acronyms.
3. The 'New Public Management' is a philosophy that took root in New Zealand in the late 1980s and spread globally. It insists on the professionalization of bureaucracy and the empowerment of citizen as customer. Reforms following this philosophy include private sector-style initiatives purporting to improve accountability through the payment of user fees, citizen charters delineating service quality standards, and institutionalized technologies and spaces for customer grievances, audits, and managed civic participation.
4. The head of the administrative arm is the commissioner, who is assisted in the everyday running of the city by various mid- to lower-level managers (chief officers, revenue officers, and so on) and engineers, a health inspector, and accountants. Councillors elected from each ward in the city for five-year terms comprise the elected arm of city government, or the council. The council and its committees create legislations, pass resolutions, and oversee budgetary allocations.
5. The IAS is a system inherited from the British for training career bureaucrats.

6. Interview with Sharadini Rath, 19 April 2007. Rath was comparing Maharashtra with Karnataka saying that in the former, politicians were much more vocal, informed, and engaged in municipal decisions than in the latter.

7. This is taken from the description of Nirmala Nagara on the website of the Department of Municipal Administration, Government of Karnataka: http://municipaladmn.kar.nic.in/NNe.htm (accessed on 8 June 2009).

8. It is a little known fact that the ADB funded Nirmala Nagara through its Karnataka Urban Development and Coastal Environment Management Project (KUDCEMP) loan. Although the state government requested the ADB to allocate loan finance from an unrelated loan to Nirmala Nagara, the ADB has no direct oversight over the reform implementation (personal communication with ADB's Indian Resident Mission, 21 November 2007).

9. Retrieved from www.egovernments.org

10. Interestingly, Gajanana Vidya Samsthe, the NGO appointed in Bommanahalli to staff the helpline (according to CMAK [2006]), was not mentioned once in interviews and focus groups I conducted in the municipality.

11. In not one of 40 focus group discussions with neighbourhood associations were streetlights mentioned as a primary concern. This is not to say that lighting, especially at night, is not valued. However, when pressed to list priority areas, associations were more likely to mention other areas of collective struggle.

BIBLIOGRAPHY

Brenner, N. and N. Theodore. 2002. 'Cities and the Geographies of "Actually Existing Neoliberalism"', *Antipode*, 34(3): 349–71.

Chandhoke, N. 2003. 'A Critique of the Notion of Civil Society as the Third Sphere', in R. Tandon and R. Mohanty (eds), *Does Civil Society Matter? Governance in Contemporary India*, pp. 27–58. New Delhi: SAGE Publications.

Chatterjee, P. 2004. *The Politics of the Governed: Reflections on Popular Politics in Most of the World*. New York: Columbia University Press.

CMAK. 2006. *Public Grievance Redressal System: Draft Report*. Bangalore: City Managers Association of Karnataka.

Coelho, K. 2005. 'Unstating "the Public": An Ethnography of Reform in a South Indian Utility', in D. Mosse and D. Lewis (eds), *The Aid Effect: Giving and Governing in International Development*, pp. 171–95. London and Ann Arbor: Pluto Press.

Dean, M. 1999. *Governmentality: Power and Rule in Modern Society*. London: SAGE.

Dixit, S. 2006. *Citizenship and Good Governance: The Sixth Annual Public Affairs Lecture*. Bangalore: Public Affairs Centre.

Ghosh, A. 2005. 'Public–Private or a Private Public? Promised Partnership of the Bangalore Agenda Task Force', *Economic and Political Weekly*, 40(47): 4914–922.

Ghosh, J. 1998. 'Development Strategy in India: A Political Economy Perspective', in S. Bose and A. Jalal (eds), *Nationalism, Democracy & Development*. Delhi: Oxford University Press.

GoK. n.d. 'Initiatives from Urban Sector of Karnataka State', Urban Development Department, Government of Karnataka, Bangalore.

———. 2006. *Initiatives from Urban Sector of Karnataka State*. Bangalore: Urban Development Department, Government of Karnataka.

Harvey, D. 1989. 'From Managerialism to Entrepreneurialism: The Transformation in Urban Governance in Late Capitalism', *Geographiska Annaler. Series B, Human Geography,* 17(1): 3–12.

———. 2005. *A Brief History of Neoliberalism.* Oxford: Oxford University Press.

Hindess, B. 1997. 'A Society Governed by Contract?', in G. Davis, B. Sullivan and A. Yeatman (eds), *The New Contractualism.* Melbourne: Macmillian.

Hindu. 2007. 'Residents Block Hosur Road Demanding Water supply', *Hindu,* 12 April. Available online at http://www.hindu.com/2007/04/12/stories/2007041 217610500.htm (accessed on 2 February 2008).

Holston, J. and A. Appadurai. 1999. 'Introduction', in J. Holston (ed.), *Cities and Citizenship,* pp. 1–18. Durham: Duke University Press.

Jayasurya, K. 2002. 'The New Contractualism: Neoliberal or Democratic?', *The Political Quarterly,* 73(3): 309–20.

Jessop, B. 2002. 'Liberalism, Neoliberalism and Urban Governance: A State-Theoretical Perspective', *Antipode,* 34(3): 452–72.

Kamath, L. 2006. 'Achieving Global Competitiveness and Local Poverty Reduction? Examining the Public Private Partnering Model of Governance in Bangalore, India', Ph.D. Dissertation, Rutgers, The State University of New Jersey, New Brunswick.

Kamath, L., V. Baindur, and P. Rajan. 2008. *Urban Local Government, Infrastructure Planning and the Urban Poor.* Bangalore: CASUMM in collaboration with CIVIC.

Kaviraj, S. 2000. 'Modernity and Politics in India', *Daedulus,* 129(1): 137–62.

KUIDFC. 2004. *Status of Urban Infrastructure in Karnataka.* Bangalore: KN Urban Infrastructure Development Finance Corporation.

Larner, W. 2003. 'Neoliberalism?', *Environment and Planning D: Society and Space,* 21(5): 509–12.

Logan, J. and H. Molotch. 1987. *Urban Fortunes: The Political Economy of Place.* Berkeley: University of California Press.

Marshall, T. 1998 (1950). 'Citizenship and Social Class', in G. Shafir (ed.), *The Citizenship Debates: A Reader,* pp. 93–111. Minneapolis: University of Minnesota Press.

McFarlane, C. 2004. 'Geographical Imaginations and Spaces of Political Engagement: Examples from the Indian Alliance', *Antipode,* 36(5): 890–915.

Nair, J. 2005. *The Promise of the Metropolis: Bangalore's 20th Century.* New Delhi: Oxford University Press.

Ong, A. 2006. *Neoliberalism as Exception: Mutations in Citizenship and Sovereignty.* Durham: Duke University Press.

Peck, J. and A. Tickell. 2002. 'Neoliberalizing Space', *Antipode,* 34(3): 380–404.

Peck, J., N. Theodore, and N. Brenner. 2009. 'Postneoliberalism and Its Mal-contents', *Antipode,* 41(S1): 94–116.

Ranganathan, M. 2010. 'Fluid Hegemony: A Political Ecology of Water, Market Rule, and Insurgence at Bangalore's Frontier', Ph.D. Dissertation, University of California, Berkeley.

Rose, N. 1999. *Powers of Freedom: Reframing Political Thought.* Cambridge: Cambridge University Press.

Sidel, M. 2001. 'New Economy Philanthropy in the High Technology Communities of Bangalore and Hyderabad, India: Partnership with the State and the Ambiguous

Search for Social Innovation', paper prepared for the conference on Philanthropy and the City, Center for the Study of Philanthropy, City University of New York. Available online at http://www.rockarch.org/publications/conferences/sidel.pdf (accessed on 5 December 2010).

Sparke, M. B. 2006. 'A Neoliberal Nexus: Economy, Security, and the Biopolitics of Citizenship on the Border', *Political Geography*, 25(2): 151–80.

Swyngedouw, E. 2005. 'Governance Innovation and the Citizen: The Janus Face of Governance-beyond-the-State', *Urban Studies*, 42(11): 1991–2006.

Vithal, B. 1997. 'Evolving Trends in Bureaucracy', in P. Chatterjee (ed.), *State and Politics in India*. New Delhi: Oxford University Press.

Wallack, J. and S. Nadhamuni. 2008. 'User Innovation and e-Governance Design', paper submitted to MIT competition on 'Hidden Successes: Urban Innovations in India'. Available online at http://ifmr-cdf.in/ (accessed on 10 December 2009).

PART 2

Protest and Claims-making in the Indian City

Chapter 6

Clean Air, Dirty Logic?

Environmental Activism, Citizenship, and the Public Sphere in Delhi

Sunalini Kumar

Citizenship—understood not as a fixed, normative ideal but as an actually existing political practice—is a complex, even protean phenomenon. On the one hand, citizenship can exert powerful egalitarian or redistributive pressure on democratic societies, and, on the other, its promise of equality and justice can often fail to materialize into real rights, immunities, and privileges for those individuals and populations who most need them. More importantly, as a growing body of literature especially in developing or post-colonial societies has documented, citizenship ideals and norms may act as counter-democratic or anti-egalitarian forces when hijacked by elite interests and sections within formally democratic political structures (Chatterjee 1998; Kaviraj 2000; Menon 2004). Citizenship also seems to have an intimate connection with the urban setting—it is within cities, with their unique pulls and pressures, their capacity to concentrate populations and fructify contradictions, to destroy settled habitats and engender new social relations that some of the defining ideals and practices of modern citizenship have taken shape. The fairytale narrative of conventional normative liberal political theory, however—which conceives of citizenship as a set of universally acknowledged rights expanding steadily under the benign gaze of the modern nation-state—serves to obscure the continuous and ongoing contestation over domains and definitions of citizenship and 'writes out' the role of cities in the history of this influential political ideal.

Put simply, and as much excellent scholarship has shown, the story of citizenship is as much a story of exclusions as inclusions; further, many of these exclusions are brought dramatically to the fore in struggles over collective life within modern cities. This essay examines one such contestation over citizenship in the context of post-liberalization urban India. In particular, it examines in detail the conversion of Delhi's transport system to 'clean' fuel—compressed natural gas, or CNG—by a 1998 Supreme Court of India order.[1] More than a decade after the CNG order, a growing body of evidence points to the fact that the 'CNG solution' was a peculiarly limited and skewed response to the serious environmental problems facing Delhi—it was ill-conceived, forcibly implemented, and ultimately proved inadequate even on its own premise as a viable, long-term solution to air pollution. Further, the CNG order premised the sacrifice of viable employment for thousands of public transport operators, specifically of autorickshaw drivers. Yet, the judgment enjoyed widespread support and a glut of celebratory reportage in mainstream national and even international media—a support that allowed a relatively ineffectual short-term policy to be portrayed as a viable long-term panacea. This essay seeks to understand how and why the complex hazards and unresolved tensions involved in this piece of environmental legislation (the question of long-term efficacy versus short-term gain, the overall impact of the policy on the urban public transport system, the infrastructural and material strain on the urban economy, or the issue of livelihood of those sections of Delhi's population rendered economically distressed or unemployed by the legislation) were ignored by judges, policy makers, and media in favour of the CNG solution.

In raising the above issues, the essay seeks to foreground the class-determined character of the CNG order as against its popular representation as a 'public'-minded order. As a growing body of literature has documented in the context of post-liberalization India, judicial activism in the field of environmental policy in India has increased dramatically in the 1990s and 2000s. A bulk of such activism has focused on urban environments; further, it has invariably manifested in anti-poor judgments which have located blame and responsibility for urban environmental degradation on the working class and otherwise marginalized urban populations. Activist environmental lawyers and judges have characterized such populations as the polluting, dangerous, and illegal elements in an urban ecological structure conceived of as 'fragile' or 'threatened' (Baviskar 2002, 2003; Bhushan 2004; Dembowski 1999; Mawdsley 2004; Ramanathan 2006; Sharan 2003; Veron 2006). In the specific context of post-liberalization Delhi, Baviskar's well-known term 'bourgeois environmentalism' and Veron's 'environmental governmentality' point to the role of middle-class biases and interests—for example, the desire for beautification, particular notions of hygiene, and fantasies of control of physical space—in shaping the new urban environmental imaginary (Baviskar 2002; Veron 2006).[2]

This essay too contributes to the critique of bourgeois environmentalism in the Delhi of the 2000s, tracing the trajectory of decision-making by which upper- and middle-class interests were able to impose their will on the shape and content of the CNG order. However, it has a more specific aim—to uncover the architecture of public debate and, particularly, the public sphere in the CNG case in order to understand how the issue of public transport in the city came to be dominated by elite interests. In particular, the essay hopes to highlight the fascination of influential sections of the public sphere for the single-point CNG solution despite, as mentioned above, its limited efficacy and significant human cost. My central argument here is that the tendentious and disingenuous use of the term 'public' in the court order, statements by judiciary and public officials, and the media allowed this order to be passed and celebrated. Further, several other structural biases and prejudices dominated the debate on the issue of public transport and environmental degradation in Delhi; these fundamentally compromised the 'publicness' of the issues being discussed, and destroyed the possibility of a democratic challenge to the juggernaut of bourgeois environmentalism. What were the material and discursive devices deployed by courts, bureaucrats, the media, and public figures that made it possible for public discourse on the CNG case to effectively become 'univocal' and drown out opposition or any real debate on the judgement? I examine these devices in some detail below, including particularly the ways in which the terms 'citizen' and 'public' were misused by influential constituents of the public sphere.

The second aim of the essay is to examine the nature and incidence of political protest around the CNG case. As is well known, Delhi has since Independence functioned not simply as the capital of the country but as the capital of political protest within a democratic nation-state. Hence, it would be fascinating to see if the CNG order—located and implemented in Delhi, with far-reaching and complex effects on the urban population here—provoked, or failed to provoke protest. In a sense, while one thread of the essay records the apparent convergence of support for the CNG order, another attempts to record the conflict and disagreement behind it. If as appears to be the case, the public sphere including public statements by judiciary in the CNG issue failed to represent all affected urban constituencies equally, the right to protest guaranteed to all citizens could arguably create a route of redressal for marginalized urban populations. In this instance, however, while opposition to the CNG order was widespread among significant sections of the affected urban population, it failed to be voiced effectively through visible protest. The reason for this, I argue, may be found in the changing landscape of protest in post-liberalization urban India. In specific terms, it appears that political protest by electorally oriented political outfits (involving displays of numerical strength through massive rallies, strikes, sit-ins, and so on) has lost much of its earlier capacity to capture public imagination, and especially the urban public sphere. On the other hand, protest by middle- and upper-class (and on rare occasions, cross-class) formations organized around ambitions of 'clean' politics, free of crime and 'corruption' has dramatically risen in the same period, and enjoyed extensive coverage in the increasingly mediatized public sphere.[3] The essay concludes with an examination of the impact of the above developments on urban citizenship, especially on de facto citizenship rights of participation, representation, and redressal.[4]

DELHI: HISTORY AND BACKGROUND

When India attained independence in 1947, Delhi became the capital of the complex and fraught democracy that India was to grow into. It was fitting therefore that its capacity for attracting and accommodating political protest did not end with the end of colonial occupation. The grand avenues and paths located in central New Delhi—built to imperial scale by the British—became unwitting hosts to massive political rallies and dissident gatherings during phases of political tumult. Following liberalization in 1991, however, and the installation of a new urban administrative regime that ironically resuscitated colonial anxieties about dissent and disorder, New Delhi was progressively 'cordoned off', thereby dramatically curtailing public assemblages at this visually and symbolically powerful site.[5] Other areas of the city have also come under tight anti-assembly regulations and ordinances, with the result that disruptive crowds of any kind are an increasingly rare sight on Delhi's streets. The political appeal of Delhi for protest has proven difficult to repress entirely, however. Central New Delhi has continued to attract motley 'protesting publics' in the 2000s—primarily middle- and upper-class groups with immediate governance agendas—to demand an inquiry into a high-profile murder or to protest corruption in an area that directly affects the affluent classes. In contrast to the restriction of traditional political groups and protest marches, these newer groups have enjoyed the indulgence of the Indian state and police along with sympathetic coverage by the influential electronic and English-language media. As mentioned in the introduction earlier, the post-liberalization 1990s mark the arrival of the middle-class citizen as a political protestor, especially within the public sphere; this point will be revisited in the following discussion.

Industry and Housing

Delhi today is a rapidly expanding urban agglomeration akin to other late modern urban counterparts. The most visible and organized economic sectors in Delhi apart from the government sector are trading (it is home to some of the largest wholesale markets and depots in India); retail (in popular imagination, Delhi is a *dukaandaaron ka shahar*—a city of shopkeepers); a small proportion of small-scale industries; and, post-globalization, a rapidly growing services sector located largely in the newly gentrified suburbs. Holston and Appadurai point out that cities in Asia, Africa, and Latin America often have little to do with industry, manufacture, or production; they can rather be military, bureaucratic, monumental or re-creative of nationalist historiographies (Holston and Appadurai 1999: 14). This certainly can be said to be true of Delhi—governed by an urban administrative imaginary which discourages the open growth of industry—industrial activity has been pushed 'underground' here, that is, to the physical and symbolic margins of the city and often into a zone of semi-legality or illegality (Nigam 2001). As the discussion below will elaborate, growing anxiety about environmental pollution in Delhi through the 1990s has intensified the anti-industrial pressure in urban planning, forcing industries further away from the legal, settled areas of the urban landscape. The invisibility of industry has in turn sanctified the invisibility, dispossession, and fragmentation of the working class here, a fact that is significant for this discussion. Recent land-use developments related to the adoption of neoliberal policies in urban planning have deepened the crisis of the working class in the 2000s. These include revaluation of urban land along commercial and speculative axes, the arrival of big capital in real estate development, and gentrification of previously low-value land (Harvey 2008; Mandel 1975; D. Roy 2007b; Smith 1996). The physical landscape of the Nation Capital Region (NCR) has undergone a dramatic transformation consequently—along with the reshaping and re-deployment of public facilities, the city has witnessed the proliferation of privatized spaces of residence, leisure, and consumption such as shopping malls, amusement parks, and gated communities (Kumar 2003). Not surprisingly, Delhi's real estate prices are now among the highest in the world, and political–administrative technologies seeking to release prime land from various uses increasingly deemed as non-productive (low-end residential and squatter colonies, urban villages, farmland, flood plains) have assumed prominence. While Delhi is by no means unique in these developments, here, the accompanying violence on the poor in the form of 'accidental' or planned slum demolition drives in recent years has been crudely direct and often physical in nature.[6] Bourgeois environmentalism has provided a ready ally for these developments. In 2006, dismissing an appeal on behalf of slum dwellers against slum demolitions, Supreme Court justices Ruma Pal and Markandeya Katju famously remarked, 'Nobody should come to Delhi if they cannot afford it.'[7]

Governance

The adoption of structural adjustment policies in India has, as is well documented, dramatically increased the role of international lending agencies like the World Bank in several areas including urban governance. These agencies have advocated the adoption of newer political and administrative techniques suited to neoliberal economic transformation; and Delhi as national capital has often taken the lead in evolving new urban governance tools. One such tool—a public–private partnership christened Bhagidari (a Hindi word that translates as stakeholdership and contains a wealth of positive connotations pertaining to a non-hierarchical, collective model of decision-making) was inaugurated in 2000. Bhagidari recently bagged a coveted UN public service award for emerging as a 'new, collective decision-making actor' in the urban context. In practice, however, as several studies have noted, Bhagidari has reinforced the clout of urban constituencies that already possessed de facto social and economic power by recognizing only those with legal residence proofs, ration cards, and professional memberships as 'citizens' groups' or 'stakeholders' for the purpose of consultative decision-making in urban governance (Mawdsley 2004; Nair 2005; Veron 2006). As Nair has argued, urban governance in post-structural adjustment India increasingly involves the installation of procedures wherein a strictly limited number of interest groups or 'stakeholders' are identified as the 'public' or the 'citizen', and services are delivered to the same (Nair 2005). As is the case with most post-colonial cities, legal residents constitute a minority of Delhi's population; hence Bhagidari is hardly innocent of class and privilege in its definitions. As Chatterjee details in his influential work on 'political society', the pre-liberalization era afforded a degree of bargaining power for poorer urban residents, either through the vote (dismissively termed in upper-class discourse as 'vote-bank politics'), the clientelistic patronage of slum lords and other local notables, or a host of quotidian micro-negotiations with power—legal, semi-legal, and even illegal (Chatterjee 1998, 2004). Bhagidari and similar schemes evidently seek the installation of a new clientelism on the urban landscape—between the State and powerful financial interests on one end, and organized, overtly

legal upper-class groups on the other. The growing clout of homeowners'/
residents' associations following the neoliberal restructuring of urban governance appears to be a worldwide trend, as noted by several studies (Davis
1990; McKenzie 2006).

Transport

Delhi is easily distinguished in transport patterns from the other three
largest metropolitan centres in India (Mumbai, Chennai, and Kolkata)
by having more cars than all of them combined, and notoriously insufficient public transport. In the mid-1980s, the Japanese car company Su-
zuki Motors almost single-handedly created the affordable car market in
a monopolistic tie-up with the Indian government. With liberalization
in the early 1990s, other car manufacturers entered the fray and the city
witnessed an explosion in personal vehicle sales. In contrast, the already
scanty bus network failed to keep up with growing demands. By the mid-
2000s, personal vehicles in Delhi (cars, jeeps, two-wheelers, and goods
vehicles) formed 95.66 per cent of the total number of vehicles owned,
while the proportion of public vehicles (autorickshaws and buses combined) was 3.81 per cent. In the early 1990s, as public pressure for an
adequate bus network rose, the government decided to partially privatize
the bus network, thus inflating the numbers of buses and routes. As of
now, Delhi has a total fleet of 12,000–14,000 buses of which the Delhi
Transport Corporation (DTC) owns approximately 3,800, while the rest
are managed by private operators. However, in this case, the solution may
have proven worse than the problem. Delhi's private buses have one of
the worst accident rates in the world due, in no small measure, to the fact
that the private bus system is run competitively, with no subsidies from
the government. Intense competition between buses for lucrative routes
and passengers leads to buses being packed dangerously beyond capacity,
and racing each other to the bus stops. Perhaps due to the fact that private
owners of public buses are powerful individuals with well-known political
connections (especially among local politicians) or because bus passengers
in Delhi are overwhelmingly working class and hence considered more
expendable, the situation with Delhi's buses has continued largely unal-
tered. Thus, there is a clear class dimension to Delhi's public transport
woes. The only exception to the class profile of public transport consumers are those who use autorickshaws (three-wheeler taxis)—these tend to
be predominantly middle class. These facts become significant in the light
of the discussion on the CNG conversion below.

Judicial Activism

As briefly mentioned above, the 1990s and 2000s have seen a massive increase in judicial activism over the urban environment. Delhi, being the location of the Supreme Court, has received a bulk of activist judgements. Two recent episodes in the city help us illuminate this starkly before we consider the CNG case. In 2001, the Supreme Court ordered the closures of 'hazardous' and 'polluting' industrial units in Delhi. Compared to the earlier instances of industrial closure (168 larger factories were closed down in 1997), however, the scale of closures was enormous in 2001, with 100,000 industrial units earmarked for closure or relocation to the outskirts of Delhi. As a result of the order, several hundred thousand workers were thrown out of their jobs. While there was a provision for compensation, this was rarely followed given the nearly non-existent bargaining power of industrial labour in Delhi.

The actual dynamics of this event are too complicated to be discussed here, but some preliminary observations are possible. First, while the judgement used the words 'hazardous' and 'polluting' together, it was obvious in the way the judgement was envisaged that it was the 'polluting' rather than the 'hazardous' nature of the industries that concerned the court. Unlike the term 'hazardous' that has an affinity with the long history of protective legislation for workers within industrial capitalism, the emphasis on 'polluting' meant that the judgement was framed within the problematic of the moral hazard of environmentalism, that polluters must pay for environmental costs to society. In simple terms, factory workers and owners—already consigned to a shadowy, semi-legal existence due to the discouragement of industry in Delhi—must sacrifice their livelihood to obtain cleaner air for 'legitimate' residents, referred to in the judgment as citizens of Delhi. Second, unlike the closures in the 1990s, during which a legacy of worker unionization and strikes did manage to influence the language of the newspaper reports, the protest against the 2001 closures was recorded in the mainstream newspapers overwhelmingly in unsympathetic terms, either accusing the protesters of disrupting the 'smooth flow of traffic' in Delhi, or of trying to evade their moral responsibility for the city's pollution. Third, in many areas, unlike earlier rounds of closures, factory owners joined workers in the protests. This was unprecedented in the history of protest in the city and could reveal the relative vulnerability of this constituency (small industrialists) vis-à-vis newer forms of capital—big finance and corporatized real estate. Fourth, there was a deliberate or accidental lack of coordination between the various legislative, executive, and enforcement agencies over the entire process of closing down non-conforming units and issuing of licenses in 2001; licenses for new units to be located in non-conforming areas were issued as recently as four days before the closures began, and the various agencies continued to blame each other for the crisis even as factory workers were killed in police firing and owners found themselves stripped of their factories overnight. The determination of the government to release land from small industry seemed to be stronger in this round of closures and it did not relent in the face of the protests, many of which turned violent in the poorer peripheral districts of the city. Thus, the breakdown of traditionally unionized protest during the factory closures paralleled a conscious fragmentation and break-down of governance.

In 2006, the Supreme Court ordered the demolition or sealing of commercial properties located in residential areas of Delhi. In this instance, there was no extenuating reason for the demolitions like pollution, except the weak one that commercial properties constitute a nuisance to the 'peace and quiet' of residential neighbourhoods. The legal-administrative support for the sealing judgment was found in an injunction in the Delhi Master-plan against 'mixed land use', or the location of commercial and residential units in the same neighbourhood.[8] According to Dunu Roy of a Delhi-based urban environmental NGO, Hazards Centre, the injunction against mixed land use is based on the outdated colonial urban policy of 'zoning'; in the contemporary urban environment there is no conceivable reason that mixed land use should be not encouraged, in fact, since it makes environmental sense to live close to one's workplace. Roy argues that mixed land use could significantly reduce Delhi's heavy dependence on private vehicles and become the cornerstone of an ecologically sustainable urban policy (D. Roy 2007a). The 'mixed land use' injunction, however, benefits big capital, since it diverts consumers away from neighbourhood shops with cheap or free parking to expensive, distant malls that have mushroomed all over the NCR.

Interestingly, the sealing and demolition affected the traditional backbone of Delhi's economy—traders and better-off petty bourgeoisie. The political and social backlash, therefore, was highly visible and vocal and received extensive coverage in newspapers and electronic media. As with the industrial closures case, fringes of the city witnessed greater violence and even deaths due to police firing on the protestors. In contrast to the industrial closures, however, the marginally greater bargaining clout of the traders secured them short-term victories from the government. The sealing exercise was postponed by a year, with the government stating officially that it would use the time to generate greater public debate. Significantly, the Bhagidari scheme has precisely defined which stakeholders may be consulted as representatives of 'the public' in closed, high-level discussions in the sealing issue—apart from traders' associations that have wrested this privilege through their protests, Residents Welfare Associations (RWAs) have been notified to make representations.

THE CNG CASE

In July 1998, the Supreme Court of India, responding to a public interest petition by activist environmental lawyer M.C. Mehta, ordered the Delhi government to oversee the conversion of public transport from conventional fuels to CNG technology. A bench comprising Justices A. S. Anand, B. N. Kirpal, and V. N. Khare quoted several international studies including a study by the Government of Australia as well as research by the Court-appointed Bhure Lal Committee and the Delhi-based NGO, Centre for Science and Environment (CSE), to conclude that CNG and liquified petroleum gas (LPG) were the most effective fuels for combating air pollution as well as global warming. Prior to the judgement, the CSE had been a vigorous votary of the CNG solution in the public domain; claiming through its highly publicized 'Clean Air Campaign' press releases that the resultant reduction in toxic emissions would be as high as 90 per cent.

The CSE's opinion was not uncontrovertible, however, within scientific and environmental circles—the scientific research organization Tata Energy Research Institute (TERI) had expressed scepticism over the feasibility of conversion of the entire public transport network in Delhi to a single (CNG) fuel and instead favoured ultra low sulphur diesel (ULSD) to reduce levels of vehicular pollution in the city. Research at TERI had shown that while CNG was a good fuel, ULSD was a better option, more suited to Delhi's road usage patterns. Moreover, TERI claimed that there was evidence that CNG produced more potent greenhouse gases than low sulphur diesel. Given that the CNG solution would cost ₹ 0.82 billion more, ULSD was also financially more viable. The most significant difference between the two organizations was that unlike the CSE's single-point one-fuel agenda, the response of TERI advocated a comprehensive transport and technology plan to be put into place over a decade—this long-term plan would include traffic management, reduction in private vehicle usage, and cross-subsidized public transport. The Delhi government-appointed Mashelkar Committee also opposed the single-fuel CNG solution, asking for a comprehensive policy that would not only include different types of fuels (including petrol-based liquid gas and ULSD) but also focus on revamping engine technology towards acceptable international emission standards.

The court, however, doggedly ruled over all counter-opinions and ordered the government to oversee the speedy transition of public transport vehicles to CNG—as mentioned above, these include buses, taxis, privately owned goods vehicles, and autorickshaws. Implementation of the court order depended on the installation of adequate infrastructure, that is, primarily uninterrupted supply of CNG through sufficient number of filling stations. The government was also directed to bear the financial burden of the conversion of government-owned public transport. However, the responsibility for conversion of privately owned public transport vehicles fell solely upon private bus/autorickshaw/taxi owners and operators. Thus, curiously for a policy that was aimed at generating greater public good, private drivers or owners of public transport vehicles were expected to install CNG engines at their own expense, without financial support from any public body. To make matters worse, the new CNG-enabled vehicles were prohibitively expensive; a CNG bus cost ₹ 1.3 million–1.5 million compared to ₹ 700,000–800,000 for the old diesel buses; and a CNG-fitted autorickshaw cost a steep ₹ 450,000 compared to ₹ 150,000 for the older diesel model.[9] Further, loans for CNG-enabled vehicles were unavailable from banks and established legal lending agencies, forcing owners to borrow at extortionate interest rates from organized cartels of private lenders.

In the absence of preparation on both fronts (government and private transporters), the CNG conversion took nearly three years to be fully implemented, causing confusion and distress to owners and consumers of public transport. Supply-side infrastructure remained inadequate for several years, with barely enough filling stations and fuel supply blockages and mile-long queues at filling stations. Monopolistic sale and hoarding of CNG kits and chassis ensued, and private bus and autorickshaw owners had to spend huge amounts of money to book new CNG vehicles or buy CNG conversion kits. As a result, drivers of public transport lost precious working hours and income waiting for the new fuel and several found themselves forced out of their livelihood by then. At one point, Delhi chief minister Sheila Dikshit decided to throw her weight behind the transporters and declared dramatically that her government was ready to face punishment for contempt of court, but that it would not allow the citizens of Delhi to suffer—she was presumably referring to passengers and operators of privately run public transport. The Supreme Court retaliated by blaming the government for 'catering to vote banks' in delaying implementation of the order. Asked by a shrill media chorus whether the government's 'defiant stand' amounted to a breakdown of constitutional machinery, Solicitor General Harish Salve warned that if this attitude persisted, *then the Center had no option but to displace the government* (Rajalakshmi and Venkatesan 2001, emphasis mine). Anomalous, biased reasoning marked the court's attitude towards the multiple constituencies affected. For instance, at one point, while ignoring the pleas of private bus operators for reconsideration of its policy, the Bench decided to arbitrarily exclude tourist buses from the CNG order, holding that tourists should not be put to any avoidable inconvenience. In another instance, while the Bench ruled that granting a relief in the deadline for conversion to CNG 'would amount to putting a premium on the lapses and inaction of the administration and the private transport operators', it granted relaxations and exemptions to 'mitigate the sufferings' of school-going children in particular. Indeed, the reference to children provided the much-needed emotional charge to the CNG argument; in an order dated 9 May 2002, the Bench stated, 'The increase in respiratory diseases specifically amongst the children should normally be a cause of concern for any responsible government…. However, children do not agitate or hold rallies and, therefore, their sound is not heard.' The Bench's attempt to claim moral high ground vis-à-vis the government also included a masterful reference to the greatest environmental disaster India has seen—the Bhopal gas tragedy. An order of the same date held that in the case of Bhopal, the 'nation rightly sought compensation' from a multinational company responsible for the tragedy; however, now 'the shoe was on the other foot' and if not prevented, the government would be responsible for 'far greater tragedies in the form of degradation of public health'.

For reasons pertaining to the lower bargaining power and visibility of the public transport operators, the political balance in the CNG fracas soon tilted in favour of the court and the Delhi government was forced to withdraw its support to transporters. As visible air pollution levels started declining from 2002 onwards, it seemed like the court's position had been vindicated. However, by 2005, despite public transport faithfully adhering to CNG, air pollution in Delhi began to outstrip its CNG 'solution'. The CSE itself notes the return of air pollution to pre-CNG levels in recent press releases. The reason for this phenomenon is so obvious that it is an absurdity that it never made its debut in the court's reasoning and public debate on the issue. As the earlier discussion on Delhi's transport structure makes clear, public transport constitutes a tiny proportion of Delhi's vehicles, whereas petrol and especially diesel-driven private vehicles have undergone an explosive growth in numbers.[10] Eventually, without a drastic change in the urban public transport policy including strict regulation of private vehicle sales, particulate matter was bound to rise and choke Delhi again, not to mention non-particulate forms of pollution that may be deadlier.[11]

In other words, Delhi's air cannot become cleaner without jettisoning the dream of every upwardly mobile urban Indian to own a car—a dream that Delhi-based environmental bulletin *Toxics Alert* evocatively refers to as involving 'excess indulgence in personal mobility' (*Toxics Alert* 2006).

Ironically, the CSE itself had foreseen the conversion of public transport as a part of a much larger series of changes in the transport habits of the average Delhi resident. Indeed, an extensive policy on CNG encompassing both private and public transport was also part of the Supreme Court's reasoning in the early 1990s. An order dated 21 October 1994 had observed:

> On an earlier occasion, when these matters came up before this Court it was suggested that *to begin with,* Government vehicles and public undertaking vehicles including public transport vehicles could be equipped with CNG cylinders with necessary modification in the vehicles to avoid pollution which is hazardous to the health of the people living in highly polluted cities like Delhi and the other metros in the country. (Emphasis mine)

The clause 'to begin with' suggests a phased CNG plan; this plan is strikingly absent from the binding 1998 order.

The selective application of the CNG policy and its short-term efficacy could be condoned if the financial and environmental costs and benefits were evenly shared amongst urban constituents. However, this was far from true in the CNG case. While long-term financial gain for middle-class autorickshaw passengers was significant in the form of reduced fares, benefits to (working class or lower middle class) bus users were negligible because of the relative inflexibility of bus fares. As for private owners and drivers of public transport vehicles, this constituency suffered considerable short-term financial distress during the conversion. My research showed that autorickshaw drivers were worst affected, suffering both in the short and long terms, as the discussion below will elaborate.[12] Most autorickshaw drivers (30 out of 34 interviewed) did not own the vehicles they drove—a pattern corroborated by Harding and Hussain's larger study (Harding and Hussain 2010). Those who did own their autorickshaws in the pre-CNG era had bought them on loan and were making just enough profit prior to the CNG order to financially survive. Since the new/refitted CNG autorickshaws cost more than double compared to the pre-CNG autos (due to the flourishing illegal market for CNG permits as mentioned in note 9; and finance being in the grip of a small cartel of extortionate lenders), autorickshaw drivers who previously owned their vehicles were forced to either discard them or sell them to a new class of autorickshaw owners who emerged at this time. These new owners, who were referred to by drivers as *seth*s (a north Indian term for merchants/profiteers), bore the cost of CNG refitting by renting the vehicles out at steep rates. The pre-CNG autorickshaw owner-drivers, on the other hand, slid down the class scale to become drivers who rented autorickshaws for a finite number of hours in a day—typically an eight-hour day or night shift, which also included the commute from the vehicle depot to the first passenger point, and the wait for fuel, which could take anything between 10 minutes and an hour depending on the station, and availability. The long wait at filling stations and the new, shorter working hours often ensured that profits were swallowed up. Further, maintenance cost for the new vehicles was almost double that of petrol vehicles. In addition, the cost of CNG had been steadily rising. From ₹ 11 per kilogram in 2000, it had risen to ₹ 16 per kilogram by 2002, and continues to rise till date. Most importantly, the overall reduction in fuel costs compared to the petrol era was accompanied by reduction in fares, thereby offsetting profit.[13]

I also found most autorickshaw drivers deep in debt, having taken loans at rates of 13–16 per cent interest in order to pay for CNG conversion kits. Drivers complained of repeated harassment and humiliation by the police and local courts on the issue of CNG fitness certificates—mandatory to operate an autorickshaw following the court order. Thus, the overall pattern that emerged from my research was that the CNG transition negatively altered the class profile and working conditions of drivers, structurally diminishing the economic prospects of this section of the working class, and turning a bulk of owners into renters of autorickshaws. It further appeared that autorickshaw drivers were highly aware of their own marginalization— one driver said that whether it was CNG or any other legislation pertaining to public transport, the courts seemed to experiment on the autorickshaw drivers before deeming the policy fit for the general public.

Turning to the question of protest, I was struck by the near-silence of private transporters regarding the CNG judgment; private taxi operators appeared to be quiet on account of their small numbers while private bus owners only briefly registered their protest. Jaswant Singh Arora, president of the Federation of the Delhi Transport Unions Congress, blamed central and State governments for not ensuring fuel availability; and M.O. Simon of the State Transporters Action Front (Delhi) complained of 'inefficient implementation' (*Times of India* 2001). On the whole, however, private bus operators did not protest the CNG policy per se. As mentioned above, this section of private transporters is economically secure and well-connected in local politics; this would explain the brief but significant support bus operators received from the Delhi government. For the same reason, they could not be counted upon to sustain the protest on the CNG issue—they switched to the CNG regime in due course and directed their financial and political clout towards intimidation of individual traffic policemen or large-scale bribing of law enforcement officials in order to escape the punitive post-CNG regime of fitness certificates, permits, and fines.

Since autorickshaw drivers were economically the worst affected constituency, it becomes important to understand why they did not use available means of protest, especially during the difficult early months of the CNG transition. In September 1998, two trade unions—the Delhi Autorickshaw Sangh and the Shiv Sena Autorickshaw Sangh—called for several large-scale strikes; however, none of these was successful. The apparent political passivity of autorickshaw drivers may be explained through class again. As mentioned above, the economic condition of autorickshaw drivers is highly precarious compared to private bus drivers, most of them being migrants from immiserated towns and villages all over North India. Thus, their freedom to strike or protest was a priori curtailed by the immediate threat of losing precious daily income and the long-term threat of returning to the hometown. All interviewees spoke of the immediate danger posed by 'hood-slashing' during strikes—the act of tearing the plastic hoods of autorickshaws by armed gangs.[14]

In contrast to the relative lack of protest by private transporters, in 2001, several NGOs calling themselves 'citizens' groups' made highly visible interventions on the issue of public transport in the print media, issuing expensive front-page advertisements in prominent English-language dailies. These advertisements took a strident anti-Delhi government stance, protesting the delay in implementation of the CNG order and the related delay in reduction of fares. They spoke in the name of the 'ordinary citizen' of Delhi and asked the government to respect the right of the citizen to be protected from autorickshaw drivers who were described in unambiguous terms in these 'public interest' advertisements as unscrupulous cheaters overcharging innocent customers. One such 'citizen's group', People's Action, concluded a diatribe against the Delhi government in one of its advertisements by saying that the government clearly 'did not care about public opinion, or the public, for that matter'.[15] Electronic news media too remained overwhelmingly sympathetic to the 'average autorickshaw user', with the result that any opportunity, however brief, to bring in the voices of the private transporters or contrary scientific opinion on the issue of public transport and CNG was lost.

In 2002, a section of autorickshaw drivers were drawn into a city-based advocacy group called NyayaBhumi—a word that translates as The Just Land, or The Land of Justice. On its website, NyayaBhumi describes itself as an NGO 'run by selfless and fairly affluent people of all age-groups who come from different walks of life'.[16] NyayaBhumi is therefore by its own definition a middle and upper class organization; in addition, it frequently refers to political corruption as the root of all problems including the problem of public transport in the city—a recognizably middle-class understanding of politics. In the years following the CNG order, the organization won the support of many autorickshaw drivers through campaigns for fare hike and an appeal to the media to reverse its 'hostile stand' towards the drivers. However, NyayaBhumi's success in reducing the distress suffered by autorickshaw drivers or giving them real bargaining power has been limited—not only have the government and judiciary not relented on any major policy concerning autorickshaw drivers, but the reputation of auto drivers and sympathy for them in the media have remained abysmal. A call for a strike by autorickshaw unions in June 2010 over fare revision drew the same vitriol from news reporters as previous calls (Basu and Rai 2010). As mentioned above, the middle and upper classes of Delhi do not generally use buses; their interaction with public transport is largely through autorickshaws. It is not surprising therefore that a formation addressing autorickshaw-related woes emerged and enjoyed benign non-interference from the state. It is notable that no comparable organization existed or was created during this time to represent other sections of public transport operators or consumers—bus passengers, for example.

CONCLUSION: BOURGEOIS ENVIRONMENTALISM, THE PUBLIC SPHERE AND CITIZENSHIP

The reasoning and statements of the Supreme Court in the CNG case reveal the skewed logic of bourgeois environmentalism well—identifying 'public good' with the creation of a clean, well-managed city for a limited, manageable number of legal residents recognized as 'citizens' (as opposed to 'populations', as Chatterjee [2004] has argued); and demonizing an increasingly illegalized working class (who are invariably saddled with operating outmoded and polluting technologies) as environmental offenders.[17] As Awadhendra Sharan has pointed out, while passing the CNG conversion order, the Supreme Court invoked the 'precautionary principle' of the court, which holds that where there is a tussle between private interest and public health, the latter shall automatically prevail (Sharan 2003). Public health could thus be opposed to private livelihood, an argument that sets up an absurd dichotomy between environment and livelihood and pretends that those seeking livelihood do not suffer from the moral and environmental consequences of their choice themselves. As Baviskar (2003) and Nigam (1997) have asked, 'Whose livelihood vs. whose environment?' The Supreme Court's definition of public health was clearly motivated by the recognition amongst judges that while the victims included 'people like us', the alleged culprits were beyond the pale of middle and upper class imagination; hence the latter could be made to bear the cost of cleaner air for all.

It is also interesting that the court at no point considered other forms of pollution during the CNG case which could have generated a more holistic or long-term discussion on urban pollution. For instance, when it referred to children as being most vulnerable to pollution it ignored the well-documented fact that the threat of water-borne diseases among urban working-class residents, especially children, is to a much greater degree than that of diseases caused by air pollution. In fact, according to an estimate by the CSE, over a million urban Indians die every year due to traditional water-borne diseases that follow from contaminated supply of drinking water, and overwhelmingly afflict the urban poor; in contrast, around a hundred thousand die per year from diseases related to air pollution. Thus, it is obvious that it was the particular nature of air pollution as a widely diffused urban risk that caught the attention of Delhi's policy makers, media, and judges, and became something of an obsession in public debate in the city. While the risk from contaminated water can be avoided by replacing public water supply with packaged drinking water or home water treatment machines, air pollution respects no class boundaries and cannot therefore be 'opted out' of. Smog, as Beck (1992) reminds us, is democratic! Indeed, the irony in the CNG case arises from the fact that the 'democratic', cross-class nature of smog allowed it to be constructed as an issue regarding 'public health' as opposed to water pollution, where, as mentioned earlier, the mortality figures are far more alarming in numerical terms but the risk can, in principle, be presented as finite. In this context, it was also particularly instrumentalist and misleading of the court to refer to the Bhopal tragedy. It is well known that in that case where the perpetrator was a multinational company and the victims were overwhelmingly working class, Indian courts have been excruciatingly slow in securing compensation for the latter. In contrast, in the case of routine urban air pollution, the apex court acted with speed and conviction.

It is important to note that the Supreme Court's reasoning in the CNG case depended on altered deployments of the idea of 'public' and 'private', the new definitions granting the court enormous legitimacy in the media and public discourse. If under the pre-liberalization era, private interest was seen to reside within society and public interest was represented by the state, under the new dispensation, it is the judiciary itself that has arrogated to itself the status of public institution par excellence. The court's new Leviathan-like self-image—a body that stands above the 'selfish babble of private interests' in society—has given judges moral high ground vis-à-vis not just society or particular organized interests, but even the government when occasion demands it. As observed by several studies, judicial activism inaugurates a vicious circle: judicial initiative hollows out governmental capacity and legitimacy; breakdown of governance justifies further judicial activism (Bhushan 2004).

The far-reaching consequences of the above developments on citizenship—both as an ideal and as a practice—are obvious. Reduced governmental legitimacy as noted by several studies threatens formal citizenship rights, diluting the power of the vote and taking crucial areas of decision-making formally out of the hands of the electorate. As far as substantive or de facto citizenship rights are concerned, a significant space for the exercise of these rights as conceptualized by normative political theory is the public sphere. Indeed, the public sphere is often valorized as a space that expresses and mediates conflicts over collective life, in the long term, helping the political community to adjudicate between respective claims or rights. In other words, the deliberative part of democracy has been hailed by theorists for its ability to fill the lacuna of the formal, representative part of democracy. In the context of our discussion, inclusive public debate may be seen as a space of redressal for marginalized urban populations.

The CNG case demonstrates, however, the susceptibility of the public sphere to hegemonic influences—in this context, bourgeois environmentalism. Writing in the context of judicial activism on environmental issues in Kolkata, Dembowski finds the construction of public sphere in that urban location similarly exclusionary, noting that the use of English and the fact that most documents related to environment and urban planning remain inaccessible to the public act as massive structural obstacles to inclusivity (Dembowski 1999: 55). As discussed above, the public discussion on CNG involved a very select section of the urban population—government officials, scientific and technical organizations, the courts, and primarily the English-language media. Further, the discussion depended on the repetitive, almost hypnotic use of scientific and technical jargon, with endless discussions on percentages, proportions, and nano-units. As Sharan notes, all of the above had the effect of producing a rather sterile and limited type of 'debate' (Sharan 2003). More to the point of our discussion, it compromised the ability of subaltern, non-English speaking and non-scientifically educated populations and voices to be heard. As a result, even the voices of the relatively more powerful private transporters were drowned in the rising chorus of technical expertise.

Further, the use of the scientific and, more specifically, technical imaginary in the CNG case allowed the complex social, economic, political, and ecological problem of air pollution to be whittled down to a neat, convenient technical solution—a neatness that suited the impoverished public sphere well. As mentioned above, the CSE's one-point 'single fuel' strategy prevailed over all alternatives including the more long-term strategies suggested by the TERI and transport researchers. The faith reposed by the judiciary in an apparently pure, apolitical phenomenon called 'technology' as the solution to intractable political and environmental problems made it difficult, if not impossible, to enter the debate from any other position—that of livelihood concerns particularly. As Sundaram effectively argues in his recent work on Delhi, abstract technical solutions and 'surgical' judicial interventions hold an overpowering fascination for urban elites in India due to their apparent promise of countering the deepening sense of risk, chaos, and disaster that characterize urban environments in the 1990s and 2000s (Sundaram 2010). The effect of this fascination on the public discussion on CNG was disingenuous and farcical, engineering a split between the apparently disinterested, 'objective' scientific voice and the messy cacophony of purely 'private' interests. As a result, demands for livelihood could be portrayed as selfish, and political constituencies organized visibly around class (private transporters) could be characterized as sectarian interests who must accede to enlightened opinion 'from above'. The middle and upper classes, on the other hand (who appeared in this debate variously as the 'citizens', 'the public', 'commuters', or simply 'the people'), retained visibility and legitimacy in public discourse, confidently exercising citizenship rights of participation and expression on the urban political landscape.

The CNG case thus demonstrates the ongoing effort of bourgeois environmentalism to reshape space in Indian cities—not merely physical space, but also the discursive space of the public sphere—in a manner that fortifies elite claims on the city, and invisibilizes subaltern ones. As mentioned in the introduction, the CNG policy ultimately proved untenable even on its grounds; the foregoing arguments hopefully illustrate how and why this short-sighted policy may be a result of the very architecture of public debate in Delhi, which failed to include all affected constituencies, let alone adequately represent them. It is tempting to wonder if the CNG case represents an aberration characteristic of post-colonial societies wherein the public sphere falls well short of its promise of inclusive public debate. Undoubtedly, political values and systems function in vastly different ways in post-colonial or developing societies; however, critics like Montag and Hill argue that the notion of the public sphere as it appears in normative Western theory inherently betrays a 'fear of the street' (Hill and Montag 2000). The public sphere may indeed be an exemplary instance of the several apparently universalist, inclusive liberal-democratic political ideals that are fated to function in selective and exclusive ways in practice due to the biases that inhere in their very construction. For example, as mentioned above, while only RWAs from wealthier, legalized colonies are recognized as stakeholders by urban government agencies, the word 'resident' has neutral, cross-class, and universalistic connotations. It is therefore a natural ally of neoliberal urban governments and upper/middle-class discourse. In rare cases, a narrow and ephemeral coalition of classes or a disempowered section within the traditional bourgeoisie could generate a new form of political action or help create a somewhat more inclusive public debate—as witnessed in the case of NyayaBhumi and the protest by traders' associations in the sealing case. But it remains to be seen how much long-term clout these constituencies and newer forms of activism are able to wield on the urban political landscape in the context of long-term neoliberal pressures, corporate interests, and organized upper-class political constituencies. NyayaBhumi undoubtedly provided a breathing space to autorickshaw drivers and an individual redressal from bureaucratic and financial corruption. It also attempted to highlight the structural issues affecting autorickshaws in Delhi, including the grip of private financiers and the collusion between politicians, local transport officials, and police in the matter of CNG permits and fitness certificates. However, NyayaBhumi is best understood not as a trade union or a pressure group in the conventional sense; its role is rather to act as a liaison force or advocacy group between primarily middle-class autorickshaw passengers and working-class drivers. Not surprisingly, in return for support on fare rationalization demands by drivers, the organization has often adopted an odiously paternalistic tone towards them, periodically running training workshops for drivers on 'orderly behaviour' and rule-mindedness. It is significant that NyayaBhumi emerged after the CNG order had been passed—it consequently helped to facilitate a smoother transition to the CNG regime rather than creating a structural alternative to the regime, or providing a long-term voice for autorickshaw drivers as a class.

How in the light of the above discussion may we assess the prospects of contemporary citizenship? Cities have always been crucial to citizenship, as the oft-repeated etymological point about the word 'citi'-zenship and its classical origin reveals. In the modern age, the connection between cities and citizenship has remained vital; the centrality of Paris in the events of

1789, or that of London's 19th century slums in generating furious debates on poverty and social citizenship rights in the British Parliament (Marshall 1950), cannot be overstated. The above has led several writers to be optimistic about citizenship in the late modern city (Holston and Appadurai 1999; Sassen 2002). The matter is not simple, however; a growing body of literature has documented the intense forms of exclusion and marginalization that seems inherent to contemporary urbanization, some going so far as to claim that modern cities remain medieval at their core in this respect (AlSayyad and Roy 2006). Other writers point to the scale and complexity of modern cities as the chief obstacle in fulfilling the promise of citizenship. According to Dagger, the requirements for civic citizenship are small size of cities; unified, non-fragmented authority; and relative physical immobility of citizens (Dagger 1981). Dagger's argument is that 'civic memory' (a fund of memories preserved and passed on inter-generationally within urban populations) is essential to politics and participation; such memory is next to impossible to create in modern cities with their shifting populations and 'publics'. In a related vein, Arendt has famously argued that since memory alone records and gives meaning to human deeds, it creates the conditions for politics in the best sense of the term (Arendt 1958). Further, Arendt argues that a truly public engagement is necessary to politics, since it is only by measuring one's deeds against others (in other words, intersubjectively and openly) that humans give meaning to political acts.

While nostalgic critiques such as those of Dagger's (some would accuse Arendt also of the same) are deeply problematic for radical or progressive-minded social theorists as they appear to defend conservative republican models of citizenship, such accounts may help us raise larger questions regarding the public sphere (including publicly expressed and recorded protest) and urban citizenship. As a growing body of literature has noted, the dynamics of the global capitalist system and global neoliberal urban restructuring have intensified in the 1990s and 2000s, displaying in dramatic fashion what Deleuze and Guattari view as capital's tendency to surpass its own limits, and become 'anti-territorial' (Deleuze and Guattari 1988). For many urban residents, these dynamics produce newer and newer forms of dislocation and invisibility, 'a series of shock experiences', as Sundaram terms it (Sundaram 2010: 5). This essay hopes to have illustrated the manner in which this dislocation is expressed in the particular ephemerality of marginalized urban populations at both material and discursive levels—brought about by an intensified assault on livelihood, residence, and public participation. Bourgeois environmentalism and similarly exclusivist, elite political discourses may thus be understood as destroying certain forms of voice and, hence, memory. If political action including participation in the public sphere or protest against marginalization depends on (civic) memory, then the consequences of the developments discussed in this essay can only be disastrous—not merely for immediately affected constituencies, but also for the *longue duree* political life of citizenship itself.

However, pessimistic accounts of urban citizenship may also be missing the mark. The modern city contains a profound ambivalence that makes any final judgment impossible—it acts as a magnet, attracting and retaining the surplus of the countryside, becoming a lodestone for the aspirations of national and increasingly international populations even as it struggles to contain itself within a recognizable centrifugal scheme, a given identity, a finite residential, cultural, and commercial axis. This ambivalence at the heart of urbanization translates into divergent, even opposing political destinies. The critical Marxist geographer David Harvey in his work strikes a balance between optimism and pessimism regarding the possibilities for meaningful citizenship in the contemporary urban context (Harvey 1982, 2000, 2008). While highlighting the intensified dispossession of the urban poor following neoliberalism, he also believes that the hope for countering this dispossession can only arise from political struggles and alliances located in the city. Echoing Henri Lefebvre, the pioneering urban theorist, he says, 'The Revolution must be urban, or fail.'

NOTES

1. The reason I put the word 'clean' in quotes is that the opinion on CNG is divided within scientific circles—evidence for the 'cleanliness' of this fuel vis-à-vis other fuels and transport technologies is not incontrovertible. The debate is represented in detail below.
2. For a fascinating parallel in colonial Banaras, please see Chakrabarty (1992).
3. The anti-backward caste reservation protests of the late 2000s, demonstrations against the Mumbai terror attack of 26 November 2009, and candlelight vigils and rallies against the murder of model Jessica Lal are emblematic examples. This form of protest has also been iconized in the climax of the popular 2007 film *Rang De Basanti*. Sundaram's recent work documents the dramatically increased role of the media in shaping urban experience in post-1990s India (Sundaram 2010).
4. The paper uses empirical material in the form of interviews with rickshaw drivers, Supreme Court judgments relating to the CNG conversion, websites, public interest advertisements in newspapers, and press releases. Thirty-four autorickshaw drivers were interviewed by the author over two years (2005–07). The paper also draws upon the research of Harding and Hussain (2010).
5. See Mitchell and Staehli's fascinating account (2005) of similar developments in Washington D.C.
6. Many slum demolitions in the 2000s have been preceded by a fire, which has in turn been preceded by a rumour about an impending fire. Since it is famously difficult in

these dense settlements to pinpoint the origin of the rumours, the government could never be officially blamed. Local authorities would, however, use the excuse of fire to bulldoze what remained of the slum. Of course, more planned demolitions have also taken place. See the extensive archive on one such legally demolished slum, Nangla Machi, available online at www.sarai.net

7. Case dated 09 May 2006, available online at http://www.nangla.freeflux.net/blog/legal-pronoucements (accessed on 12 September 2010).

8. The Delhi Masterplan—an urban planning document created in 1962—embodies an imaginary whose proximity to colonial urbanism is even more 'sustained than is commonly assumed' (Sundaram 2010: 65). As a result, it has proved incapable of keeping pace with the demands of a booming post-colonial metropolis, and has been observed more in breach during its life. Sundaram argues that it was, however, 'phantasmatically recalled' in the 1990s by activist courts and civic groups in order to 'relive the mythic moment of liberal urbanism' that marked its birth.

9. In fact, a bulk of the cost for the new CNG autorickshaws goes towards bribes for obtaining permits for owning and operating a rickshaw; after a Supreme Court cap on autorickshaws in 1997, permits for new autorickshaws have to be applied for. This process is controlled by powerful private financiers and government officials who make a killing on the permits.

10. According to the CSE, the share of diesel cars, a mere 4 per cent of the total new car registration in 1999, climbed to nearly 20 per cent in 2006. Diesel is more polluting compared to the commonly available lead-free petrol according to standard parameters.

11. Compressed Natural Gas as a fuel does not counter all forms of pollution, but only particulate matter that causes visible pollution and respiratory ailments; in fact, there is evidence to suggest that CNG technology may be carcinogenic.

12. While bus owners had suffered too, most buses tended to be owned by influential and politically well-connected individuals who were able to bear the burden of the conversion with their ample funds.

13. For an excellent, detailed exegesis of these issues, see Harding and Hussain (2010).

14. The demonic reputation of Delhi's autorickshaw drivers among Delhi's residents is legendary and unique in India; for an exploration of how and why this reputation was formed, and whether it is deserved, see Harding and Hussain (2010).

15. 'Sorry Delhi, You Lose', advertisement by 'People's Action' in *Indian Express*, 26 August 2003.

16. See the Nyayabhumi website: http://www.nyayabhumi.org

17. This illegalization has been doubly disastrous, as it affects the urban poor both in dwelling and in livelihood. See Ramanathan (2006).

BIBLIOGRAPHY

AlSayyad, N. and A. Roy. 2006. 'Medieval Modernity: On Citizenship and Urbanism in a Global Era', *Space and Polity,* 10(1): 1–20.

Arendt, H. 1958. *The Human Condition.* Chicago: University of Chicago Press.

Basu, I. and R. Rai. 2010. 'Auto Unions All Set to Arm-twist Government', *Times of India,* Delhi, 18 June.

Baviskar, A. 2002. 'The Politics of the City', *Seminar,* 516(August) 40–42.

———. 2003. 'Between Violence and Desire: Space, Power, and Identity in the Making of Metropolitan Delhi', *International Social Science Journal*, 55(175): 89–98.

Beck, U. 1992. *Risk Society: Towards A New Modernity.* London: SAGE.

Bhan, G., and K. Menon-Sen. 2008. *Swept Off the Map: Surviving Eviction and Resettlement in Delhi.* Delhi: Yoda Press.

Beiner, R. (ed.). 1995. *Theorising Citizenship.* New York: SUNY Press.

Bhushan, P. 2004. 'Supreme Court and PIL: Changing Perspectives under Liberalisation?', *Economic and Political Weekly*, 39(8): 1770–774.

Bridge, G. and S. Watson (ed.). 2000. *A Companion to the City.* London: Blackwell.

Chakrabarty, D. 1992. 'Of Garbage, Modernity, and The Citizen's Gaze', *Economic and Political Weekly*, 27(10/11): 541–47.

Chatterjee, P. 1998. 'Community in the East', *Economic and Political Weekly*, 33(6, Feb. 7–13): 277–82.

———. 2004. *The Politics of the Governed.* Delhi: Permanent Black.

Dagger, R. 1981. 'Metropolis, Memory and Citizenship', in *American Journal of Political Science*, 25(4): 715–37.

Davis, M. 1990. *City of Quartz: Excavating the Future in Los Angeles.* London: Verso.

Deleuze, G. and F. Guattari. 1988. *A Thousand Plateaus.* London: Athlone Press.

Dembowski, H. 1999. 'Courts, Civil Society and The Public Sphere: Environmental Litigation in Calcutta', *Economic and Political Weekly*, 34(1/2, Jan. 2–15): 49–56.

Dupont, V., E. Tarlo, and D. Vidal (eds). 2000. *Delhi: Urban Space and Human Destinies.* New Delhi: Manohar Publishers.

Featherstone, M., S. Lash, and R. Robertson (eds). 1995. *Global Modernities.* New Delhi: SAGE.

Gupta, N. 1998. *Delhi Between Two Empires 1803–1931.* Delhi: Oxford University Press.

Habermas, J. 1991. *The Structural Transformation of the Public Sphere*, pp. 255–282. Cambridge, MA: MIT Press.

———. 1995. 'Citizenship and National Identity: Some Reflections on the Future of Europe', in R. Beiner (ed.), *Theorising Citizenship.* New York: SUNY Press.

Harding, Simon and Arshad Hussain. 2010. *On the Road to Nowhere? Auto-rickshaws in Delhi: The System, Problems and Recommendations* (Monograph). Report commissioned by the Aman Charitable Trust, New Delhi.

Harvey, D. 1982. *Limits to Capital.* Oxford: Basil Blackwell.

———. 2000. *Spaces of Hope.* Berkeley: University of California Press.

———. 2008. 'The Right to the City', *New Left Review*, 53(September–October): 23–40.

Hill, M. and W. Montag. 2000. *Masses Classes and the Public Sphere.* London/New York: Verso.

Holston, J. and Arjun Appadurai. 1999. 'Introduction', in James Holston (ed.), *Cities and Citizenship*, pp.1–17. Durham: Duke University Press.

Ignatieff, M. 1995. 'The Myth of Citizenship', in R. Beiner (ed.) *Theorising Citizenship*, pp. 53–78, New York: SUNY Press.

Kaviraj, S. 2000. 'Democracy and Social Equality', in F. Frankel, R. Bhargava, Z. Hassan, and B. Arora (eds), *Transforming India*, pp. 88–119. Delhi: Oxford University Press.

Kumar, S. 2003. 'Nostalgia, Secession and the Absurdity of It All', *Himal South Asian*, June, 64–69.

Lahiri, T. 2009. 'The Ground Beneath Our Feet', *Tehelka*, December 12, pp. 26–37.

Lefebvre, H. 1991. *The Production of Space*. London: Blackwell Publishers.

Majumdar, I. *Unorganised Workers of Delhi and the Seven Day Strike, 1988*. (Monograph), V. V. Giri National Labour Institute of India, Noida.

Mandel, E. 1975. *Late Capitalism*. London: Verso.

Marshall, T. H. 1950. *Citizenship and Social Class*. Cambridge: CUP.

Mawdsley, E. 2009. 'Environmentality in the Neoliberal City: Attitudes, Governance and Social Justice', in H. Lange and L. Meier (eds), *The New Middle Classes: Globalising Lifestyles, Consumerism and Environmental Concern*, pp. 237–51. Berlin: Springer Press.

———. 2004. 'India's Middle Classes and The Environment', *Development and Change* 35(1): 79–103.

McKenzie, E. 2006. 'The Dynamics of Privatopia: Private Residential Governance in the USA', in G. Glasze, C. J. Webster and K. Frantz (eds.), *Private Cities: Local and Global Perspectives*, pp. 9–30. London: Routledge.

Menon, N. 2004. 'Citizenship and the Passive Revolution: Interpreting the First Amendment', *Economic and Political Weekly*, 39(8): 1812–819.

Menon, N. and A. Nigam. 2007. *Power and Contestation: India since 1989*. London: Zed Books.

Mitchell, D. and L. Staehli. 2005. 'Permitting Protest: Parsing the Fine Geography of Protest in America', *International Journal of Urban and Regional Research*, 29(4): 796–813.

Mukherjee, R. and M. Singh. 2009. *Delhi: The Making of a Capital*. Delhi: Roli Books.

Nair, J. 2005. *The Promise of The Metropolis: Bangalore's Twentieth Century*. New Delhi: Oxford University Press.

Narain, S. 2002. 'Changing Environmentalism', *Seminar,* Issue 516, August, available online at http://www.india-seminar.com/2002/516.htm (accessed on 27 October 2010).

Nigam, Aditya. 1997. 'Whose Delhi Is It Anyway?' *Revolutionary Democracy*, Vol. III, No. 1, available online at http://www.revolutionarydemocracy.org/ (accessed on 13 July 2011).

———. 2001. 'Dislocating Delhi: A City in the 1990s', *Sarai Reader 2001: The Public Domain*, Delhi: Sarai CSDS.

Rajalakshmi, T. K. and V. Venkatesan. 2001. 'Commuters' Crisis', *Frontline,* 14–27 April, available online at http://www.hindu.com/fline/fl1808/18081190.htm (accessed on 27 October 2010).

Ramanathan, U. 2006. 'Illegality and the Urban Poor', *Economic and Political Weekly*, 41(29): 3193–197.

Roy, D. 2006. *The Delhi Master Plans in Perspective* (Monograph), The Hazards Centre, New Delhi.

———. 2007a. *Delhi Master Plan 2021: What Is to Be Done* (Monograph), Hazards Centre, New Delhi.

———. 2007b. *World Class Cities? Poverty, Inequality and Displacement—Civil Society Responses to Poverty Reduction* (Monograph), Hazards Centre, New Delhi.

Roy, A. 2009. *Listening to Grasshoppers: Field Notes from a Democracy*. London: Penguin.

Sassen, S. 2002. 'The Repositioning of Citizenship: Emergent Subjects and Spaces for Politics', *Berkeley Journal of Sociology,* 46: 4–25.

Sharan, A. 2003. 'Governing Technology: The City in the Age of Environmental Crisis', *Sarai Reader 03: Shaping Technologies*. New Delhi: Sarai-CSDS.

Smith, N. 1996. *The New Urban Frontier.* London: Routledge.

Singh, K. (ed.). 2001. *City Improbable : An Anthology of Writings on Delhi.* New Delhi: Viking.

Soja, E. W. 1997. *Postmodern Geographies.* London: Verso.

Sundaram, R. 2010. *Pirate Modernities: Delhi's Media Urbanism.* London: Routledge.

Times of India. 2001. 'More fingers point at government's impractical moves', *Times of India,* New Delhi, 26 February.

Tarlo, E. 2001. *Unsettling Memories: Narratives of the Emergency in Delhi.* London: C. Hurst and Co.

Toxics Alert, December 6, 2006; available online at www.toxicslink.org (accessed 27 October 2010).

Veron, R. 2006. 'Remaking Urban Environments: The Political Ecology of Air Pollution in Delhi', *Environment and Planning A,* 38(11): 2093–2109.

Chapter 7

Who Operates and Who Agitates?

A Class-wise Investigation of Contentious Action and Citizenship in Varanasi, India

Jolie M. F. Wood

Scholars of Indian politics and society have been deeply engaged in the global debate over applying historical 'Western' concepts of civil society to developing, post-colonial societies. One point of contention concerns the ability of the lower classes, the working poor, or the subaltern to participate in this realm of public life. Complicating this question is how the concept of civil society is to be understood: should one adhere to its original formulations in the interest of theoretical 'purity' or modify the concept to suit particular social, political, and economic conditions? The eminent Indian scholar, Partha Chatterjee, has argued that the concept of civil society is of limited relevance to India, where it is manifested as a closed, modern, bourgeois realm that excludes most Indians, who are poor, uneducated, unable to exercise the rights of citizenship, and preoccupied with the struggles of daily life. As they cannot participate in civil society, the argument goes, their engagement with the state is necessarily more contentious and politicized, and their claims frequently must transgress legal boundaries. According to Chatterjee, such engagement constitutes a separate realm of action, which he labels 'political society'. The 'modern elite', on the other hand, participates in civil society and engages with the state in an orderly, rational, and contained manner. The lower and middle classes interact with the state in separate realms, according to different modes of engagement, and make different kinds of claims (Chatterjee 2001, 2004).

I explore and challenge this argument with an empirical study of occupational groups in the north Indian city of Varanasi (also known as Benaras or Kashi), addressing the following questions: How do associations representing groups at different class levels make demands upon the state?

ey use more confrontational tactics when making demands upon the st.. than bourgeois associations? Do middle-class associations necessarily make demands upon the state in a more orderly, contained fashion? What do these patterns tell us about applying the concepts of 'civil society' and 'urban citizenship' in India?

My investigation revealed a surprising pattern: associations representing two middle-class occupations (traders and lawyers) were highly contentious, carrying out far more protests and strikes from 1998 to 2008, than the associations representing two lower-class occupations as a whole (boatmen and weavers), which tended to prefer formal, institutionalized, or more contained means of making demands upon the state. Breaking down the weaver category into lower-class handloom weavers and middle-class powerloom weavers adds further nuance to these findings. These findings directly challenge the conclusions drawn by Chatterjee and other scholars (particularly John Harriss), and should provoke a deeper examination into contentious politics and civil society in India.

While any full explanation for these findings would involve a countless number of factors, economic resources appear to play a critical role: institutionalized, contained modes of engagement are less costly and less risky than contentious modes, which is why lower-class associations prefer them. However, they are also less efficient and more time-consuming in the long run, which is why middle-class associations abandon them and move on to protest and strike more quickly. The middle-class associations have the resources to successfully use contentious action against institutions of the state to gain immediate response to their grievances.

However, because these findings run counter to the empirical findings of scholars who have studied contentious politics and civic engagement in other Indian cities (Chatterjee 2001, 2004; Harriss 2006; Roy 2003), factors peculiar to Varanasi—political culture, political opportunity structure, and physical environment—will also be considered. Structural and environmental factors presumably would affect all occupational groups somewhat equally and thus cannot by themselves account for the differences observed among the groups. These factors however, can shed some light on why protest and strike might be such attractive options for those groups that can afford them, that is, the middle class.

These findings contain several implications for the existing literature on civil society in India. While the lower-class associations tend to rely on formal, institutionalized means of making demands, the middle-class associations frequently resort to contentious action, which raises the question of who is and who is not acting within civil society and whether civil society can be viewed strictly as a bourgeois realm of orderly, contained, 'civil' be-haviour. It suggests that there is indeed a considerable disconnect between historical Western theories of civil society and the way in which people actually participate in public life and engage with the state in India. How-ever, this disjuncture may exist not for the reasons that Chatterjee describes: rather, I find that, to the extent that civil society in India is bourgeois, it is not always orderly and contained; and to the extent that it is orderly and contained, it is not exclusively bourgeois. Civil society in India—or at least in some Indian cities—may be more inclusive than the historical Western concepts allow, and more contentious than some scholars have recognized.

CIVIL VERSUS UNCIVIL SOCIETIES

Those who analyse the meaning and relevance of the concept of civil society and its applicability to non-Western, post-colonial societies, often begin by invoking the idea as it was developed by political philosophers in Britain and continental Europe in the 18th and 19th centuries (Chatterjee 2004; Kaviraj and Khilnani 2001). However, as Taylor, Seligman, Cohen, Arato, and many other scholars have demonstrated, the traditional Western con-cept of civil society is far from unified or fully developed, even with regard to its application in the West, let alone elsewhere (Cohen and Arato 1992: 91; Seligman 1992: 50). To the extent that something like a 'Western concept' of civil society exists, Hegel is widely credited with having developed and integrated it most fully. As Kaviraj and Khilnani write, 'Hegel's intervention in the discussions on civil society is considered crucial by most interpreters' (Kaviraj and Khilnani 2001: 3). Hegel described civil society as the space between the family and the state, where the 'particular' and 'universal' are integrated and where individuals pursue strictly private, as opposed to com-munal, interests (Hegel 1996: par. 182). It is where individuals separated from their ascriptive identity and families come together out of mutual need, seeking to fulfil their individual interests in relationships of exchange. Hegel divides society into 'estates': the agricultural estate, the business estate, and the universal estate (the last concerned with bureaucratic or administrative functions) (Hegel 1996: pars. 201–05, Wood 1996: xix). Most closely as-sociated with civil society is the business estate or bourgeoisie (Jones 2001: 107–18; Seligman 1992: 45–51). Notably missing from this scheme is the working class. 'This is a serious omission,' write Cohen and Arato, 'espe-cially because Hegel claims that his estates correspond to economic dif-ferentiation.' His failure to fully recognize the 'specifically modern form of stratification' of social class led him to disregard the working class 'as being unable to integrate into, and unable to contribute to the integration of, civil society' (Cohen and Arato 1992: 98–99).

Following Hegel's lead, Habermas also viewed citizenship and the sphere of public rational-critical discourse as essentially bourgeois. For Habermas, 'civil society' is the larger realm of commodity exchange and social labour, within which lies the 'bourgeois public sphere', the social and cultural space within which private citizens (that is, educated property owners) came together as a 'public' to debate society, culture, and politics (Habermas 1991). The public sphere is 'bourgeois, because in it independent owners of property…are capable of generating, at least in principle, a collective will through the medium of rational, unconstrained communication' (Cohen and Arato 1992: 211). Initially shaped by 'class-structured exclusion', the public sphere became transformed and its characteristic 'rational-critical discourse' degenerated when it expanded to include the working classes (Calhoun 1993: fn.9).[1]

Several post-colonial scholars have adopted the Hegelian concept of civil society as a predominantly bourgeois realm in their critiques of the concept's applicability in the developing world. Chatterjee writes:

> I have favored retaining the old idea of civil society as bourgeois society, in the sense used by Hegel and Marx, and of using it in the Indian context as an actually existing arena of institutions and practices inhabited by a relatively small section of the people…' (Chatterjee 2004: 38)

Accordingly, he argues that in post-colonial, developing countries, the civil society concept is of little use in understanding public life (Chatterjee 2001, 2004). 'Most of the inhabitants of India', that is, the poor, the peasantry, the subaltern, are 'only tenuously, and even then, ambiguously and contextually, rights-bearing citizens in the sense imagined by the constitution. They are not, therefore, proper members of civil society' (Chatterjee 2004: 40). Kaviraj extends Chatterjee's argument thus:

> Elite groups, educated in Western style, understand the advantages of social individuation and have the skills of association—i.e., the subtle and, in some ways, culturally unfamiliar art of getting together and committing themselves partially and transiently to others with the same sectional interests. People belonging to other social groups do not. (Kaviraj 2001: 317)

Along similar lines, Harriss identifies class-wise variation in people's civic engagement in the south Indian cities of Chennai and Bangalore and finds that '"civil society" is the arena for middle-class activism and assertion;

and to a significant extent, the middle classes engage in such activism whilst people of the informal working class engage in politics' (Harriss 2006: 461). These observations echo Chatterjee's argument regarding a separate, more disorderly, and more politicized realm of activism among the poor called 'political society'. In an epigraph, Harriss quotes a civil society activist who asserts, 'Only the poor agitate; the rich operate.' Harriss illustrates this maxim with descriptions of two types of citizens' groups. The first type is 'distinctly elitist' and 'run by upper-middle class people'. These organizations are concerned with 'participation in budgeting, and of transparency and accountability in local government'. 'Many of these organizations are run with large budgets, drawn partly at least from overseas funders, with a high degree of genuine professionalism' (Harriss 2006: 455). He compares this category of associations with those that 'typically originate with or are focused on the informal working class, that mobilize and organize people to make demands upon the state' (Harriss 2006: 455). 'These two types of organizations engage with government in very different ways,' Harriss writes. The upper-middle-class organizations 'have adopted the paradigm of "public–private partnership" and champion the notion of "collaborative change"'. On the other hand, the 'mass movements' that represent the interests of slum dwellers

> [...] have consciously adopted 'protest' and see their methods as being successful in protecting the rights of the poor and the marginalized. 'Partnership' with the state is inconceivable to most of these organizations, and the way they seek to obtain political representation is usually through entering into mainstream politics. (Harriss 2006: 456)

Hegel's disregard of the working classes' potential for participation in civil society and Habermas's view of the degeneration of the public sphere with its eventual inclusion of the masses—not to mention Shils's (1991) insistence that civil society is characterized by 'civility'—provide an explanation for the views of Chatterjee, Kaviraj, Harriss, and others, who in their theoretically purist zeal adopt a rather narrow, historically specific, and, by contemporary standards, elitist concept of civil society and then discard it as ill-suited to India because of the broad, mass-based nature of Indian public life. However, I would urge against a strictly historical, Euro-centric theory of civil society that effectively requires the creation of new categories and labels in order to consider the public engagement of the lower classes, or of non-Western and/or post-colonial societies. Theorizing separate public spheres (civil society, political society) according to types of action and different socio-economic groups is not of much analytical use, because as a growing body of empirical evidence shows, including the evidence presented herein, urbanization, increased participation in the institutions of democracy, and globalization are having profoundly transformative effects upon people's experience and practice of 'citizenship'.

My concept of civil society is more in line with Tocqueville's vision of associational life. Tocqueville argued that a vibrant associational life was essential for preserving individual freedom against both the 'demands of the government' as well as the 'tyranny of the majority' (Tocqueville 2003: 811, 223). He saw a tumult of associational activity in America, with meetings called and committees formed for every purpose. Stepan and Linz take a Tocquevillian approach when they define civil society as the sphere of action where 'self-organizing and relatively autonomous groups, movements, and individuals attempt to articulate values, to create associations and solidarities, and to advance their interests'. It can include 'social movements (e.g., women's groups, neighborhood associations, religious groupings, and intellectual organizations), as well as associations from *all social strata* (such as trade unions, entrepreneurial groups, and professional associations)' (Stepan and Linz 2001: 298–99; emphasis added).

Viewing civil society as associational life in the Toquevillian sense allows for a more neutral application of the concept of civil society to a variety of political and social contexts and does not require an a priori exclusion of the uneducated, non-property-owning working classes. With regard to India, there is an abundance of detailed empirical studies portraying a diverse associational life (Bhargava and Reifeld 2005; Bhattacharyya et al. 2004; Elliot 2003; Jayaram 2005; and so on). A recent example is Coelho and Venkat's study of neighbourhood associations in Chennai, which examines the activities of 197 associations at various class levels, including resident welfare associations, self-help groups, youth groups, dalit (scheduled caste or 'untouchable') associations, traders' associations, religious groups, and local units of unions or political parties (Coelho and Venkat 2009: 359). Despite the traditional equation of civil society with bourgeois society and the acceptance by several major scholars of Indian politics of this concept, an associational life that is not limited to the bourgeoisie or educated middle classes appears to be thriving. However, what kind of associational life is it? Despite the expectations of Hegel and Habermas, it is not exclusively bourgeois, and despite the injunctions of Shils, it is not always civil. Further, despite the findings of Chatterjee, Kaviraj, and Harriss, it is not entirely true that the middle to upper classes engage in an orderly, contained civil society while the lower classes are relegated to agitating on a disorderly, politicized fringe, what Chatterjee calls 'political society'.

THE RESEARCH

Varanasi, also known as Banaras, is a city of over one million people located in north India, in the state of Uttar Pradesh (UP) (Government of India 2001). It is one of the oldest living cities in the world, having been continuously inhabited for at least 3,000 years (Singh and Rana 2006: 30). Located on the Ganges River, it is regarded as a sacred city among Hindus, Buddhists, and Jains. While it is popularly regarded as having a strongly 'Hindu' identity, its historically large Muslim population, about 27 per cent of the total population according to the 2001 census, has also had an important influence on local history and culture. It has been a commercial capital since at least the late 1700s (Bayly 1983: 104–06; Freitag 1992: 1–22). Its economy continues to be based largely upon commerce, as well as tourism and pilgrimage-related services and small industries, principally silk weaving. It is also a district administrative centre and thus is the site of a large district court complex. Therefore, while chosen somewhat randomly, the occupational groups under study—boatmen, handloom weavers, traders, and lawyers—represent a fairly large portion of the city's population.

Varanasi is not yet a 'global' city comparable to Mumbai, Bangalore, and some of the other locations studied in this volume, and signs of its direct encounter with contemporary globalization have only recently become obvious: the arrival of national and international chain stores, the opening of indoor malls, and the inevitable intrusion of McDonalds. However, while Varanasi might not yet be considered a global city, its transformation into a larger, more modern urban centre is having new effects upon patterns of associationalism and conceptions of citizenship, along the lines of what Holston and Appadurai have described: 'Cities remain the strategic arena for the development of citizenship… With their concentrations of the nonlocal, the strange, the mixed, and the public, cities engage most palpably the tumult of citizenship' (Holston and Appadurai 1999: 2–3). The salience of occupational identity and the strength of interest-driven occupational associations, as opposed (or in addition) to caste or religious identity and caste or *biradari* councils in a city popularly regarded as strongly tradition-bound, and the urban centre of a region where caste loyalty is still a powerful social and political force, shows the impact that urbanization can have upon the reconstitution of interests and the re-shuffling and re-layering of identities.

It is not that caste no longer matters; what Sassen describes as the 'unmooring of identity' in globalized cities is not evident in Varanasi, at least not yet (Sassen 1999: 191). Traditional social hierarchies are still a powerful force. However, heavy migration of workers from the countryside, various economic pressures, and other factors have forced many people to take up new and unfamiliar occupations in the cities, or allowed them to take advantage of opportunities that they did not have before. Thus, many occupations in Varanasi are no longer 'owned' by particular castes or religious communities, and are in fact quite diverse. Even in occupations that are still largely dominated by particular communities, the task of defending the occupational or economic interests of the group no longer belongs primarily to traditional caste or *biradari* councils. In the case of the boatmen and to some extent the weavers, these functions are served by associations that have little to do with the social concerns of the community and are mainly concerned with the professional interests of the occupation. Traders' and lawyers' associations, representing occupational groups that are quite diverse in terms of their members' caste and religious affiliations, are likewise entirely focused on occupational interests and have no evident connection to any caste or religious councils. Occupational associations represent a form of collectivity that has not been studied much, if at all, in India and offer a new perspective on broader claims made by Chatterjee and Harriss about class-wise differences in participation in civil society and civic associations, as they are generally (though imperfectly) coterminous with class. These particular occupational groups together represent a large portion of the population in Varanasi (though getting exact numbers was impossible). Daily perusal of local newspapers yielded a strong impression of their high level of activity in Varanasi. This study is based on several sources of original data, including extensive interviews conducted between October 2006 and December 2007 and from September to October 2008; an informal survey taken of ordinary members of each of the occupational groups (30–60 questionnaires completed among each group); and a survey of newspaper reports covering the years 1998–2008.

WHO AGITATES AND WHO OPERATES?

This study began with a general inquiry into forms of engagement between occupational associations and the state. I conducted research on six occupational groups, but only four groups will be discussed here due to limited space: handloom weavers and boatmen, representing the urban lower class, and traders and lawyers, representing the urban middle class. I also include some discussions of the middle-class powerloom weavers, comparing them with handloom weavers, which allows for an imperfect 'control' of additional social and religious factors (the other two occupational groups studied were teachers and doctors).

Through open-ended interviews I sought to learn how each of these groups accesses the administration, influences policy decisions, and gets benefits, concessions, and special favours from the government. I became particularly interested in their use of contentious action to make demands upon the state. When an unexpected pattern in contentious action began to emerge, I undertook a large-scale survey of newspaper coverage of strikes and protests by each of these groups, which for the most part confirmed my impressions. As the data in Table 7.1 suggest, the lawyers' and traders'

TABLE 7.1. REPORTS OF CONTENTIOUS PUBLIC ACTION BY OCCUPATIONAL
ASSOCIATIONS IN VARANASI, 1998–2008

Year	Traders	Lawyers	Boatmen	Weavers* Handloom or unknown	Powerloom
1998	5	4	0	3	3
1999	9	5	0	0	0
2000	18	17	0	2	2
2001	9	18	0	5	0
2002	21	8	0	2	0
2003	58	11	0	10	14
2004	14	11	0	17	0
2005	55	7	2	6	1
2006	19	7	1	7	0
2007	26	21	1	5	0
2008	27	6	18	1	0
Total	261	115	22	58	20

Source: These numbers refer to the number of reports that appeared in the Varanasi local edition of the popular Hindi daily *Dainik Jaagran*, of organized contentious action including strikes (*hartaal*), shutdowns (*band*), sit-ins (*dharna*), processions (*juluus*), and other rallies and demonstrations (*pradarshan*) carried out by organizations representing the occupational groups under study. I recognize the limitations of relying on newspaper reports to make firm conclusions and use these numbers only to augment extensive qualitative data.

Note: * The weavers are a complicated case, as explained below. I divide them into lower-class handloom weavers and middle-class powerloom weavers and compare their mobilization efforts. Most of the handloom weavers' 58 contentious actions represented here were small, brief rallies organized by outside activists, NGOs, and political parties on handloom weavers' behalf. Most powerloom weavers' actions were costly, lengthy strikes and major demonstrations.

groups resorted far more frequently to strikes, sit-ins, and other forms of contentious, and occasionally even illegal, public action, while the boat-men's and weavers' groups tended to prefer formal, institutionalized, and/or contained means of making demands.

These results are quite at odds with the arguments of Chatterjee, Ka-viraj, and Harriss and suggest that a re-examination of how many have viewed popular participation in associational life, or civil society, in India is necessary. While these findings might be surprising in the context of the work by these and other scholars, they are consistent with the literature on resource mobilization and social movements in the West (for example, McAdam et al. 1996; McAdam et al. 2001; Oberschall 1973; Tilly 1978; Zald and McCarthy 1979). According to a resource mobilization perspec-tive, contentious action becomes attractive when sufficient resources and adequate mobilizing structures, a favourable political opportunity structure, and perhaps the assistance of influential allies, all become available at the right time. I found that resources and mobilizing structures (associations) are factors that are critical for explaining the varying levels of participation among the groups under study. Building durable and influential mobilizing structures and organizing members to participate in contentious action is not easy for groups with fewer economic resources. Thus, they have weaker, more loosely established associations and have more difficulty in mobiliz-ing others in their occupational group to participate in time-consuming meetings and demonstrations. Strikes are particularly costly and almost im-possibly so for most lower-class workers. Therefore, they tend to use less costly, less risky means of making demands upon the state: filing petitions, using the judicial system, making appeals to district and state-level admin-istrative authorities, voting in elections, and so on. The middle-class oc-cupational groups, on the other hand, have the resources necessary to build up powerful associations, attend organizational activities like meetings, and participate in contentious action. They do use formal, procedural means such as those listed above, and utilize informal channels such as personal connections. However, they also frequently lose patience with such time-consuming processes and resort to agitation, as it usually brings a quicker and more satisfactory response.

That the lower-class associations understand the 'art of getting to-gether and committing themselves partially and transiently to others with the same sectional interests' (Kaviraj 2001: 317) and are capable of pursuing regular administrative channels to press their demands is consistent with what Holston found among the poor residents of several 'auto-constructed' communities on the urban periphery of São Paulo, Brazil, who struggled for many years for land rights. In the past, they would respond to challenges to their property rights with violence, which would escalate when the police would get involved. Over time, residents learned to organize into associations and use the law to challenge attempts to take their land. He describes how they were 'converted' from violence to 'law talk' and how their associations became involved in the legal defense of their residential rights (Holston 2008: 234). He writes that 'the difficult conditions of illegal residence…motivated people to pursue new articulations of citizenship', which 'generated a new urban citizenship' among residents (Holston 2008: 234–235). Coelho and Venkat's findings are also consistent with both Holston's and my work. They argue that 'the urban poor increasingly resort to civil associational forms to claim urban citizenship, and middle class associations are more deeply engaged with the sphere of formal politics than their own or scholarly accounts convey' (Coelho and Venkat 2009: 358).

However, Coelho and Venkat as well as Kamath and Vijayabaskar (2009) caution against 'over-schematization' and 'over-homogenization' when making generalizations about the civic activism and political relationships of middle and lower classes. The pattern I discovered in class-wise participation in contentious action is not evident in all Indian cities, as suggested in studies by Harriss and others. Additionally, there is the question of why even middle-class associations would prefer agitation to 'operation' or more institutionalized ways of making demands, when agitation would appear to be the costlier option for any group, in terms of time spent away from work or leisure activities and the risk of getting arrested or injured. A political opportunity structure and/or political culture that is specific to Varanasi might help explain these puzzles. In social movement literature, political opportunity refers to the set of exogenous conditions that makes contentious action possible (Eisinger 1973; McAdam et al. 1996; McAdam et al. 2001; Meyer 2004; Tarrow 1998). In Varanasi, statements frequently made by leaders of occupational associations indicate that protest and strike are viewed as highly effective means of making demands upon the state. Institutional channels, such as submitting memos, applications, or petitions to administrative officials and resolving grievances through the court system are viewed as time-consuming and as ultimately yielding unsatisfactory resolutions. Meetings with political figures and government officials are an important means of making demands upon the state, but these do not always result in a positive outcome either. Therefore, the traders and lawyers associations often resorted to agitation, claiming that institutional channels would yield little benefit and justifying—even valorizing—their actions in terms of their 'rights' in a democracy, and invoking the heroism of freedom

,hters during the Independence Movement who practiced civil disobedience and courted arrest for a worthy cause. Institutions of the state, such as the administration and police, effectively encouraged the use of agitation by ultimately making or at least promising concessions desired by the associations. Proving association leaders' cost–benefit calculations right, they appear to respond to association demands in a far speedier manner than they would have if associations had followed normal procedural channels. While it is an annoyance to city residents whose daily routines are disrupted by strikes, blocked roads, and so on, I would speculate that agitation in Varanasi may have less of an image of subversion or dysfunctionality than it might in other cities. Furthermore, it evidently works. Agitation is an attractive, effective, and perhaps even 'heroic' option for those who can afford it.

Furthermore, Varanasi's physical environment may also encourage and enable the use of contentious action, rendering it more effective than it might be in other cities. Holston (1999) discusses the impact that physical public space has upon the 'political domain of social life' and argues that modernist urban design encourages separation and discourages active citizenship. The 'modernist traffic system…eliminates the urban crowds and the outdoor political domain of social life that the street traditionally supports. Estranged from the no-man's land of outdoor public space that results, people stay inside' (Holston 1999: 162). Such modernist urban planning has definitely not been undertaken in Varanasi. The city proper is largely unplanned, its narrow roads and alleys forming a tight, organic network around the riverbank. In Varanasi, one of the most densely populated cities in India, streets are an extension of private living and working space.[2] Homes and places of business open directly onto the street, with no gardens or gates separating them from the hustle and bustle of street life. People work, socialize, and linger in front of their homes and businesses, in constant contact with each other and passing traffic, which is usually congested and slow. If one wants to publicize one's grievances to the public or send a message to government authorities by creating a spectacle or disruption, the streets of Varanasi offer the ideal environment. There it is nearly impossible to avoid the spectacle and inconvenience of a procession, effigy-burning, or *dharna pradarshan* (sit-in demonstration). It is possible that in Varanasi agitation has become a favoured means of making demands upon the state because it affects residents and businesses more directly than it would in a city where streets have been planned with speedy, efficient transportation and 'orderly' public spaces in mind. Below, I present empirical evidence gathered about each of the occupational groups and discuss the implications of these findings in the conclusion.

CASE STUDIES

Traders

Traders include small shopkeepers, wholesalers, and other vendors, and while they represent a broad range of socio-economic categories (for example, income, caste, and religion), they are almost entirely within the broader middle class. As Varanasi is chiefly a city of commerce, the associations that represent traders are, in the estimation of several local community leaders, the most prominent occupational associations in the city.[3] There are dozens, if not hundreds, of small traders' associations organized by commodity (for example, ready-made apparel, grain, and stationery), locality, retail versus wholesale, and so on. Most of these small associations are members of one of two large umbrella associations, the Kashi Vyapar Pratinidhi Mandal (Kashi Traders Representative Association, or KVPM) and the Varanasi Nagar Udyog Vyapar Mandal (Varanasi City Industry [and] Traders Association, or VNUVM). These local umbrella organizations are well established with published by-laws, frequent meetings, regular elections, means for collecting dues, and budgets. Each umbrella organization is also the city-level chapter of a larger state-level organization whose officers interact with state-level administrative and elected officials on a regular basis.

Traders associations are probably the most politicized of all the associations under study. The KVPM and VNUVM used to be a single organization until leadership struggles, differences in strategy, and conflicting political ambitions caused them to split several years ago. Now, the leaders of VNUVM are closely connected to the Bharatiya Janata Party (BJP), while KVPM tends to be more closely associated with the Samajwadi Party (SP). The KVPM general secretary served as the city president of the SP for several years and was the party's candidate for a seat in the state legislative assembly in the 2002 Vidhan Sabha election. Association leaders appear to use these political connections to win individual favours and concessions, as well as special consideration for the business community. The KVPM general secretary was in an especially advantageous position when the SP was in control of the UP government. He claimed that as long as the SP was in control of the government, he could go directly to state leaders and state his case.

So, do these close connections to the state government reduce the need for protest? As shown in Table 7.1, traders are the most contentious occupational group among the four shown here and among all six in the original study. From 1998 to 2008, *Dainik Jaagran* published 261 reports of strikes, shutdowns, sit-ins, rallies, processions, and other forms of public protest. One of the major issues concerning the traders' associations in the last few years has been whether the UP state government should implement value-added tax (VAT), and if so, in what form. Traders associations successfully prevented adoption of the VAT in 2003 and 2005 through intense agitation involving several shutdowns (*bandh*s). *Dainik Jaagran* reported a total of 58 contentious actions in 2003 and 55 in 2005, more than any of the other groups in any year under study. The anti-VAT movement continued in 2007 with state-wide shutdowns, demonstrations, and processions (see Figure 7.1). Despite all these efforts, the state finally implemented the tax in January 2008.

The KVPM general secretary said that when the SP was not in control of the state government, he had to rely more on protests to influence

FIGURE 7.1. MEMBERS OF THE BHELUPUR BUSINESS ASSOCIATION PROTEST THE PROPOSED VALUE-ADDED TAX (VAT) IN STATE-WIDE SHUT-DOWN IN VARANASI ON 11 SEPTEMBER 2007

Source: Photo by author.

state leaders on the VAT issue. However, according to our newspaper survey, there is no evidence that KVPM carried out fewer protests when the SP was in power from September 2003 to May 2007 than after the Bahujan Samaj Party (BSP) won control of the state government in May 2007. Indeed, KVPM carried out many such contentious actions while the SP was in power. Taking a different line, another KVPM leader said that one reason the 2005 anti-VAT movement was so much more vigorous than the 2007 movement was that, in 2005, Chief Minister Mulayam Singh Yadav of the SP was sympathetic to traders and supported them. Traders were emboldened by his support to protest, believing that their efforts were more likely to make a difference. This might be one reason why one sees a much higher number of contentious actions in 2005 than in 2007 (the 2007 anti-VAT protest was launched after the BSP took control of the state government).

Thus, it is evident that the occupational group that resorts to agitation most frequently also has possibly the strongest political connections of any of the occupational groups under study. The frequency of their protest is not reduced when they have greater access to government and thus more opportunities to 'operate'. This illustrates one of the central puzzles of our inquiry: while Chatterjee and Harriss both expect those who protest to be lacking institutional access, the traders represent a group that is middle class and well connected, but that nonetheless carries out more protests and strikes than any other group under study. This suggests that under certain conditions some groups may be more likely to protest when they have more, not less, access to state institutions, or when they believe there is a greater chance that authorities will be responsive to their efforts.

Lawyers

As the administrative seat of Varanasi district, the city is the site of the district court complex (*kaccheri*), where the district magistrate's (DM) office and most, if not all, of the other district administration offices are located. Hundreds of lawyers work here daily, preparing court papers, petitions, and other documents for the thousands of people who come every day. Their incomes range widely, placing them anywhere from the lower-middle to the upper-middle class.

In Varanasi district, there are two major associations that defend the interests of lawyers, the Central Bar Association (Varanasi) (CBA) and the Banaras Bar Association (BBA). Both are very old and well established: the CBA, now the larger, more powerful organization, was founded in 1903. The BBA dates back to the mid-19th century and is said to be the oldest bar association in India. Many lawyers are members of both. Both organizations are highly formalized, with constitutions, articles of association, annual elections, and so on. The CBA has its own building that houses a legal library, offices, and meeting rooms. As mobilizing structures, these associations are highly effective. They coordinate their positions on issues of interest to lawyers and cooperate when carrying out any kind of contentious action. They are also highly unified: when they go on strike, they effectively shut down the district court.

Because of the nature of their work, lawyers—especially the association leaders—have well-established, routinized, professional relationships with district-level administrative officials and judicial authorities. When a dispute or other issue concerning lawyers arises, bar association leaders may call district level officials to try to iron it out informally. If such conversations are inconclusive, bar associations leaders may call a meeting among members to discuss further steps. The bar associations also interact with state government officials regarding legislation under consideration, offering recommendations and occasionally attempting pressure (often through protest) on officials to accept their recommendations. However, it is important to note that the CBA and BBA do not involve themselves in electoral politics. Indeed, association leaders took great pains to stress their independence from political parties.

As the lawyers are intimately familiar with the workings of the administration and judiciary and have direct lines of communication with government officials, one might expect them to be successful 'operators', to borrow a term from Harriss's source. However, not only are they the second-most contentious group according to our newspaper survey (*Dainik Jaagran* printed 115 reports of contentious public actions from 1998 to 2008), it is the lawyers' protests that most frequently turn violent, resulting in occasional property damage and, in at least one known instance, bodily injury to administration employees. In August 2007, a small band of lawyers and their supporters stormed the administrative office of the Pindra *tehsil* (an administrative unit) in Varanasi district, upset furniture, and beat up employees in protest against a *tehsil* employee who had assaulted a lawyer the day before. Charges were filed by both sides, but the police made no arrests. In response, CBA and BBA called a strike that lasted about two weeks and was accompanied by a daily *dharna* in front of the DM's office (see Figure 7.2). The lawyers demanded that the DM and another official be transferred, and that the official accused of the initial attack against the lawyer be arrested and/or suspended. Intensive negotiations among the lawyers' leaders, the DM, and the commissioner during the strike resulted in

FIGURE 7.2. STRIKE AT THE DM'S OFFICE IN AUGUST 2007. SITTING AMONG THE LAWYERS IS FORMER MEMBER OF THE STATE LEGISLATIVE ASSEMBLY (MLA), HARISHCHANDRA SRIVASTAVA, IN A SHOW OF SOLIDARITY

Source: Photo by author.

the transfer of the Pindra official. The lawyers dropped their other demands and claimed a victory. Afterward, many lawyers continued to defend the actions of their colleagues who had wreaked havoc at the *tehsil* office, arguing that it was a justifiable response to 'sudden provocation'.

This was one of the more dramatic protests carried out during the course of fieldwork; however, interviews and media reports reveal that it was not unusual. When one asks association leaders why they resort to protest and strike so often and so quickly, the general response is one of frustration and impatience with the unresponsiveness of the administration. One CBA official said:

> The administration is not as transparent as they should be, so this is a problem from time to time. There are complaint procedures, like submitting applications, but these are not heeded. So the only way to get the administration to listen is to go on strike. *Jab tak bachha nahin rota, maa usko doodh nahin pilati hai* [not until a child cries will the mother give it milk].

Yet it is not only the unresponsiveness of the administration that causes so many lawyers' strikes to happen; after all, if the administration is unresponsive, it is unresponsive to many kinds of groups, not only lawyers.

y the privileged position of lawyers and their considerable resourc-
llow them to resort to contentious action to force a response from
the administration. When I asked the general secretary of the CBA why
demonstrations and strikes were so effective, he said it was because the CBA
is 'an association of intellectuals', and that lawyers had 'respect in society'.
This sense of privilege and high status appears to lend considerable impatience. When explaining why lawyers moved so quickly from dialogue with
the administration to strike in the August 2007 incident described above,
the general secretary of the BBA said, 'People didn't want to compromise,
they wanted results.' Lawyers have the means, in terms of resources and
excellent mobilizing structures, to act on their frustration and impatience
and to take advantage of an environment that rewards contentious action.
This group of respected middle-class 'intellectuals' does not see protest and
strike as being outside the realm of proper civic behaviour.[4]

Boatmen

As one of the holiest cities in India, Varanasi is a major pilgrimage destination for devout Hindus as well as a popular tourist attraction for Indians
and foreigners alike. An estimated 2,000 boatmen ply their trade on the
Ganges, taking pilgrims and tourists out on the river for religious rituals and
sightseeing. The boatmen of Varanasi have been integral to the economic,
social, and cultural life of the city for centuries. They constitute both an occupational group and a caste or *jati*—Mallah, classified by the Government
of India as a Most Backward Caste (MBC). However, these two identities
do not overlap perfectly: 'The majority of all Mallahs in Banaras are engaged
in occupations not connected to the river economy' (Doron 2008: 16). The
boatmen are overwhelmingly lower class; though a few successful ones have
moved into the middle class by acquiring fleets of boats and hiring others to
ply them, most boatmen either row their own boat or a boat belonging to
another and take home what they earn each day.

Boatmen have at least one well-established mobilizing structure aimed
at defending their occupational interests, the Mallah Samuday Sangharsh
Samiti (Mallah Community Struggle Committee, or MSSS), founded in
1976. The general secretary is the committee's driving force, and, while
controversial, he is also regarded among boatmen throughout the city as the
community's most active organizer. The MSSS calls for a general meeting
whenever an issue affecting boatmen's interests arises. There are other small
committees as well, but none as durable and well known as the MSSS. With
his fellow officers, the general secretary frequently visits administrative

offices such as the DM, the state forestry department, and municipal corporation offices. On rare occasions, the MSSS organizes rallies and processions
(*Dainik Jaagran* reported a total of four from 1998 until 2007). However,
MSSS's days as the primary association among boatmen may be numbered:
in January 2008, the most successful strike held by the boatmen in at least
a decade was organized by young upstarts from the community who were
dissatisfied with the MSSS's leadership, working in cooperation with the
Congress Party, as will be further discussed below.

Despite this recent, perhaps temporary, partnership with the Congress, neither the MSSS nor the community as a whole is much involved
in politics. In fact, one surprising finding was that despite representing a
population of about 50,000 in a city of one million, the Mallahs do not
have any stable, strong links to any one political party. One might expect
that in an electoral system widely regarded as being based on patronage relationships between parties and caste/religious groups (for example, Chandra
2007), such a large caste-based community would carry considerable political clout. However, community leaders have not established a long-term,
mutually beneficial relationship with any party or individual politician, nor
does the community vote as a bloc: on the evening before the 2007 state
assembly election, the *chaudhary* or chief caste elder of the largest boatman
locality called a meeting to discuss which candidate the community might
endorse. No agreement was reached; the final consensus was that each person should vote for whomever he wished.

The main issues of concern to the boatmen of Varanasi in recent years
were the bans both on fishing and on the use of motorboats within the city.
The entire length of the river passing through the city has been designated
as a wildlife sanctuary. As in all wildlife sanctuaries, all fishing and boating
is technically banned (officials enforce the ban only with regard to motor-
boats, not rowboats). Since these activities are central to their livelihoods,
boatmen have been working to overturn this ban since 1989, making frequent trips to the DM's office and the local forest department office, and
one trip to visit officials in the state capital, Lucknow. In this way they have
succeeded in winning temporary periods of non-enforcement of the ban.

Whenever the administration occasionally decides to enforce the ban,
the MSSS organizes large processions and demonstrations at the DM's and
commissioner's offices and wins another temporary reprieve. However, such
actions have taken place only four times in recent memory: in 1991, 1993,
2006, and 2008 (the 2008 action lasted 10 days and garnered 12 stories
in *Dainik Jaagran*). The MSSS general secretary, while the primary organizer of the first three actions, portrays himself as more of an 'operator' and

prefers negotiating with the administration to calling strikes and protests. Generally, whenever there is an issue of concern to the boatmen, the leaders of the committee meet up with government officials. They are quite familiar with the formal channels of approach to administration officials and use these channels regularly. When the forest department re-asserted the ban in January 2008 and announced steep new taxes on passenger fares, the MSSS sought to negotiate a better deal for the boatmen, but some aspiring young leaders among the boatmen decided that the time was ripe for a strike. They were soon in touch with a local Congress politician and began planning an action. The MSSS general secretary opposed this plan, claiming that after 18 years of fighting this battle, he was on the verge of winning permanent concessions and that a strike would bring them back to square one and be harmful to boatmen. He also complained about the involvement of a political party in organizing the strike, labelling it a political demonstration. He maintained that the final outcome—the compromise that the strike leaders reached with the forest department—was less beneficial to boatmen than the deal he believes he could have gotten without the city's boatmen having to lose 10 days' earnings. While it is possible that he also opposed this strike because he was not the initiator of it and had lost control of the situation, his opposition to this action is consistent with his past statements and actions. When I asked whether he would be organizing a protest with regard to a boating restriction imposed in October 2007, he expressed resistance: 'Meetings are going on, dialog is happening, so why do *dharna pradarshan* (sit-in, demonstration) now? The need for *dharna pradarshan* comes when communication breaks down or demands are not being fulfilled.' The lack of economic resources within the community appears to play a major role: many boatmen and their leaders complain about the difficulty of maintaining a unified front. When faced with the choice between striking and continuing to earn, many boatmen will choose the latter. Therefore, the MSSS has pursued more contained means of making demands and negotiating compromises.

In the case of the January 2008 action, the new taxes announced by the forest department were so uniquely onerous (for example, foreign tourists— boatmen's most lucrative customers—were to pay ₹ 350 [US$7] tax on a ₹ 50 [US$1] boat ride, and boatmen additionally were to pay ₹ 50–100 [US$1–2] per day just for the privilege of plying their boats) that most boatmen seemed to agree that there was little option but to strike. This combined with the mobilizing assistance of a major political party may have inspired boatmen with enough confidence to put down their oars. After 10 days of strike, the forest department shelved its plan.

Weavers

The weavers present a complicated case. As with the boatmen, this is not only an occupational group, but largely a *biradari* (caste or *jati*) and religious community as well. Most weavers in Varanasi (estimates range from 60 to 95 per cent) are Muslims, of the Momin Ansari *biradari*, and most Ansaris in Varanasi are weavers and increasingly, in the last couple of decades, textile merchants. For analytical purposes I divide weavers into two occupational sub-groups—the traditional handloom weavers, who are extremely poor and marginalized, and the powerloom weavers, who are far more prosperous, having moved up the economic ladder by purchasing powerlooms. The handloom weavers have faced major obstacles in advancing their interests through contentious action, while the powerloom weavers have been fairly successful in this regard. In this section I will compare the two groups in terms of their resources and mobilizing structures, their use of protest and strike, and their use of more contained means of making demands.

Handloom weaving is one of the most important traditional occupations of Varanasi; handloomed Banarsi silk saris are famous throughout India and used to be considered an indispensable part of a bride's trousseau. However, it is also an industry in decline, and handloom weavers are enduring extreme hardship. Therefore, despite being highly skilled craftsmen, handloom weavers are among the poorest, least (formally) educated workers in Varanasi. Powerloom weavers, who can produce a less artful and cheaper version of the traditional Banarsi sari in a fraction of the time, are in a considerably better financial position than the handloom weavers. Most are comfortably middle class to upper-middle class. The interests of handloom weavers and powerloom weavers and shopkeepers conflict to some extent, though not entirely: handloom weavers compete with powerloom weavers (at a great disadvantage) and are routinely under-compensated by the shopkeepers. Many end up going to work for powerloom owners as operators of the powerlooms.

To some extent, the traditional social organizations of the Ansari community as a whole serve as occupational associations, and their role must be seriously considered. Rudolph and Rudolph (1984) make a strong argument for viewing traditional caste associations as serving 'modern' political and economic functions, so I follow their lead. The Ansari community of Varanasi is divided into smaller communities known as *tanzim*. The functions of the *tanzim* leader, known as the *sardar* or *mahato* depending on the *tanzim*, include counselling people within the community concerning marriage, divorce, and other family matters, resolving intra-community disputes, and so on. However, there is evidence that some of these leaders and their councils serve not only to provide social guidance, but to fight for weavers' economic interests as well. Furthermore, several interviewees have suggested that the *sardar* and *mahato* are the only leaders in the weavers' community with the power to call a large-scale strike, and newspaper reports from the years 1998–2008 bear this out: every report of a strike by groups identified as weavers or Ansaris mentions the *tanzim* leadership as one of the main forces, if not the principle force, behind the action. However, the *tanzim* leadership appears to exercise this influence on behalf of powerloom owners more often than handloom weavers. When making demands upon the state, it uses more contained means (for example, lobbying and negotiating with government officials) when the issue is one of greater concern to the handloom weavers, and more contentious means (for example, calling for work stoppages) when the issue is of greater concern to the powerloom weavers. As the *tanzim* leadership is usually dominated by particular elite families that have become powerloom owners and silk merchants, the use of different strategies could be due to either the pursuit of personal economic interest, or the plain fact that powerloom weavers can better afford to strike than handloom weavers.

While the *biradari tanzim* serve some of the functions of occupational associations, this is not their primary purpose. When it comes to organizations devoted exclusively to occupational interests, the handloom weavers have not been able to create any stable, strong occupational associations of their own. Some handloom-weaver activists have attempted to organize their fellows, calling meetings and organizing small rallies, but their efforts have been hindered by the challenges of organizing a profession so poor that it is desperate for any work, underpaid or unsteady as it may be. Therefore, the handloom weavers' most successful mobilizations have heavily depended upon outside assistance: grassroots activists from the Ansari community who are not themselves handloom weavers, such as one member of an elite family who leads the Bunkar Bachao Andolan (Save the Weavers Movement, or BBA); externally funded non-governmental organizations (NGOs) such as the Bunkar Dastakar Adhikar Manch (Weaver and Artisan Rights Forum, or BDAM), associated with Oxfam; and an organization connected to the Communist Party of India–Marxist (CPI-M), the Bunkar Dastakar Morcha (Weaver and Artisan Popular Front, or BDM). With the exception of the BBA, which is no longer active, these organizations organize frequent small rallies and conferences, 'street corner' meetings, and visits to administration officials such as the DM and assistant director of handlooms, a state-level official whose office is located in Varanasi. They employ handloom weavers as organizers and liaisons, but are not created or directed by handloom weavers.

Powerloom weavers, on the other hand, have had a fairly strong self-organized association working in defense of their interests, the Banaras Powerloom Weavers Association (BPWA), founded in 1985. The association became fairly well known during one general secretary's tenure from 1995 to 2003–04. The association is not continuously active, but is reconvened whenever there is a perceived threat to powerloom weavers' interests. This former general secretary says that he could call a meeting and reassemble the group 'in an hour'.

A comparison of the frequency and type of contentious action by handloom weavers and powerloom weavers is illuminating. As shown in Table 7.1, *Dainik Jaagran* contained 58 reports of contentious public action by handloom weavers. A closer analysis of these reports in Table 7.2 reveals that almost all the handloom weavers' actions were sit-ins, rallies, processions, meetings, and other less costly actions, while seven of them involved strikes. These actions were almost entirely organized by NGOs such as BDAM, BDM, and other outside activists. The BDAM holds conferences, rallies, and an occasional small demonstration before the DM's office. The BDM activists conduct 'street-corner meetings' and rallies intended to educate weavers on their rights vis-à-vis government benefits and programmes, and formulate additional demands of the government. These actions usually last about an hour or two.

Three-quarters of the powerloom weavers' actions, however, were self-organized strikes. In 2003, the BPWA, with support from the *tanzim* leaders, called for a costly three-week shutdown of all powerlooms in protest

TABLE 7.2: REPORTS OF ACTIONS BY HANDLOOM WEAVERS VERSUS POWERLOOM WEAVERS, 1998–2008

	Handloom weaver actions	Powerloom weaver actions	Total actions in weaver community
Strikes	7	15	22
Sit-ins, rallies, processions, meetings, and other non-strike actions	51	5	56
Total actions	58	20	78

Source: From *Dainik Jaagran.* See note below Table 7.1.

against the excise duty on powerloom products. According to the former BPWA general secretary, the owners of powerlooms gathered 50,000 powerloom workers and staged a massive rally at the DM's office. The strike continued for three weeks, during which time a series of rallies and sit-ins occurred. The excise duty was finally lifted for those who owned fewer than 10 powerlooms, which the former BPWA general secretary says accounts for almost all powerloom owners in Varanasi. This leader recounted three more agitations carried out during his tenure, all in protest against a new tax policy or import barrier.

Both handloom weavers and powerloom weavers also make demands in more contained ways, through formal, institutionalized channels as well as informal 'operating'. When it comes to these contained means, perhaps the most effective mobilizing structures that both handloom and powerloom weavers have are the *biradari tanzim*. While the *sardar* and *mahato* share more economic interests with the powerloom weavers, some of these leaders claim to be responding to a moral obligation to protect the welfare of handloom weavers as well, as the *sardar* and *mahato* are traditionally responsible for protecting and holding together the Ansari community as a whole. Therefore, they meet with government officials to make demands for subsidies and other forms of assistance for handloom weavers, and for infrastructural improvements in neighbourhoods where poor Ansaris live. The most active in this regard is the *sardar* of the *chaudhavi* (fourteenth) *tanzim*, known as the *chaudahon*. He and his council have been pressing for government benefits and concessions, and have met with prominent state- and national-level political figures regarding issues such as special electricity rates for weavers and several assistance schemes for handloom weavers. The *chaudahon* says he generally resists calling strikes among handloom weavers, arguing that meetings are more effective than strikes, and that strikes only result in losses to the weavers. It may be that *tanzim* leaders refrain from calling strikes in order to protect their own economic interests and are incapable of putting up a genuine fight for the interests of poor weavers. However, the *tanzim* leadership's 'operating' among powerful political figures appears to have yielded concrete benefits to the handloom weavers in the form of assistance schemes. Working on behalf of handloom weavers, the BDM, BDAM, and other NGO workers have also been active in making demands upon the state in more contained ways, frequently meeting with administrative officials regarding benefit schemes such as special medical insurance plans, silk yarn subsidies, reduction in electricity rates, and so on. They also work for infrastructural improvements in localities dominated by handloom weavers.

The handloom weavers, being poor and without strong, enduring mobilizing structures of their own, have been incapable of organizing and executing many protests and strikes. They have, however, been able to participate in small, low-cost, low-risk rallies and other actions organized by outside organizations. This can be contrasted with the success of the powerloom owners in mobilizing on several occasions, including a three-week long movement that would be unimaginable among handloom weavers. The weavers' most powerful mobilizing structures, the *biradari tanzim*, prefer 'operating' when making demands upon the state, particularly with regard to issues of concern to handloom weavers. On the rare occasion when the *tanzim* leadership gets involved in 'agitating', they are acting on behalf of powerloom owners.

CONCLUSIONS

Clearly, characterizing class-wise patterns of engagement with the state, or participation in civil society, is no simple, straightforward matter. I have suggested that greater economic resources and better developed mobilizing structures enable middle-class groups to take advantage of a political opportunity structure and a physical environment that enables contentious action. Local political culture also appears to encourage protest, which appears to be imbued with a special moral legitimacy, an almost inherent 'righteousness', that may be an enduring legacy of the Indian Independence Movement.

Much of what goes on in civil society in India is contentious, and most of this is directed at the state. However, this is not a peculiarly Banarsi or Indian characteristic; political theorists such as Montesquieu, Tocqueville, Hegel, and others conceived of civil society as a space where people form associations in order to check the power of the state or the 'tyranny of the majority', which necessarily involves conflict and contention. Furthermore, if civil society is conceived in terms of a Tocquevillian model of associational life, it is also clear that the lower classes are fully capable of participating in it. Therefore, excluding either contentious action or the poor working classes from the realm of 'civil society' seems an unnecessarily rigid interpretation of a theoretical concept that might not be as relevant in an age when urbanization and globalization are reconstituting interests and identities, and democratic consolidation is offering people new means of participation and mobilization. To theoretically place particular classes or groups outside the boundaries of civil society is no longer tenable, and Holston's concept of 'insurgent citizenship' (Holston 2008) illustrates how the very act of fighting for one's formal rights creates the reality of citizenship. Finally, purist interpretations of the civil society concept further disregard the varying compulsions and incentives offered by different political cultures and political opportunity structures, which unnecessarily limits the concept's usefulness and applicability.

However, there is a twist: my findings suggest that civil society in Varanasi, and perhaps elsewhere in urban India, does not only permit contentious, disorderly action, it privileges it. If contentious action is the preferred mode of making demands upon the state, where does this leave groups that cannot afford to carry out protests and strikes? By having to rely more on formal, institutionalized, contained means of making demands— by being forced to behave in a more 'civil' fashion—are they actually being excluded from civil society? Clearly, they would be at a disadvantage in an environment that privileges protest. However, as the boatmen have shown, when the stakes are really high, they find allies who can help them mobilize. The handloom weavers, likewise, readily take the assistance of outside organizations. As Holston (2008) rightly argues, in no democracy is citizenship ever evenly or consistently realized across groups. Not only do inequalities of resources and capabilities exist within every society, but the meaning, manifestation, and developmental trajectory of the very concept of citizenship vary across societies and are shifting constantly.

NOTES

1. However, as Cohen and Arato point out, Habermas does not view an exclusive public sphere as truly public: 'The public sphere of civil society stood or fell with the principle of universal access. A public sphere from which specific groups would be *eo ipso* excluded, was less than merely incomplete; it was not a public sphere at all' (Habermas 1991: 85; see also Cohen and Arato 1992: 226).
2. According to 1991 Census of India figures, population density of the city proper was 11,227 persons per square kilometre (http://www.varanasi.org/statistics.html, accessed on 10 August 2009). A local historian and preservation activist estimated that population density in the 'old city center' currently reaches 500–700 persons per hectare (Singh 2007).
3. Retail and wholesale trade accounts for the largest portion of the workforce in Varanasi, accounting for over 30 per cent of total main workers, according to the 2001 census.
4. The question of whether it is actually legal for lawyers to strike is murky. A legal scholar cites several court opinions to show that 'the judiciary has practically banned the strikes/ hartals by advocates' while one Supreme Court decision states:

It is the duty of every advocate who has accepted a brief to attend trial, even though it may go on day to day and for a prolonged period. He cannot refuse to attend court because a boycott call is given by the Bar Association. (Jain 2006)

BIBLIOGRAPHY

Bayly, C. A. 1983. *Rulers, Townsmen and Bazaars: North Indian Society in the Age of British Expansion, 1770–1870*. Cambridge: Cambridge University Press.

Bhargava, R. and H. Reifeld. 2005. *Civil Society, Public Sphere, and Citizenship: Dialogues and Perceptions*. New Delhi: SAGE Publications.

Bhattacharyya, D., N. G. Jayal, B. N. Mohapatra, and S. Pai (eds) 2004. *Interrogating Social Capital: The Indian Experience*. New Delhi: SAGE Publications.

Calhoun, C. 1993. 'Civil Society and the Public Sphere', *Public Culture*, 5(2): 267–80.

Chandra, K. 2007. *Why Ethnic Parties Succeed: Patronage and Ethnic Head Counts in India*. Cambridge: Cambridge University Press.

Chatterjee, P. 2001. 'On Civil and Political Society in Post-colonial Democracies', in S. Khilnani and S. Kaviraj (eds), *Civil Society: History and Possibilities*, pp. 165–78. Cambridge: Cambridge University Press.

———. 2004. *The Politics of the Governed: Reflections on Popular Politics in Most of the World*. New Delhi: Permanent Black.

Coelho, K. and T. Venkat. 2009. 'The Politics of Civil Society: Neighbourhood Associationism in Chennai', *Economic and Political Weekly*, 44(26/27): 358–67.

Cohen, J. L. and A. Arato. 1992. *Civil Society and Political Theory*. Cambridge: MIT Press.

Doron, A. 2008. *Caste, Occupation, and Politics on the Ganges: Passages of Resistance*. Surrey: Ashgate.

Eisinger, P. K. 1973. 'The Conditions of Protest Behavior in American Cities', *The American Political Science Review*, 67(1): 11–28.

Elliot, C. M. 2003. *Civil Society and Democracy: A Reader*. New Delhi: Oxford University Press.

Freitag, S. B. 1992. 'Introduction: The History and Political Economy of Banaras', in S. B. Freitag (ed.), *Culture and Power in Banaras: Community, Performance, and Environment*, pp. 1800–980. Berkeley: University of California Press.

Government of India. 2001. 'Census of India 2001: Basic Data Sheet, District Varanasi (67), Uttar Pradesh (09)'. New Delhi: Ministry of Home Affairs, Government of India.

Habermas, J. 1991. *The Structural Transformation of the Public Sphere*, T. Burger with the assistance of F. Lawrence (trans.), Paperback edition. Cambridge: MIT Press.

Harriss, J. 2006. 'Middle-class Activism and the Politics of the Informal Working Class', *Critical Asian Studies*, 38(4): 445–65.

Hegel, G. W. F. 1996. 'Editor's Introduction', in A. W. Wood (ed.), H. B. Nisbet (trans.), *Elements of the Philosophy of Right*, pp. vii–xxxii. Cambridge: Cambridge University Press.

Holston, J. 1999. 'Spaces of Insurgent Citizenship', in J. Holston (ed.), *Cities and Citizenship*, pp. 155–176. Durham: Duke University Press.

———. 2008. *Insurgent Citizenship: Disjunctions of Democracy and Modernity in Brazil*. Princeton: Princeton University Press.

Holston, J. and A. Appadurai. 1999. 'Introduction: Cities and Citizenship', in J. Holston (ed.), *Cities and Citizenship*, pp. 1–18. Durham: Duke University Press.

Jain, S. 2006. 'Of Advocates' Strike. The Practical Lawyer: The Practical Legal Information Service', *The Practical Lawyer: The Practical Legal Information Service*, May 13, Available online at http://www.ebc-india.com/practicallawyer/index. php?option=com_content&task=view&id=147&Itemid=54 (accessed on 18 January 2008).

Jayaram, N. 2005. *On Civil Society: Issues and Perspectives*. New Delhi: SAGE Publications.

Jones, G. S. 2001. 'Hegel and the Economics of Civil Society', in S. Khilnani and S. Kaviraj (eds), *Civil Society: History and Possibilities*, pp. 105–30. Cambridge: Cambridge University Press.

Kamath, L. and M. Vijayabaskar. 2009. 'Limits and Possibilities of Middle Class Associations as Urban Collective Actors', *Economic and Political Weekly*, 44 (26/27): 368–76.

Kaviraj, S. 2001. 'In Search of Civil Society', in S. Khilnani and S. Kaviraj (eds), *Civil Society: History and Possibilities*, pp. 287–323. Cambridge: Cambridge University Press.

Kaviraj, S. and S. Khilnani. 2001. 'Introduction', in S. Khilnani and S. Kaviraj (eds), *Civil Society: History and Possibilities*, pp. 1–7. Cambridge: Cambridge University Press.

McAdam, D., J. D. McCarthy, and M. N. Zald (eds). 1996. *Comparative Perspectives on Social Movements: Political Opportunities, Mobilizing Structures, and Cultural Framings*. Cambridge: Cambridge University Press.

McAdam, D., S. Tarrow, and C. Tilly. 2001. *Dynamics of Contention*. New York: Cambridge University Press.

Meyer, D. S. 2004. 'Protest and Political Opportunities', *Annual Review of Sociology*, 30: 125–45.

Oberschall, A. 1973. *Social Conflict and Social Movements*. Englewood Cliffs: Prentice-Hall.

Roy, A. 2003. *City Requiem, Calcutta: Gender and the Politics of Poverty*. Minneapolis: University of Minnesota Press.

Rudolph, L. I. and S. H. Rudolph. 1984. *The Modernity of Tradition: Political Development in India*. Chicago: University of Chicago Press.

Sassen, S. 1999. 'Whose City Is It? Globalization and the Formation of New Claims', in J. Holston (ed.), *Cities and Citizenship*, pp. 177–94. Durham: Duke University Press.

Seligman, A. B. 1992. *The Idea of Civil Society*. Princeton: Princeton University Press.

Shils, E. 1991. 'Civility and Civil Society', in E. C. Banfield (ed.), *Civility and Citizenship in Liberal Democratic Societies*, pp. 1–15. New York: Paragon.

Singh, R. P. B. 2007. 'Varanasi (India): Perspectives and Visions of Strategic Urban Development of a Heritage City', case study presented at ISOCARP [International Society of City and Regional Planners] Congress 2007: Urban Trialogues, Antwerp, September 19–23. Available online at http://www.isocarp.net/Data/case_studies/1015.pdf (accessed on 19 July 2011).

Singh, R. P. B. and P. S. Rana. 2006. *Banaras Region: A Spiritual and Cultural Guide*. Varanasi: Indica Books.

Stepan, A. C. and J. Linz. 2001. 'Toward Consolidated Democracies', in A. C. Stepan (ed.), *Arguing Comparative Politics*, pp. 295–314. New York: Oxford University Press.

Tarrow, S. 1998. *Power in Movement: Social Movements and Contentious Politics*. Cambridge: Cambridge University Press.

Tilly, C. 1978. *From Mobilization to Revolution*. Reading: Addison-Wesley.

Tocqueville, A de. 2003. *Democracy in America and Two Essays on America*. G. E. Bevan (trans.). London: Penguin Books.

Taylor, C. 1990. 'Modes of Civil Society', *Public Culture*, 3(1): 95–118.

Zald, M. N. and J. D. McCarthy (eds). 1979. *The Dynamics of Social Movements: Resource Mobilization, Social Control, and Tactics*. Cambridge: Winthrop Publishers.

Chapter 8

Linking Urban Vulnerability, Extralegal Security, and Civil Violence

The Case of the Urban Dispossessed in Mumbai

Jaideep Gupte

THE PHYSICAL PERPETRATION OF CIVIL VIOLENCE[1]

Sumatha,[2] a housemaid, refuses to bandage her leg. She would rather let the wound from a rat bite fester, than show that she is injured. To her, a bandage is a sign of weakness; a sure way to signal that she is losing whatever footing she has in her day-to-day survival in the neighbourhood. By rushing through the housework in several middle-class households, Sumatha supports her older sister as well as a mentally challenged cousin. She says there are vultures out to get her and her jobs; she must not allow them to get near. During the last riots, she had got hurt and lost all her jobs.

David, a handyman who has taken on a Christian name since he works for both Hindus and Muslims, and is presently a member of one of the large Mumbai gangs, asks why people are so frightened of bullets—'after all, the [local] word for a bullet and a sweet candy is the same!' While showing me a bullet, he says he sometimes coats his *goli* (bullet) with jaggery to make it a proper *goli* (candy). 'I am then no different from the shopkeeper who sells candies; we both make a living from candies, no?'

Tamima Iqbal, a practicing lawyer and social worker, is lovingly called '*Apa*' or elder sister. She also runs the Mahila Takrar Nivaran Kendra (Women's Conflict Resolution Cell) just across the road from the neighbourhood police station. In it, *Apa* holds her own court twice a week to primarily hear cases of triple-*talaq*. However, it is not just women who bring their grievances before *Apa*, but also men—complaining of harassment by the local musclemen, neighbours—with their disputes over the use of common areas, and even local political party representatives and shop owners.

No fees are charged, and officially the court has no legal or police backing. After all parties have been heard, *Apa* delivers judgment, which is noted on her *parchi* (letterhead) by her trusted office aide. A woman who has just received her judgement clasps the *parchi* tightly—it says, 'The husband will pay ₹ 5,000 to the wife and rent a flat in the neighbourhood for the family.' No signatures or stamps are necessary.

Civil violence, used in this chapter to refer primarily to rioting, is a term that has received much academic attention in the urban Indian context. A significant contribution is Varshney's study of 'Ethnic Conflict and Civic Life' (Varshney 2002). Pathbreaking in its detailed analysis of civil society, the study treats civil violence as something ever-present and only dampened by institutionalized inter-communal civic engagement. That is, Varshney's thesis provides insights into the causes of peace, rather than the origins of violence. Another major scholastic contribution is Brass' characterization of an 'Institutionalized Riot System' (Brass 1997, 2003), which exposes the mechanisms by which endemic communal violence is deliberately provoked and sustained. The study implicates the police, criminal elements, members of the business community, as well as leading political actors in the continuous effort to 'produce' communal violence (Brass 2004: 4840). Other important contributions to the literature include works by Engineer (1994a, 1994b, 2005) and Wilkinson (2004). Similar to Brass' thesis on riot production, Engineer and Wilkinson also explore the links between political aspirations, electoral incentives, and the incidence of communal violence.

Most studies have rejected the understanding of communal violence, or violence in which people are targeted based upon the community they belong to, in terms of religious strife between two unified 'Hindu' and 'Muslim' sides by arguing that it is 'untenable to interpret...the history of communalism in terms of the development of unified and cohesive community consciousness' (Gooptu 1997: 918). While these studies have provided key and important insights into the dynamics of civil violence, a gap that still exists in the literature pertains to why it is that some of the most vulnerable individuals choose to partake in civil violence and/or perpetuate it, even when the alleged political incentives do not directly accrue to them. In other words, while Brass' riot production system explains how any particular socio-economic event can be mutated by the political motivations of key leaders to trigger a full-scale outbreak of violent rioting, the grassroots question of why the common person would buy into such a system of violence remains unanswered.

In this chapter, I recognize two separate types of involvement in urban civil violence in Mumbai. The first type includes those involved purely in the mobilization of violence, by arousing ethno-religious sentiments, for example. This is repeatedly seen to be the precursor to, or the context in which, communal riots in India take place. There is a second type of involvement, which is more rudimentary, in that it encapsulates the physical perpetration of violence. Here, studies show us that those who physically perpetrate civil violence tend to be from the most vulnerable sections of society, for example, an overwhelming majority of those arrested for physically perpetrating civil violence in and around Mumbai are below the poverty line (cf. Khopade unpub.; Saraf 1995 among others).[3]

With reference to the second type of involvement, I argue that in Mumbai, the relationship between infra-power and urban vulnerability, in a context of inadequate provision of security by the state, is such that it incentivizes the physical perpetration of violence. More specifically, that the physical perpetration of violence might also be seen as an urban survival strategy for the more vulnerable sections of the urban population. The chapter concludes by questioning whether in a context of urban vulnerability coupled with the inadequate provision of state security, inter-communal civic engagement necessarily equates to continued communal harmony. Consequently, it asks whether policies targeting urban vulnerabilities could be a sharper way to reduce the incidence of urban communal violence.

SECURITY PROVISION AND HOW 'SLUMS' SHAPE THE URBAN ECOLOGY OF THE DISPOSSESSED

What Is a 'Slum'?

Urban areas which show certain characteristics of destitution are often described as 'deprived' areas and classified as 'slums'. There is often a presupposition that 'slums' are places of 'dirt, criminality, pilferage' and those who dwell there are 'squatters and encroachers' whose rights are therefore tainted by 'illegality and ineligibility' (Ramanathan 2005: 2905). However, there are multiple realities associated with terms such as 'slum' or 'poor' or 'dispossessed', and, arguably, these meanings are of immense significance to questions of urban citizenship. Slums tend to experience the most severe bouts of civil violence, which brings into further question the impact such systems of violence can have on notions of citizenship for the urban dispossessed and disenfranchised. More often than not, the manner in which government aid and development efforts, infrastructural provisions, including electricity, water, sanitation, as well as policing and security, are experienced can be linked closely to how one is classified—as a 'slum dweller' or a 'poor person', for example. It is therefore necessary to first elaborate briefly upon the various definitions used when categorizing an area as a 'slum' and the nature of deprivation in such an area.

The Material and Spatial Dimensions

The magnitude of the slum statistics for India presents a bleak picture: the most recent census reveals that nearly 43 million Indians live in slums. In other words, 15 per cent of India's total urban population are slum dwellers. At least 17.7 million people live in slums in the 27 largest cities of India.[4] Of these, the largest number of slum dwellers in any one city (approximately 6.5 million) is found in Greater Mumbai, accounting for an astonishing 54 per cent of the city's population (Census of India 2001). Few countries around the world are so blighted by urban deprivation as India is. The socio-economic costs of rapid urbanization are plainly evident in the continued and heavy dependence of urban dwellers on illegal slum settlements where asset and physical vulnerability is typically very high, the heavy reliance on an unprotected informal economy, and, therefore, the dependence on extralegal means for survival. It is important to note, however, that the label of 'poor' or the language of poverty might not be entirely adequate in this context since not all vulnerable people in Mumbai are poor—people might move in and out of poverty, but be continuously vulnerable. It might also be the case that those who could be classified as 'poor' do not necessarily identify with any such label. When the stakes are so intense and protracted, and the numbers so vast, the very basic exercise of defining a 'slum' has great implications.

It is important to flag-post here that around the world, there are several different criteria used when classifying an area as a slum. One of the most popular definitions is that of the UN-Habitat which classifies a slum as 'a heavily populated urban area characterized by substandard housing and squalor' (United Nations Human Settlements Programme [UN-Habitat] 2003: 8). The central aspects of this definition point to very high density of housing, low service provision, and an unhygienic environment. Local variations may include minimum size requirements. For example, the 2001 Indian census uses an operational definition according to which a 'slum' constitutes 'a compact area of at least 300 population [*sic*] or about 60–70 households of poorly built congested tenements, in unhygienic environment usually with inadequate infrastructure and lacking in proper sanitary and drinking water facilities' (Census of India 2001).

The National Sample Survey Organization's (NSSO) notes for the 49th round of the 2001 census render a slightly different definition. In it, a slum or a *bustee* is defined as:

> [A] compact area with a collection of poorly built tenements, mostly tempo-rary in nature, crowded together usually with inadequate sanitary and drink-ing water facilities in unhygienic conditions. An area, as defined above, is considered as 'slum' if at least twenty households live in the area. Slum dwell-ings are commonly known as '*Jhopad patti*' in Mumbai and '*Jhuggi Jhopri*' in Delhi. Some of the slums in the urban areas only may be found to be declared slum [*sic*]. The remaining slums are considered as undeclared slums. (NSSO 2001: Round 49/8.4/105–06).

Earlier rounds of the NSSO census had slightly varying definitions. These did not place any restrictions on the number of households in an area, and did not classify slums into 'declared' or 'undeclared' (as in the 44th and 28th rounds). In the 31st round, an undeclared slum was defined as an area unit having 25 or more structures mostly of temporary nature, or 50 or more households residing mostly in temporary structures, huddled together, or inhabited by persons with practically no private latrine or inad-equate public latrine and water facilities.

While the NSSO definition is unclear as per the meaning of impor-tant terms such as 'compact area' or 'poorly built', it is a narrowed down version of an earlier conceptualization from the 1956 Slum Areas Improve-ment and Clearance Act (SAICA). The 1956 SAICA broadly defined a slum as an area in which buildings are

> in any respect, unfit for human habitation; and are by reason of dilapidation, overcrowding, faulty arrangement and design of such buildings, narrowness or faulty arrangement of streets, lack of ventilation, light, sanitation facilities or any combination of these factors, detrimental to safety, health and morals. (GoI 1956: Section 3/1)

Under these broad criteria, much of the government-provided and even privately built housing in Mumbai, outside of certain high-income districts, can be classified in the least as 'slum-like', satisfying some, if not all, of the defining criteria mentioned above. This raises an interesting issue of comparability which is picked up on in the 2003 UN-Habitat report—that 'slum' is, in effect, a relative concept, in that what is considered as a slum in one city might be regarded as adequate housing in another city. Nevertheless, much like the 2001 Census of India framework and the earlier 1956 SAICA, most definitions worldwide are at their basic level based on material and spatial parameters only such as the structural conditions of the living environment, be they of buildings or of infrastructural provisions such as roads, sanitation, and electricity. For this reason, many definitional frameworks struggle to cope with the high degree of fluctuation in the spatial nature of slums; for example, they may be vulnerable to sudden changes in jurisdiction or spatial aggregation.

What about Vulnerability and Insecurity?

The spatial and material aspects of a slum, namely the 'dilapidated and infirm housing structures, poor ventilation, acute overcrowding, faulty alignment of streets, inadequate lighting, paucity of safe drinking water, waterlogging during rains, absence of toilet facilities, and non-availability of basic physical and social services' (Chandramouli 2003: 82) are rightly captured in the definitional frameworks mentioned above. These aspects are the static components in the definition of slums—static because each describes the inadequate provision of tangible infrastructure or services, which could conceivably be alleviated by their provision. In addition to these material and spatial dimensions, however, a slum also possesses several important dynamic characteristics. First, the changing spatial nature of a slum: it can 'come up', grow, or be demolished overnight. By simply eluding to the material or spatial parameters, like poor construction or non-existing infrastructure, no definition can capture the high degree of vulnerability caused by the non-permanence of one's circumstance. In slums, this non-permanence can be all-encompassing, ranging from the uncertainty over one's living space and personal security to uncertainty over one's livelihood options, and, hence, uncertainty over one's life-choices.

Another vital component missed by static definitions of slums is physical vulnerability such as vulnerability to disease. In one sense, disease might also be captured in material and spatial terms—that is, the probability of disease might be gauged by poor hygiene levels, lack of access to clean drinking water, sanitation or electricity, poor ventilation systems, high cohabitation often in very close proximity to livestock, and so forth. However, at the micro-level it also becomes important to characterize the reproductive and recursive nature of physical vulnerability. Not only is it more likely that diseases will occur in a slum, it is also more likely to spread. If a slum dweller falls ill, it also means that he or she will take longer to recover. As slum dwellers are more likely to be dependent on the informal or day-wage sector, their falling ill would probably mean losing their entire daily income, which would further deplete their resources, limiting access to medicine. It is of particular interest to this research that, in a context of severe civil violence, the probability of disease and its spread is intensified: the heightened physical trauma of civil violence obviously affects the most physically vulnerable first. Normal day-to-day support structures like clinics, access to medicines and doctors may get suspended during violent episodes, while death and decay also intensify the spread of disease.[5]

Physical vulnerability and insecurity are different from the spatial or material under-provision of infrastructure or services because they incorporate reproductive and recursive elements. Thus, they can be just as crippling, if not more, to the livelihood options and life-choices of slum dwellers, as are the spatial and material constraints. It is important to note here that by including this dynamic component in the definition of what constitutes a slum, vulnerability becomes the operative concept as opposed to poverty. That is to say that poverty, in and of itself, is not a defining characteristic here. As mentioned earlier, slum dwellers may dip in and out of poverty, but be continuously vulnerable. Indeed, slum areas in Mumbai generate and sustain a substantially large informal and semi-formal sector. They house people of varied professions, from shop or small business owners, to well-paid lawyers and call-centre professionals, right through to mechanics, day-wage labourers, and the unemployed. The point here is that by virtue of their living environment, and regardless of their poverty status, slum dwellers endure a greater degree of vulnerability than those who do not live in slums.

Interestingly, this focus on the micro-level—physical vulnerability and individual insecurity—does not decontextualize the individual from their socio-political and economic surroundings. As I have already argued, because these processes are recursive and reproductive, they in fact link the individual to wider dynamics in the local and non-local. Here, the individual is not isolated as in a utilitarian or rationalist framework. Instead, individuals are viewed as an important part of a system, which they influence and which influences them. This thesis argues that the material, spatial, as well as recursive components can constructively be taken into account under one framework and therefore the term slum is used to refer to a set of five particular characteristics, namely: (*a*) a high degree of vulnerability due to insecure or non-existent tenures and imminent threats of eviction; (*b*) a high degree of physical insecurity; (*c*) a lack of basic state service provision coupled with unhealthy living conditions and hazardous locations; (*d*) very low space-per-person, and cohabitation of several families; and last (*e*) social exclusion from citywide services and networks.

Asset and Physical Vulnerability

The experience of vulnerability in Mumbai then is a dynamic, complex, and multi-dimensional one. The specificities of the mega-city imply a greater degree of contestation for space and resources, coupled with a normalization of violence that is now ubiquitous in cities across Asia, Africa, and Latin America. Once again, it is important to note that not all vulnerable people in Mumbai are poor—people might move in and out of poverty, but be continuously vulnerable. It is also the case that those who could be classified as 'poor' might not identify with any such label. Sumatha, introduced at the start of this chapter, could easily be described as one living in poverty—she lives in a makeshift semi-*pucca jhopad patti* (made of rusty sheets of corrugated tin and plastic tarp), and has no savings. But on hearing about my research, she immediately gives me ₹ 50 (a very large sum compared to her daily expenditure) to 'donate towards this research'. 'It is my way to help poor people,' she tells me.

For a sizeable majority in Mumbai, the vulnerability they experience can be seen to have three interdependent 'asset' dimensions (as in Moser [1998]). The first is an income dimension, where the vulnerability results from a high susceptibility to income shocks, caused by an almost total dependence on day-wage labour. The second dimension is environmental, where vulnerability arises from a constant subjugation to the environmental hazards of noise, water, and air pollution; lack of adequate sanitation; and insecure living space, all extenuated by an urban infrastructure grossly incapable of withstanding climatic disasters. This is a particularly intensified reality in the city's slums.[6] The third is a social dimension, where social fragmentation due to the 'greater social and economic heterogeneity associated with wider distributional ranges of incomes, opportunities, and access to infrastructure, services, and political influences' (Moser 1998: 4) found in a mega-city, cuts out community, or at times even familial, support networks to heighten vulnerability.

Vulnerability might also be looked at through a more fundamental lens by focusing on the physical aspects of urban survival. Borrowing from criminological studies (Pantazis [2000], among others), vulnerability might simply be defined as: the inability to protect oneself—'either because they cannot run fast, or lack the physical prowess to ward off attackers, or because they cannot afford to protect their homes, or because it would take them longer than average to recover from material or physical injuries' (Hale 1996: 95). As seen through the contrasting realities of the lives of Sumatha and David presented at the start of this chapter, this simple and matter-of-fact definition has the ability to capture even the nuanced and variant experiences of urban vulnerability in Mumbai. That is, at some fundamental level, physical vulnerability is intertwined with, and even underwrites, all three dimensions of asset vulnerability.

The Conceptual Failure of Policies Based on Material and Spatial Parameters

It is important to take a step back at this stage and consider why a definition of a slum based on recursive vulnerability and insecurity could be problematic for those frameworks which define slums in material and spatial dimensions only. My argument is that it would pose problems in two ways.

First, rehabilitation and relocation programmes which use material and spatial definitions to define their target areas, might, for example, find that while the relocation sites rectify the static under-provision of infrastructure by providing, for example, tenements in a concretized structure, the recursive components of vulnerability and insecurity continue, or even proliferate, in the relocation sites. Often, the relocation sites are on the fringes of the city, in previously underdeveloped areas characterized by minimal police outreach and, therefore, an environment where legal boundaries and norms are feeble. They are also characterized by isolation from medical (for example, clinics) and municipal (for example, sewage systems and garbage collection) services. Being on the city fringes also means that certain avenues for income, like selling food or shoe-polishing, tend not to be viable given the dearth of office-goers in the newly urbanized sites. Thus, while the relocation site might provide its inhabitants with concretized structures to live in, it may also subject them to greater levels of insecurity and vulnerability—that is, the relocation from slums to slums. Importantly, this would imply that a relocation exercise goes from being regarded as successful to being ineffective or even detrimental to the overall exercise of reducing slums. In addition to this, areas previously not regarded as slum areas on account of their tolerable spatial and material parameters, could conceivably be classified as slums owing to heightened levels of vulnerability and insecurity.

Second, a definition based on vulnerability and insecurity might be problematic for frameworks which rely solely on material and spatial definitions because it would redefine the question of whose responsibility slum eradication is. Traditionally, dealing with slums falls under the purview of urban planning boards, the municipality, the legislature, or related non-governmental organizations, but falls outside the direct purview of the police and judiciary. Including vulnerability and insecurity parameters, however, implies the direct involvement of the police (or other private agencies providing security) within slum eradication efforts, and in the context of Mumbai, for example, this would imply a drastic reworking of the way in which slum policies are devised and implemented. Currently, the police are brought in only as secondary actors at three distinct stages of rehabilitation or resettlement—first, to provide backup during municipality demolition drives and to evict any non-cooperative dwellers; second, to enforce law and order in the transit site (if any); and last, to reinstate police authority at the resettlement site. Similarly, the judiciary is used as an aggressive tool to either dispense the state's legal authority to usurp land, or to enforce private property development rights. It is evident that these interjections by the police and judiciary are, and by their design can only be, very violent and oppressive in nature. If physical security and vulnerability mitigation were parameters used to measure the success of slum rehabilitation schemes, then it would become clear that such police and judicial involvement is tantamount to a failure of the schemes. Challenging slum eradication policies in this manner is arguably a positive step forward, and the following sections further elaborate on how this reworked definition of slums might also be a central force in policies dealing with civil violence.

THE *MOHALLA* (NEIGHBOURHOOD)

Muslim dominated areas of South Central Mumbai were particularly affected in the 1992–93 riots. Not only are these areas densely populated with extremely poor infrastructural provisions in terms of inadequate access to electricity, clean water, sanitation, as well as structurally unsafe housing, but they also suffer from ghettoized segregation from the rest of the city. Nevertheless, these areas have a long history, being some of the oldest districts in Mumbai, and most residents choose to continue to live in vulnerable conditions (cf. Chadha 2005).

In the neighbourhood which I studied, the police station describes its jurisdiction as 'predominantly a Muslim area, with Hindus and other minorities making up only 30 percent of the population'. The area is dotted with mosques and Islamic schools. There are a variety of businesses based in the locality, ranging from heavy metal and frame works, to tile shops, tailoring, and leather works. There are also certain *chawls* (slum-like concrete buildings with several one or two room tenements on each storey linked by a common hallway, usually with shared latrines and water taps) where there is a mixed population of Hindus and Muslims. This is one of the most communally sensitive areas and has seen frequent communal riots. Significant occurrences of communal activity were reported here during the rioting of 1992–93 (Srikrishna 1998). Following those riots, there has been a steady exodus of Hindus from the area, leading to the further ghettoization of the neighbourhood.

Infra-power

Aside from the spatial dimensions, it is the 'non-obvious, non-formal, and often ephemeral forms of organization, knowledge, connections, solidarity, and mythology that organize and weave together urban localities, if not entire cities' (Hansen 2005: 1). There is tangible power resident in these networks of knowledge, solidarity, and even mythology. It is this power that Tamima *Apa* draws on to run her court. While there are no laws that make her judgements binding, in the neighbourhood, her decisions are respected by all parties. Because such power is achieved through individual and/or social agencies outside of the state apparatus, these networks have been referred to as 'infra-power', or power from below (Hansen 2005).

These non-traditional forms of legitimacy challenge, or at times even collude with, traditional forms of power and control. Importantly, they have come to be more accessible and dependable in delivering services to the vulnerable. People choosing to put their grievances before *Apa* is evidence of this, as well as a loosening of the state's monopoly on imparting legal justice. Her court also directly challenges the authority of the local *maulana*s (Islamic scholars/leaders) and their call to bring civil and other disputes to the mosques.[7] I asked Tamima Iqbal if she faced any direct competition with *fatwa*s (an Islamic decree) issued by the local *maulana*. She tells me:

> We make it clear to the people who come to us that we [her court] have also read the Koran, so they have to decide whether they want to go by the *maulana's fatwa* or what is actually written in the Koran…. When we started, three or four *maulanas* came here saying 'you have gone and opened this place [the conflict resolution cell] but what do you know about the *shariat*? We will come and sit here.' To that I simply said no! You have got your shop [the mosque] and I have got mine. If someone insists on [their case being judged as per] the *shariat*, they will be referred on to the mosque…let the *maulana* say whatever…we are also working for the community…in fact I challenge anybody, because no one does the work I do…and no one has the connections I have.

But of course, infra-power and state or religious authority are not always in competition, they also collude: during communally tense situations, such as local tensions between the Deobandi Muslims and the Barelvi Muslims, or in a Hindu–Muslim mixed *chawl*, the police rely on Tamima *Apa* to ease the situation (see Thakkar 2004: 583–84). One such example is from a small riot that had broken out in the neighbourhood because a passing *Ganesh Chaturthi* (a Hindu festival) procession mistakenly believed that some Muslim boys had thrown an egg at them. A Mumbai Police inspector was caught in the middle of this, and was being overpowered by the mob. To the inspector's good fortune, Tamima Iqbal managed to pull him out and pacify the mob before any serious injuries were sustained. This incident has now achieved a near myth-like quality for those who know Iqbal—not only in the local police stations into which Iqbal enjoys ready access, but also in the eyes of those who attend her court. Following this incident, Iqbal has often been called upon by the local police to mediate communal tensions, be they between Hindus and Muslims, or between different Muslim sects.

On one occasion, a lawyer practicing in the Small Causes Court in Mumbai admitted to the corrosion of legal authority of the state. He described to me that a significant proportion of his clientele are landlords with cases of illegal tenancy, requesting court orders to evict the difficult tenants:

> Due to the Bombay Rent Act it is virtually impossible to evict an illegal tenant… the only way to solve the matter efficiently is to hire a *goonda* [the local thug or goon], little bit of *mara-mari* [fist-fight type violence] and get the tenant out first, once the landlord is back in the property *then* the legal proceedings can go on forever, but you *have to* initially use force. I'm a lawyer and I'm telling you that, just see!…the experience is the same for tenants facing evictions, where the most secure rent agreements are not the ones on all the fancy officially registered stamp paper and all…but the verbal contracts with the local *goonda*.

In fact, there are entire *chawls* where none of the residents have a tenancy agreement. Their only agreement is a verbal one with the local *goonda*. An important question poses itself at this juncture: why do people choose to bring their disputes to *Apa*'s court or get into verbal contracts with a *goonda*, when the Small Causes and Family Courts have been set up particularly to hear civil cases, cases relating to tax, family matters, property disputes, and other such cases? In other words, why is it that infra-power can compete so readily with traditional authority of the state? The answer is evidenced in that fact that the frequent instances of long drawn-out tenancy battles show legal proceedings to be arduous and impotent in contrast to the *goonda* who 'delivers as promised and paid for'. The Family Court is also largely non-functional, straining under approximately 8,000 pending cases in 2001, with an average of 25 new petitions filed daily. The only way around the pending cases is to pay a tout, who charges substantial fees for a speedy and favourable judgement (Garari 2001).

It is interesting to note that Tamima Iqbal's judgement scribbled on a chit of paper delivers a greater sense of security than the presence of the beat constable, who works close to 18 hours per day in an effort to achieve the same. A woman who had brought forth a case of husband-harassment described to me her relief that *Apa*'s judgment had fallen favourably for her—she now felt safe. When asked why she didn't instead go to the police, she dismissively smirked at the ability of the local police to protect her inside her house. In a similar vein, another case brought to the Women's Conflict Resolution Cell was of a small time thug, who calls himself 'The Lizard' and was threatening to extort money from a family. He had on several occasions broken in through the front door and ransacked the family's tiny living quarters. Instead of taking their grievance to the police, the eldest daughter in the family had brought the complaint to *Apa*. As the case proceedings unfolded, it became increasingly clear that it was in fact not the daughter, but her husband who was approaching the court through his wife. Just as with the earlier case, he too felt that approaching the police would either not be possible, or would be ineffective.

These examples highlight two important points: first, that the under-provision of credible state security contributes to urban vulnerability as defined above. And second, that there is a subsequent growing reliance on non-state, at times extralegal, channels to supplant the under-provision of state security.

Powertoni

In the context of Mumbai, a particular notion prevalent at street level provides good insight into the systems of infra-power: *Powertoni* is a Mumbai-street slang term abbreviating Power-of-Attorney to a colloquial understanding of 'the wherewithal to get things done'[8]—an ability to bend or break the rules (laws) as one sees fit. Shiv Sena musclemen often use the term to describe the free hand they are given to carry out their duty—they are working for Bal Thackeray (the Shiv Sena supremo), and so have *powertoni* from him. Thus, *powertoni* signifies a power that does not originate in oneself, but a power that one holds usually by virtue of violence, on somebody else's behalf. Who the 'someone else' is, is at times unclear: David, the handyman in the neighbourhood (introduced at the start of the chapter), claims his *powertoni* from his past acts of violence. '*Shuru mein mene saat supari khaya hein,*' he tells me, which literally translates to 'In the beginning, I ate seven beetel nuts', but actually means that what gave David his initial *powertoni* were the seven murders he was paid to commit. Now no one even bothers to find out whom he killed or at whose behest (or whether he actually killed anyone at all); everyone simply knows he has *powertoni*. This goes back to the definitional core of infra-power: it is non-obvious, non-formal, and ephemeral—invisible to the casual passer-by.

Individuals, like the local hoodlum, or a gang member might possess *powertoni*, as might groups like gangs.[9] Being in possession of infra-power signifies an agency outside of the formal channels, a sovereignty beyond the state, a know-how of the city not only to get things done, but importantly also to provide security in times of need. Infra-power can mean access to the benign—getting front seats at a local cricket match, or the material signs of 'the good life: cellular phones…air-conditioning, visits to [the local] red-light area' (Hansen 2000: 266), as well as the more critical aspects of urban livelihood—protection from violence and harm, a secure space to live, or access to employment.

Lastly, it is important to re-state that even though infra-power refers particularly to non-state and extralegal channels of agency, the potency of infra-power is also tapped into by state (or 'legitimate') actors such as policemen, labour union leaders and politicians.[10] In sum, infra-power not only competes with the authority (monopoly) of the state, but it can also collude or even have a corrosive effect on it.

LINKING CIVIL VIOLENCE, INFRA-POWER AND VULNERABILITY

Thus far, I have aimed to illustrate that the under-provision (or failed provision) of credible and accessible state security can lead urban folk to rely upon systems of infra-power in order to counteract vulnerability. In this section, I will further unpack the interface between vulnerability and violence.

The individual rioter bears the most direct risk and cost of the riot. Horowitz (2001) asks why then do we not see more 'free-riding', that is, more people with ethnic grievances just letting others be violent on their behalf. He theorizes that participants grossly underestimate the risks of partaking in ethnic rioting, since rioting is a mob or a group phenomenon, which reduces individual risks. However, by using asset and physical vulnerabilities to cross-section the urban population, a paradox becomes apparent: it is evident that those who riot or are involved in communal violence tend to be the most susceptible to the resultant violence. That is, it is the most vulnerable who tend to partake in the violence. This susceptibility is different from Horowitz's risk assessment because a rioter might feel it less risky to be violent in a mob, but physical and asset vulnerabilities of the rioter mean that the rioter is also less likely to recover quickly from wounds sustained, more likely to lose all income from regular day-wage labour, much more likely to be left homeless, and a lot less likely to have the connections (which money can buy) to get access to fair justice if arrested. In short, those who riot seem to have the most to lose. So why then do they riot?

Sultan Hafeez, who runs a local paper recycling business and is deeply connected within the social organization of the neighbourhood, tells me that those who have been imprisoned invariably come out with stronger criminal networks, and even if they do not, there is always some weight attached to quoting one's experiences in jail. This is emphatically echoed right through David's career as an odd-jobs man: he boasts that he too has 'cut his time in jail', and this is almost like a qualification to get into certain circles. The point I am highlighting here, however, is larger than the criminal networks within jails: partaking in violence and having some way to showcase it appears to be a significant means to signal deservedness, even merit, to enter into those systems of infra-power which seem most effective in providing protection against vulnerability. Sultan Hafeez explains:

> During the riots there were big rumours going around that they [the Hindus] were travelling around in ambulances so as to go unnoticed, and then ambushing Muslim neighbourhoods… suddenly someone would shout out that they had spotted a suspicious ambulance… we were all of course working extra hard to dispel these silly rumours, but the boys who got up to track down the ambulances were seen as the saviours… same thing with those who went out to take part in the riots. They might have been petty criminals, but after the riots, people did favours for them…they looked after them…

The small day-to-day struggles[11] for the boys mentioned by Hafeez tended to ease after their involvement in the riots. The story is much the same in Hindu (Shiv Sena) neighbourhoods where the rioters were instead seen as warring parties, and so later reaped in the awards for their gallantry—a better living space, or better connections to the inner circles of the Shiv Sena, for example. In this view, physically perpetrating violence and publicly displaying strength therefore take on the characteristics of an urban survival strategy for those involved at the grassroots level.

Militant Politics

Appadurai describes the Shiv Sena's growth and survival, from being 'mainly a group of urban thugs...to [becoming] a regional and national political force' (Appadurai 2000: 646), as being fuelled essentially through violent and criminalized efforts of 'urban cleansing'. For parties and individuals alike, accessing infra-power therefore has much to do with showcasing physical fitness. For Sumatha, this involves not wearing a bandage to show that she is physically capable of protecting her livelihood, while David needs to work off of a reputation of extreme violence. Sumatha and David are of course two extremes in the full range of urban vulnerabilities, but the point remains that involvement in violence can give access to systems of infra-power that prove elusive to those who are not willing to partake in the violence.

Another episode elucidates the point from a different angle, showing how the context of communal violence can lead to tangible long-term benefits for those involved. Imamwada, in the jurisdiction of the J. J. Marg Police Station in South Mumbai, has two Hindu *chawls* next to which are three contiguous Muslim ones. This location witnessed widespread and intense communal disturbances during the 1992–93 riots. After five days and nights of continuous work, the Mumbai Police uncovered the group of Hindu and Muslim youth at the centre of the rivalry. After much negotiation, it was found that all five *chawls* had an overlapping need—reliable water supply. The squalid conditions in the *chawls* had caused much strife amongst residents, and the inadequate supply of water had been the latest addition to their worries. It was agreed that the municipal commissioner would immediately be approached to help ease the tensions. Concrete plans were made and water supply was increased, and eventually reinforced by laying broader pipes.

The vulnerabilities addressed in Imamwada were broader than the simple provision of a water connection. It was about community members witnessing a commitment on part of the municipal corporation to provide a service, made authentic by quick action on part of the Mumbai Police.[12] Once these vulnerabilities which arose primarily out of a lack of credible service provision were addressed, it appears that space for communal civic engagement (or 'inter-communal engagement' as in Varshney [2002]) opened up quite readily in the locality.

However, it needs to be noted that the context of imminent city-wide rioting and the further threat of intensified street fighting between neighbouring *chawls* seem to have provided the catalyst to spark otherwise inefficient state services into prompt action. And even so, much depended on individual officers with foresight and capacity, rather than an institutional response. Therefore, while being temporarily effective at controlling the violence at hand, such instances of 'the militant crowd as a manifestation of people's power' (Tambiah 1997: 260), successfully achieving results, paradoxically contribute to the continued reliance on militant politics in the long run. Here, infra-power is intertwined with the creation of myths of violence and auras of fear or respect, and, further, this dynamic between urban violence and infra-power shares a particular closeness to rioting, communal violence, as well as gang violence, in that these public displays of bravado and strength are not only seen by all, but also prove easy for other community members to associate with. Thus, even though the core grievances may arise out of physical and asset vulnerabilities, showcasing involvement in public displays of violence appears to be a particularly good access route into systems of infra-power.

PROMOTING CIVIC ENGAGEMENT OR ADDRESSING VULNERABILITIES?

This chapter has raised questions around the continued involvement of vulnerable sections of the urban population in a system in which violence is used instrumentally. The field evidence I have presented here in brief suggests that physical participation in violence at the grassroots level might also be seen as the cycle of vulnerable urban folk using their involvement in communal violence as a means of accessing infra-power, which in turn supplants for the failed provision of credible state security. That is, vulnerable urban folk readily rely upon extralegal channels of authority, legitimacy, and security, when state provision of the same is inadequate. At this level, themes of ethnicity and religiosity appear to play a lesser role than do the day-to-day vulnerabilities faced by urban folk.

It is during mobilization, as well as the process of building myths and auras, however, that ethnicity and religiosity seem particularly relevant— the perpetrators are immediately associated with one ethno-religious community, while the victims are associated with another. When Tambiah characterizes ethnicity as 'the most potent energizer, embodying and radiating religious, linguistic, territorial, and class and caste identities and interests', whilst also being 'the umbrella under which personal, familial, commercial, and other local scores are settled' (Tambiah 1997: 261), he too is hinting at the dual levelled nature of such violence. Varshney's focus on inter-communal associational engagement (Varshney 2002: 11–12) therefore continues to remain cogent insofar as it is a measure of the causes of peace. It is likely that civic engagement would help dampen violence once it erupts, and encouraging a healthy inter-communal associational civic space is therefore an important consideration. However, even in the presence of such inter-communal engagement, it needs to be recognized that given their extreme circumstances of vulnerability and a reliance on violence as a survival strategy, urban folk may not refrain from killing one another in continued spates of communal disharmony. In other words, while a strong inter-communal associational space can lessen the ferocity of riots (even to the extent where there are no casualties), on its own it might not be able to prevent communal disharmony from sparking riots in the future.

A young Muslim mechanic chose to remain anonymous when he told me:

> I know and understand my neighbour…I even call him 'brother' when I come across him on my way home from work some nights…he happens to be Hindu, but if I am to lose my job because of him, then what? I will do anything to keep food on the table for my family, right?

The impassioned pathos of the mechanic's narrative would suggest that inter-communal engagement might not always equate to continued communal peace. And, further, that asset and physical vulnerabilities operate closer to the core of reasons that spark communal violence in and around the neighbourhood I studied. This corroborates Brass' findings that 'it is pure diversion to invest resources in promoting civic engagement, when attention and resources should be directed towards uncovering the system and process of riot production and the producers thereof' (Brass 2004: 4839–840).

Police as Drivers of Urban Development?

It is also necessary to ask whether city police can contribute to the success of a policy framework which looks to disincentivize *ex-ante* the physical involvement in civil violence through specific (long-term) policies to reduce asset and physical vulnerability. Given that uniformed and usually armed police form the most public arm of the state's machinery in cities today, their role goes far beyond the traditional paradigms of policing crime or simply carrying out violent interjections on behalf of the state. The police are also the domestic caretakers of the prevailing legal system, and in this capacity, should constitute a monopoly on the legitimate use of force. At the same time, a growing reliance on non-state and extralegal actors is a reality faced in many cities around the world. A recent study on slums in Cairo found the following:

> What characterizes the social life of the urban dispossessed is not simply anomie, alienation and a 'culture of poverty', nor a particular penchant for embracing [extremists/violent] politics, but primarily the practice of 'informal life'—a social existence characterized by autonomy, flexibility, and pragmatism, where survival and self-development occupy a central place. The urban disenfranchised person tends pragmatically to lend support to diverse political trends and movements, both governmental and oppositional, including [extreme/violent ideologies], so long as they contribute to those central objectives. (Bayat 2007: 580)

It is evident that this kind of reliance on informality and infra-power can scarcely be controlled by top-down approaches to policing which prioritize crime-control through enforcement and arrests. Alternatives to viewing informality and infra-power as 'crime', that is, the further disenfranchisement of already dispossessed urban citizens, can only be achieved by initiating a dialogue amongst equals, between those reliant on infra-power and those responsible for the legal provision of security. At the same time, it also becomes necessary to rethink how 'slums' and 'poverty' are defined, since both are heavily subjective conceptualizations that at times can hide the recursive impacts of vulnerability and insecurity.

Since the riots of 1992–93 in Mumbai, there has been a lot of emphasis on building inter-community civic bodies—one such example is the Mumbai Police requiring every police station to form neighbourhood committees, with representations from all communities as well as the police. These committees are to be consulted and relied upon to maintain inter-community peace. While this kind of institutionalized civic engagement no doubt has the capacity to dampen violence once it has erupted, an environment where credible channels of legally provided security are easily accessible breaks down the incentive structures for the physical perpetration of communal violence, thereby dismantling the riot-production system from the bottom up. That is, targeting asset and physical vulnerability and reducing the reliance of urban folk on extralegal channels, together with the promotion of inter-communal civic engagement, would form a more holistic and sustainable strategy to counter trends in urban communal violence.

It would be interesting to learn whether the analysis presented here holds true in different neighbourhoods in Mumbai, and indeed in other cities around the world. Recognizing the interconnectedness among extralegality, infra-power, and civil violence in this manner can greatly contribute to our present understandings of what it means to be an urban citizen, of vulnerable or insecure urban environments, as well as add to the manner in which urban development is conceptualized.

NOTES

1. The ethnographic fieldwork for this study was conducted over eight months in a Muslim locality in South Central Mumbai. Comments and guidance from Dr Nandini Gooptu and Professor David Anderson have been invaluable, but any faults are mine alone. I am grateful for the support received from the Harold Wingate Foundation, the Carr, Stahl, JCR Grant, and the Norman Chester Award. I am also grateful to the organizers and participants of the Symposium on Cities and Citizenship: Interrogating Urbanism in Contemporary South Asia, 14 February 2008, at the Center for South Asia Studies, UC Berkeley, for their comments and suggestions. An earlier version of this paper was also presented at the 9th Global Development Conference on Security for Development: Confronting Threats to Survival and Safety, 29–31 January 2008, in Brisbane, Australia.

2. Names of all interview respondents have been changed to maintain anonymity, and most interviews have been translated from local dialects of Marathi/Hindi/Urdu.

3. Suresh Khopade in his study on rioting in Bhiwandi, a few kilometres north east of Mumbai, finds that out of 962 individuals charge-sheeted for rioting, 63 per cent were below poverty line, while 95 per cent of those killed were also below the poverty line (Khopade unpub.). Similarly, V. K. Saraf (1995) finds that in the mid-1990s the majority of gang members in Mumbai were young adults, between the age of 19 and 28 (66.5 per cent), with the average life span of a gang member being 35 years, while most of them had at least a secondary school education (42.5 per cent). Interestingly, Saraf also found that gang members were predominantly Maharashtrian, but from outside of Mumbai, while about 30 per cent of those he sampled were from other states.

4. These are cities with a population of more than 1 million.

5. The link between disease and riots is not a recent phenomenon by any means. For example, Chatterji and Mehta (2007) document the link in early 20th century riots in colonial India.

6. During the flooding in 2005, more than 500 people died in Mumbai alone. The floods brought large sections of Mumbai to a complete standstill under neck-deep water. The severity of the problem was evidenced by two features: (*a*) even though Mumbai city is completely coastal, the flooding was caused primarily by the inability of rainwater to reach the sea, and not by the sea encroaching into the city; (*b*) the worst hit areas were the slums and suburbs, while the high-income areas of South Mumbai were almost completely spared any disruption.

7. See Hansen's discussion of how the Ulema Council promoted itself as an authority better suited to interpret Muslim Personal Law than any other court in Mumbai (Hansen 2000).

8. For a powerfully crafted colloquial expression of *powertoni*, see Mehta (2004: 39–110).
9. See, for example, Hansen's discussion of the individual capacity of 'K' as compared with the wherewithal of Dawood's gang (Hansen 2000: 266–67).
10. See, for example, Hansen's discussion of Shiv Sena's 'plebian' political culture as undermining democratic rule (Hansen 2001).
11. Day-to-day struggles might involve, for example, a threat of eviction from their living quarters.
12. The hands-on involvement of the then commissioner of police Mr Satish Sahney, who was present on location and spoke to the youth of all *chawls*, contributed significantly to the authenticity of the state's actions.

BIBLIOGRAPHY

Appadurai, A. 2000. 'Spectral Housing and Urban Cleansing: Notes on Millenial Mumbai', *Public Culture*, 12(3): 627–51.
Bayat, A. 2007. 'Radical Religion and the Habitus of the Dispossessed: Does Islamic Militancy Have an Urban Ecology?', *International Journal of Urban and Regional Research*, 31(3): 579–90.
Brass, P. R. 1997. *Theft of an Idol: Text and Context in the Representation of Collective Violence*. Princeton: Princeton University Press.
———. 2003. *The Production of Hindu–Muslim Violence in Contemporary India*. New Delhi: Oxford University Press.
———. 2004. 'Development of an Institutionalised Riot System in Meerut City, 1961 to 1982', *Economic and Political Weekly*, 39(44): 4839–848.
Census of India. 2001. *City-wise Total Population and Slum Population in Million Plus Cities (Municipal Corporations)*. Delhi: Office of the Registrar General and Census Commissioner.
Chadha, M. 2005. 'Inside Mumbai's Dilapidated Sprawl'. Available online at http://news.bbc.co.uk/2/hi/south_asia/4176738.stm (accessed on 2 March 2009).
Chandramouli, C. 2003. 'Slums In Chennai: A Profile', in M. J. Bunch, V. M. Suresh and T. V. Kumaran (eds), *Proceedings of the Third International Conference on Environment and Health, Chennai, India, 15–17 December, 2003*, pp. 82–88. Chennai: Department of Geography, University of Madras and Faculty of Environmental Studies, York University.
Chatterji, Roma and Deepak Mehta. 2007. *Living with Violence: An Anthropology of Events and Everyday Life*. New Delhi: Routledge India.
Engineer, A. A. 1994a. 'Communal Violence and the Role of Law Enforcement Agencies', *South Asia Bulletin*, 15(2): 16–23.
———.1994b. *Lifting the Veil: Communal Violence and Communal Harmony in Contemporary India*. London: Sangam Books.
———. 2005. 'Communal Riots, 2004', *Economic and Political Weekly*, 40(6): 517–20.
GoI. 1956. Slum Areas Improvement and Clearance Act (SAICA). Available online at http://www.commonlii.org/in/legis/num_act/saaca1956329/ (accessed on 2 March 2009).
Garari, K. 2001. 'Family Court Has 8,000 Pending Cases'. *Times of India*, Mumbai, 2 November. Available online at http://timesofindia.indiatimes.com/articleshow/674105472.cms (accessed on 2 March 2009).

Gooptu, N. 1997. 'The Urban Poor and Militant Hinduism in Early Twentieth-century Uttar Pradesh', *Modern Asian Studies,* 31(4): 879–918.

Hale, C. 1996. 'Fear of Crime: A Review of the Literature', *International Review of Victimology,* 4(2): 79–150.

Hansen, T. B. 2000. 'Predicaments of Secularism: Muslim Identities and Politics in Mumbai', *The Journal of the Royal Anthropological Institute,* 6(2): 255–72.

———. 2001. *Wages of Violence: Naming and Identity in Postcolonial Bombay.* Princeton and Oxford: Princeton University Press.

———. 2005. 'The Anthropologist and the Hustler. Introductory Notes on Infra-power and Legibility in the City', paper presented at conference on Urban Charisma: On Reputations, Hustlers, Big Men and Other Forms of Urban Infra-Structure, Yale University, New Haven, USA, September 23.

Horowitz, D. 2001. *The Deadly Ethnic Riot.* Berkeley: University of California Press.

Khopade, S. Unpublished MS. 'The Bhiwandi Danga'.

Mehta, S. 2004. *Maximum City: Bombay Lost and Found.* Hardcover edition. New Delhi: Penguin Books India.

Moser, C. 1998. 'The Asset Vulnerability Framework: Reassessing Urban Poverty Reduction Strategies', *World Development,* 26(1): 1–19.

National Sample Survey Office (NSSO). 2001. *The National Sample Survey of India.* Delhi: Government of India.

Pantazis, C. 2000. '"Fear of Crime", Vulnerability and Poverty: Evidence from the British Crime Survey', *British Journal of Criminology,* 40(3): 414–36.

Ramanathan, U. 2005. 'Demolition Drive', *Economic and Political Weekly,* 40(27): 2908–912.

Saraf, V. K. 1995. 'Formation of Criminal Gangs in Major Cities', PhD Thesis, Bureau of Police Research and Development, BPRD, Delhi.

Srikrishna, Justice B. N. 1998. *Report of the Srikrishna Commission Appointed for Inquiry into the Riots at Mumbai during December 1992 and January 1993: Volumes I and II.* Mumbai: Government of Maharashtra.

Tambiah, S. 1997. *Levelling Crowds: Ethnonationalist Conflicts and Collective Violence in South Asia.* New Delhi: Vistaar Publications.

Thakkar, U. 2004. 'Mohalla Committees of Mumbai: Candles in Ominous Darkness', *Economic and Political Weekly,* 39(6): 580–86.

United Nations Human Settlements Programme (UN-Habitat). 2003. *The Challenge of Slums: Global Report on Human Settlements.* London: Earthscan.

Varshney, A. 2002. *Ethnic Conflict and Civic Life: Hindus and Muslims in India.* London: Yale University Press.

Wilkinson, S. I. 2004. *Votes and Violence: Electoral Competition and Ethnic Riots in India.* Cambridge: Cambridge University Press.

Chapter 9

Displaced Borders

Shifting Politics of Squatting in Calcutta

Romola Sanyal

The migration of people to cities has influenced the ways in which urbanization has taken place. In addition to expanding the periphery, immigrants have influenced the culture and politics of cities through their own practices and beliefs. While there is much work done on rural–urban migration, the impact of cross-border migration—particularly that of refugees on cities—remains under-investigated. This is primarily due to the fact that refugees are often put in camps and viewed as temporary 'guests' in a host nation even if they remain within its borders for a long time. Yet, increasingly, refugees are moving to cities and moving into their slums and squatter settlements. This has caused dilemmas for humanitarian aid agencies as well as local and national governments as they feel the need to separate refugees from locals in order to diffuse any possible tension that may flare up between them. Refugee camps, through their expansion over time, become cities as well. The relationship between refugees and cities is therefore increasingly important as refugees have the capacity to impact the politics of their host state and also the local cities within which they are located. This chapter looks at the politics of refuge in Calcutta (or Kolkata, as it is now known) in the aftermath of the 1947 partition and how the migration of refugees and their demands to be resettled has continuously impacted the urbanization of the city as well as the articulation of citizenship rights.

The material for this chapter draws upon historical sources as well as on interviews carried out with residents from former refugee colonies in Jadavpur, Calcutta. The interviews were part of a larger project of understanding the process of urbanization of refugee spaces. Interviews were conducted with approximately 45 refugee households in Netaji Nagar, Bijoygarh, and Azadgarh colonies in Jadavpur between 2006 and 2007.

A BRIEF BACKDROP TO THE PARTICULAR
PARTITION OF BENGAL

Calcutta, or Kolkata, is a city that has been shaped out of migrations of people from various parts of the world through its history. From such distant groups as Armenians, Iraqi Jews, and Afghans to migrants from more proximate locations such as Gujarat, Rajasthan, Orissa, and Bihar, Calcutta's urban history and geography through its colonial period has been continually reshaped by the flows of people that have come through and often remained within it.

While many of these migrations have been prompted by economic opportunities, many also have been a result of natural and political disasters (and a combination of both), and have reached crisis proportions. During the Bengal famine in 1943, for example, thousands of people from East Bengal (now Bangladesh) came to Calcutta in search of food. The famine was a product of administrative failure that did not adequately respond to the loss of crops and grains in cyclone-hit East Bengal. This was in conjunction with the British government's decision to divert grains from the countryside to the city during the Second World War. It was a man-made famine in which upwards of 2 million people died of starvation or malnutrition (Metcalf and Metcalf 2001). Many left the countryside for major urban areas such as Calcutta in search of food. The movement of such large numbers of people to the city of Calcutta put intense pressure on its infrastructure. A few years after the famine, another political disaster, this time the partition of India, also prompted vast flows of migrants into the city. On the eve of independence in 1947, India was divided into its Muslim majority regions and Hindu majority regions. The former became the state of Pakistan with the larger part of the state lying to the west of India (West Pakistan) and the smaller part becoming what was previously East Bengal (East Pakistan). The Hindu majority regions became the state of India. The border has since come to play an important role in the urbanization of Calcutta and other cities in India. Border imagery is invoked in the security rhetoric of the state (when evicting illegal Bangladeshis from Delhi) and in spates of urban violence in cities such as Mumbai. The production of the border also reconfigured what was once rural–urban migration from the villages of East Bengal to the city of Calcutta as it now entailed much more significant movement across a newly formed international boundary. The possibilities of movement across the boundary became more limited and the reception afforded to migrants, now 'refugees', became much more complicated after 1947.

The partition of India was neither clean nor clinical. As Joya Chatterji has pointed out, multiple partition plans, negotiations, and political manoeuverings took place to gain more land both by the Congress (for the Indian side) and the Muslim League (for the Pakistani side) (Chatterji 1999). However, what partition would entail for the ordinary person was not carefully considered by either politicians or bureaucrats who poured over maps and plans. Gyan Pandey notes that in fact political leaders did not imagine that partition would cause people to leave their homes or their livelihoods and neither did they desire it (Pandey 2001). However, that is precisely what happened. As news of an impending partition of Hindus and Muslims began to spread, ordinary people living in border regions and in the parts of the country where partition was to take place began to find ways to leave for wherever they would be part of the religious majority. Violence on an unprecedented scale marked this period and it began its journey in East Bengal where the first Hindu–Muslim riots took place in the villages of Noakhali and Tippera in 1946. Hindu peasants left and moved to West Bengal in search of safety. A few months later, as a backlash to the Noakhali and Tippera violence, riots took place in Calcutta. The three-day mayhem dubbed 'The Great Calcutta Killing' became one of the first major urban communal riots in India.

Tensions between Hindu and Muslim communities spread through the subcontinent and found its worst materialization in the northwest, in Punjab. Here, partition violence led to carnage on an unprecedented scale as people were killed, raped, forcibly converted, and women were abducted by members of the Hindu, Muslim, and Sikh communities. The result was one of the largest mass displacements of people in modern history. An estimated 10 million people became refugees and crossed what was to become the border between India and Pakistan from both sides. Of this, approximately 3 million refugees moved across the India–East Pakistan border.

The movement of people as a result of partition took place for several months across the border between West Pakistan and India. Eventually, the border was sealed and the migration of refugees stopped. However, on the eastern side, the border was not so easily manageable and the concomitant politics was also complicated. The Bengal border, being one of the longest in the world, runs through a difficult topography of jungles, rivers, densely populated villages, and farmland, making it difficult to monitor and control. The partition politics in this part of the world has also had a complex history for the past 60 years. First, partition violence in Bengal never took place on the same scale as that in the Punjab. As a result, the Indian government was also less willing to rehabilitate refugees coming from East

Pakistan, an issue this essay will elaborate further on. Second, the relationship between East Pakistan and West Pakistan was also fraught. Political and linguistic discrimination coupled with economic neglect led to popular uprisings in East Pakistan. It eventually fought for and won independence from its western part and became Bangladesh in 1971.

The Indian government, in lieu of these conditions, also believed (rightly or wrongly) that Hindus coming over the border from East Bengal/ East Pakistan (and later Bangladesh) should 'go back'. Both states, India and Pakistan, made assurances to their publics that religious minorities would be protected, but it is evident that the minorities themselves were made to feel as social outcasts in both countries. Such promises by the leaders did little to placate the fears of the Hindus who arrived in India with no intention of returning. For the middle-class refugees in particular, the fear stemmed not only from the concern of physical harm, but also of losing the dignity of one's family or social standing. As noted in the Punjabi case, many women were abducted in the ensuing violence and mayhem. Women were seen as the upholders of family honour. Therefore, a woman abducted was linked to the loss of manhood (because of the inability of men to protect their womenfolk against others) and subsequently the loss of family honour. In addition to this was the fear of ruptures within the social structure. In East Bengal as in many other places, caste systems operated such that most Muslims had largely been peasants and sharecroppers, at the bottom of the social and economic hierarchy. With the creation of the state of Pakistan, premised on a Muslim majority population, it was expected that Muslims would gain greater rights in the state, and Hindu upper-caste power would decline. Upper castes, middle classes and affluent Hindu families realized this and they constituted the majority of those who chose to move to India in the initial stages of partition.[1] They wanted to be part of a nation in which they would not only be part of the numerical majority, but also continue to exercise their social practices. 'Going back' therefore was not an option in a variety of different ways (N. Chatterjee 1992).

JABAR DAKHAL–HUKUM DAKHAL: RESPONSES TO DISPLACEMENT AND SHELTER

The movement of refugees from East Bengal to West Bengal in the aftermath of partition had significant repercussions for the processes of urbanization in Calcutta, as well as for the shifting ways in which citizenship was articulated. The Indian government did make some efforts to rehabilitate/ resettle refugees, although most schemes appear to have benefitted the poor and the lower classes of refugees. Hiranmoy Bandhopadhyay, a former Indian Civil Service officer who was in charge of a significant part of the refugee rehabilitation in Bengal, wrote in his book *Udbastu* that the government of West Bengal provided two types of assistance to refugee groups. One set of refugees only approached the government for help in securing shelter. Within this group, one lot had the money to pay rent and was only looking for a house to live in. For them, the government took over (*hukum dakhal*) a number of vacant houses. These houses would then be divided into small flats and given to families on rent. The second lot of people within this same rentier category was not so well off economically. The government had to not only find places for them, but also carry the burden of the rent themselves (Bandhopadhyay 1970). The government housed such people in government camps such as Relief and Transit camps, as well as Permanent Liability (PL) camps for old and infirm refugees and unattached women. These camps were set up in a number of different places. Many are still in existence including Coopers Camp (the largest) that is located approximately 200 kilometers away from Calcutta. Most camps and relief and rehabilitation sites were scattered in various parts of the state away from each other.

The conditions of the camps were described by many as appalling and unfit for human habitation. Inadequate aid from the central government of India not only strained relations between the state and national governments, but also made life difficult for those living in the refugee camps as many could not afford basic services and goods because of the lack of income (Chakrabarti 1999). Several of these camps continue to be in existence today and remain burdened by financial problems and concerns over creating income-generating schemes.

Hukum dakhal, or government take-over of land also included such legal moves as The Waste Lands (Requisition and Utilization) Act of 1951 which sought to recover waste lands for certain public uses that would better utilize the space. These lands were often given to refugees as their lack of shelter was of public (government) concern and fell within its purview. Similarly, the West Bengal Evacuee Property Act of 1951 sought to not only protect the properties of those who had left, but also to dispose of them if the individual or family had clearly stated intentions of not returning to India (Sen 2000: 53–55). In these ways, the government attempted to provide adequate shelter options for refugees.

The other set of refugees was made of those who the government could not help at all because they were neither so destitute to be cared for completely, nor were they wealthy enough to carry the burden of rent.

These were the people who became squatters and took over private and public land around the city of Calcutta (Bandhopadhyay 1970). This process of acquiring land forcibly and through invasions is what is referred to as *jabar dakhal* (which in Bengali loosely translates into forcible occupation). The colonies are therefore also referred to as *jabar dakhal* colonies by locals. The squatters who invaded and occupied these areas were comprised of middle and lower classes of refugees from different caste backgrounds. The involvement of middle-class *bhadralok*[2] refugees in the squatting movement in Calcutta is particularly interesting as it created a unique set of dynamics between the squatters and the state. Usually an illegal act, carried out by poorer and lower classes, squatting is not associated with *bhadralok* classes. In fact, the act of squatting by these *bhadralok* classes was seen as a matter of shame because they felt they had been compelled to trespass on private property in order to acquire a sense of security and respectability. They were therefore often ashamed to disclose their locations and were keen to regularize and legitimize their colonies (N. Chatterjee 1992: 207). Arguably, the class dimension of these squatters played a key role in mediating the response of the state to the illegal occupation of land, a situation that was not repeated with later migrants who came from low class and caste backgrounds.

Squats began once refugees realized that help from the government was inadequate or not forthcoming at all. Self-styled leaders from amongst the refugees (largely men) led squats in different parts of Calcutta with a particularly large concentration in the south. This area known as Jadavpur used to be a largely peri-urban area consisting of farmlands as well as privately owned land by small and large landowners living in Calcutta. A significant number of Muslims lived in this area as well. Refugees in the process of squatting displaced the Muslims and took over land owned by both small landowners as well as large land developers who had bought the land in hopes of making substantial profits at a future time.

While the displacement of Muslims by refugee squatters is an issue that has gone largely unnoticed, the invasion of squatters on private property did have repercussions on urban politics as it led to scattered altercations between refugee-squatters, private landowners, and the state government acting on behalf of the private landowners. Resistance ranged from clashes between squatters and privately hired thugs, as well as the police and refugee-led resistance against legal attempts to evict them. For example, the State attempted to pass an Eviction Bill in 1951 but came up against stiff resistance from the refugee organizations. Refugee committees from various parts of West Bengal had by now organized under several umbrella groups, the most prominent of which was the United Central Refugee Council (UCRC). The UCRC, along with a rival faction, the Refugee Eviction Resistance Committee, led mass protests in the city and demanded that all colonies be recognized. Faced by the embarrassment of the bill, it was quickly withdrawn and redrafted. The new version of the bill titled 'The Rehabilitation of Displaced Persons and Eviction of Persons in Unauthorized Occupation of Land Act' included a pledge to accommodate displaced persons who had engaged in the unauthorized occupation of land (Deb 2000: 76). Such a reversal by the government indicates a reluctant recognition of the refugees' rights to urban services and infrastructure. This included the right to remain in the city and the right to housing.

In addition, a new definition for the term bona fide refugee was expanded to include those who had arrived in West Bengal before 31 December 1950. This redefinition of refugee status extended the deadline of qualification for this status for those who were displaced, which according to a West Bengal Government Press Note had been set for 25 June 1948 (Chakrabarti 1999: 18). The extension of refugee status meant that more people who had arrived in India after partition qualified for relief and resettlement from the government rather than being treated as illegal immigrants.

These revisions were considered major victories for the refugee movement in Bengal who subsequently continued organizing and demanding greater rights for refugees to the city and to citizenship. The Communist Party of India (CPI) which had been championing their cause and helping them organize also gained electoral and political success as a result of refugee victories. The party and the refugees worked in tandem with each other to extract concessions from the state and national governments (Chatterji 2001: 74–110). Such political successes are premised upon acts of insurgent citizenship, in which the urban poor stake claims to the city through protest. However, this case is unique because the urban poor consist of middle-class refugees, a class group and a migrant group that does not usually demand the right to squat in cities. In some ways, therefore, this case study complicates the distinction between civil society and political society that Partha Chatterjee has discussed (P. Chatterjee 2004). *Bhadralok* refugees who were once part of civil society shifted between that category and political society in their efforts to secure resettlement rights in Calcutta. These contradictory positions (*bhadralok* yet political society) thus expose the complex configurations of social, political, and class categories in Indian cities and invite a rethink of the ways in which post-colonial conditions can unsettle commonly held views and categorizations on urbanism and urban societies.

Another interesting point to note from this case study is that the right to the city in this case is synonymous with the right to national citizenship and the right to belong to the Indian state. Feldman amongst others have noted how East Bengalis who migrated to West Bengal after partition did so because they felt they were moving to a place where they 'belonged'. Partition had deconstructed previously held ideas of 'belonging' (to a homogenous and indivisible Bengal, both East and West) and exposed and reified the heterogeneity of identity that actually existed (Feldman 2003). Hindu East Bengalis who chose to migrate to West Bengal saw their acts of squatting (in the face of limited or no resettlement help from the Indian government) as a right they had acquired by (*a*) being an active part of the Indian national movement, (*b*) by being the unfortunate victims of a partition that was not of their volition, and (*c*) by promises that were made (and not held true) by Indian national leaders who promised them shelter if they felt the need to leave (N. Chatterjee 1992). Space, and in this case, urban space became the container within which the right to resettlement was exercised. By acquiring one (the right to squat), the refugees were essentially demanding the other (the right to remain) and, by extension, the right to Indian citizenship.

SHIFTING DEFINITIONS OF REFUGEE AND MIGRANT

There were many and often conflicting positions that the government took in relation to refugees and their resettlement in India. Conflicts that took place between the state and central governments manifested themselves on the landscape. For example, the state government was more willing than the central government to receive and resettle refugees. However, it also had to contend with the meagre amounts of money it received for the process, and hence many of the schemes put in place were poorly executed. In other cases, the government gave tacit approval to refugees to invade a piece of vacant property and set up their colony on their own. This was how, for example, Bijoygarh colony was set up in the abandoned US military barracks in Jadavpur. In still other situations, the State government also had to balance its own interests and those of the elite of society against those of the refugees. Thus, when refugees began invading private property, much of which was owned by the middle and upper classes of Calcutta, the government had to act in the interests of private property and attempt to evict the refugees through legal action. For later refugees, the government at both the State and national levels pressed on them to resettle outside of West Bengal. Often, coercion was used to send people to the notorious Dandakaranya Project.[3] Inhospitable living conditions compelled many to leave and attempt to return to West Bengal under very difficult circumstances.

The contradictions in relief efforts mirror the contradictions in providing refugee status as well. Largely, the term 'displaced' has been used in official literature, but this has not remained consistent. Those displaced prior to 15 October 1947 were not considered displaced.[4] This essentially meant that those who were displaced from Noakhali and Tippera, or even during the Calcutta riots, would not be considered displaced. An Inter-dominion Agreement in April 1948 attempted to settle the problem of minorities in India and Pakistan through the secure return of people to their countries as well as the protection and restoration of their properties. Minorities Boards were set up to provide relief to minorities. Evacuee Property Management Boards, composed of minority community members, were also established in districts or areas from where substantial numbers of people had left. The 1950 Nehru–Liaquat Ali Pact (Delhi Pact) also aimed to restore properties to returning migrants (Sen 2000: 50).

Until 1952, the movement of people between India and Pakistan was largely unrestricted to allow people to make a choice about where they would settle. In 1952, passports were introduced. This led to panic and a rise in the number of people crossing the border between East Pakistan and the adjoining Indian States. The Indian government classified those who crossed the border between 1946 and 1958 as 'Old Migrants', while East Pakistanis who sought asylum in India between 1964 and 1971 were called 'New Migrants'. This had three significant consequences: first, though they were called 'new migrants', for all practical purposes the people coming into India were treated like refugees. They were offered the possibility of resettlement so long as they agreed to be resettled outside of the State of West Bengal. Second, the usage of the term 'migrant' was a contradiction as it generally refers to voluntary movement, while the literature on movement of people, particularly Hindus between East Pakistan and West Bengal, notes that they were forced out rather than 'volunteering' to leave. Third, by defining 'Old Migrant' and 'New Migrant' by linking it to their year of entry into the country, the government excluded many of those who came in between 1958 and 1964 from the possibility of acquiring official assistance (Dasgupta 2001).

The terms 'migrant', 'refugee', and 'displaced' were used interchangeably in the official writings over the course of decades following

Independence. It is clear that from the mid-1960s the term 'migrant' was more widely used in official literature than 'displaced' or 'refugee'. A large number of official reports that deal with definitions are replete with such ambiguities and inconsistencies. In 1971, in the face of large numbers of people who were displaced as a result of the Bangladesh War of Independence, the central government eventually chose to use the term 'refugee' to define them. It is debatable whether the government chose to use differing and often contradictory terms for its convenience or for the sheer inability and incompetence to deal with a particularly complex situation.

BORDER POLITICS AND THE GROWING PROCESS OF ILLEGALITY

The politics of the border has not only affected the resettlement of people in India, but the ways in which the cities have urbanized as well. Many who came later were from lower class and caste backgrounds and were only given the option of resettlement in Dandakaranya or no help at all. Faced with these limited and difficult choices, many either tried to settle themselves with no help from the state, or reluctantly went to Dandakaranya in order to receive any amount of state aid (Kudaisya 1996). From the 1970s, these options also evaporated.

Since 1971, the border between India and Bangladesh has not quite remained the same. Although there have been previous attempts at trying to control and monitor the border, the task has proven quite difficult for security forces and indeed for the State (Van Schendel 2005). Radcliffe's line that divided a region into two independent nation-states also divided the lives and livelihoods of people who lived on the border and depended on its dynamic economy to sustain their existence. As a result, locals living on the border often flouted the demarcation line and continued to cultivate their fields (that often lay on the other side) and go to the village *haat*s (marketplace) to exchange goods. In recent years, an increased effort has been made by the Indian government to secure the border. The Indian government currently treats people coming over the border as illegal immigrants rather than as refugees. Yet, as scholars such as Ranabir Samaddar have pointed out, many of the reasons why these families continue to come to India are not any different from 1947. Hindu families often cross the border because they face discrimination and harassment in Bangladesh and the state does not provide them with adequate, if any, help. They are thus forced to migrate in order to preserve a livelihood. Muslims also migrate from Bangladesh as the state is one of the poorest in the world and acute poverty drives people off the land. Samaddar points out that one of the problems with international humanitarian discourse is that it defines refugees as those who escape political violence, and that too mainly, when there is a founding moment. Those who flee structural violence are thus left to the vagaries of the international migration and economic regimes that fail to recognize the increasingly blurred distinction between political violence and structural violence. Those who do manage to migrate are then criminalized and driven into underground economies and into the margins of urban societies (Samaddar 1999).

In India, such controversies over border management have been linked to a growing concern over terrorist activities (from Pakistan and Bangladesh), and the Indian government has attempted to not only deport 'illegals' from India, but has proceeded to build a fence between the two countries.[5] The result of that is deeply problematic as the Indian government has been accused of deporting Indian Muslims under the pretext of sending back 'Bangladeshis'. The deportation process itself entailed nothing more than dumping people at the border, only to have them make their way back again (Ramachandran 2005). Further, the fence that is being built between India and Bangladesh will only make the lives of the people living at the border ever more difficult. Aside from the varied terrain of the Indo-Bangladesh border, political miscalculations and complications during the partition process led to Indian enclaves being located inside Bangladesh and vice-versa. Often these enclaves (may be one or two villages) of one country would be located inside another country with no way of accessing the resources of their own country or that of the country which surrounds them. Today, security personnel need to negotiate with each other over such mundane issues as allowing someone from one enclave to 'cross the border' in order to go to the hospital many miles away. Thus, while a tremendous anxiety exists in India with regard to the border and the daily transgressions across it, the state (aside from security forces) is largely absent at this border and no attempt has been made thus far to rectify the situation (Cons 2007; Jones 2009).

If we assume that the border does not replay its politics within the body of the nation-state, we would be mistaken, as studies have shown how participants in urban violence can also use the rhetoric of national border conflicts when displacing and segregating communal 'others' from themselves (Chatterji and Mehta 2007). The discourse of national security in this case also brings the politics of the border to the politics of urbanization, and shapes the ways in which urban citizenship is articulated amongst the urban poor.

THE HISTORIC LEGACY OF PARTITION ON THE URBANIZATION OF CALCUTTA

As mentioned earlier, many refugees settled on the peripheral areas of Calcutta, forcibly taking over private and government land to build settlements for themselves. Initial attempts by the government at trying to evict refugees gave way to slow formalization and an overall approach of benign neglect. Refugees built much of their squatter settlements through their own sweat equity. This included everything from their own homes to roads, infrastructure, schools, markets, and so forth. Many of the brick structures that are seen around the colony today only came into existence some 15–20 years ago when they finally began receiving titles to the land they were on. The process was such that the government initially gave them a 99-year lease and later turned these to freehold titles. The provision of a legal title to land was a blessing to the refugees in a number of different ways. They could use this land as collateral for loans from the government or financial institutions, something they could not afford to do earlier (R. Roy 1972: 7). In addition, the security of tenure allowed people to upgrade to permanent structures without the fear of losing their investments. Once the land titles were provided, it was also possible to sell the land to developers and profit from its sale.

Class plays a significant role in the success of the early squatter colonies established by partition refugees. Most refugees who squatted, as noted earlier, were middle class, educated, and often white-collar workers. Their initiative to squat stemmed from their refusal to be accommodated in government resettlement schemes which in their view were abysmal. Earlier it was mentioned that the refugees believed it was their right to be resettled appropriately in India. In demanding such rights to resettlement, the refugees operated two contradictory logics simultaneously. On the one hand, they demanded the right to citizenship and the right to be treated as equals to other Indian citizens. They resented the label of refugee and instead saw their predicament as a product of the political manoeuverings of the Indian and Pakistani states. It is noteworthy that many of the discussions with refugees with regards to the gradual upgrading of their colonies are cast in the narratives of *koshto* (hardship and suffering) and *cheshta* (struggle). Interviewees repeated these metaphors to describe the process of becoming social and economic equals of local West Bengalis/Calcuttans. On the other hand, the refugees also demanded preferential treatment for their resettlement. They saw their right to the city and the right to the state as superceding that of Muslims in India (and in fact this acted as an impetus for them to displace Muslims from the colony areas). They also saw 'appropriate' resettlement as a form of repayment from the state of India for their contributions towards the struggle for independence.

It is evident therefore that refugee politics conflated the right to the city with the right to the nation-state. The act of squatting was not merely a means of acquiring shelter on the margins of the urban environment. The politics of self-housing challenged the discrimination of the state which sought to deny refugees the right to remain within the borders. Urban citizenship discussions often place the politics of rights to the city in opposition to the rights to the state. The city is seen as the site within which citizenship is re-made while the nation-state recedes into the background (Holston and Appadurai 1999). While cities do in fact provide the fertile ground within which new forms of urban politics are created and contested, these processes can and often are linked to larger questions of rights and privileges within the nation-state itself. What is achieved and acquired within the city can have implications for how the state and its laws respond to people as well. As Massey has pointed out, the global is always implicated in the local (Massey 1994: 110–21). In this instance, the national is also implicated in the urban. The choice of moving to West Bengal was predicated on the notion of a Hindu-Bengali identity whose status had to be maintained. Refugees imagined themselves as belonging to an imagined community of Hindu Bengalis, and hence their rightful place was amongst their co-religionists on the Indian side of the border. The poor reception they received was undoubtedly a shock, but it also served as a catalyst for them to claim their place in the nation. The struggles over urban space and resources was not simply about the specificity of the urban but rather the city was the specific local site within which struggles for larger rights (linked to the nation and the state) were carried out.

The Calcutta case is admittedly a more unusual example within the broader scope of refugee literature, in which refugees engage in civil protest (usually reserved for the public of a nation-state) to demand specific rights to citizenship. However, it opens up possibilities of unsettling ideas of displacement at local and international levels and allows new ways of imagining belongings in an era of globalization. The case study, for example, is illustrative of the point that the distinction between refugees and economic migrants are tenuous at best. Separating the two into distinct categories, one to be pathologized and contained within limited spaces (refugees) and the other to be demonized and deported (economic migrants), fails to recognize the ways in which the two categories of people are very similar to each other. Refugees and 'economic migrants' leave their home countries because of a complex web of reasons in which economics and political and social repression often blend into each other. Their migration and settlement strategies are also often quite similar and this is more so the case now as greater numbers of refugees are moving to urban areas and living in slums. Refugees therefore need to be recast from being paralyzed victims of violence and oppression to being proactive agents of change in cities.

CONCLUDING THOUGHTS: CONTEMPORARY URBANIZATION AND CHANGING WAYS OF CLAIMING THE CITY

The unusual aspect of class clearly plays an important role in the process of urbanization of refugee colonies in Calcutta. Those who came in the late 1950s, 1960s, and onwards and were from lower class and education backgrounds did not often have the means to contest the state in the same ways. As the politics of the border had also changed, they also could not take advantage of the generally sympathetic atmosphere of the 1947 partition to argue for right to shelter. These later refugees who came to Calcutta did not engage in vocal protests against the government for not resettling them appropriately. Either they were resettled in Dandakaranya, or they squatted by railway lines and on the expanding periphery of Kolkata in what can perhaps be described in Asef Bayat's terms as the 'quiet encroachment of the poor' (Bayat 2000). For those who came before 1971, it was important to be in an urban environment to be able to engage in wage labour and earn a decent livelihood. They therefore took the risk of not receiving aid from the state by resettling themselves.

For those who came after 1971, there was the double burden of not only self-settling, but also avoiding detection. In being considered 'illegal' immigrants or 'infiltrators' the fear of being caught and deported has largely driven present-day refugees underground in a variety of ways including taking on fake identities, bribing officials, and hiding within the urban milieu (Ramachandran 1999). Such practices have significant implications for the continued urbanization of Kolkata (the gateway for much of the migration from Bangladesh to India) as well as for its politics. It could be argued that in fact, national and border security interests have spelled the death of popular politics of shelter in Kolkata. The legal ambiguities of the border and the refugees over the past 60 years have pointed to the fact that the state has always had a troubled relationship with those coming across from East Pakistan in search of refuge.

In the contemporary moment however, with the rise of globalization and subsequent securitization, these practices have only become more exacerbated and ushered in an era of accelerated urban informality and urban marginality. The moral claim to the right to citizenship that refugees demand against the backdrop of partition or the structural violence that accompanied it on both sides of the border can no longer be made. Admittedly, the reasons for coming across the border are somewhat different now from what the *bhadralok* refugees made out after partition. Contemporary migration across the border is a result of economic hardship and discrimination and less of a choice than what the refugees exercised after partition. Lower caste and class Hindus had chosen to stay on in East Pakistan until the 1970s because their lot was not significantly different from their Muslim counterparts. However, with structural violence increasing, they are compelled to seek refuge across the border in India where they are also not welcome and are treated as illegal immigrants. The border now appears to mimic the nature of the US–Mexico border, where a physical fence between India and Bangladesh is part of a broader anti-immigrant rhetoric. The politics of the border, however, continue to inform the urbanization of the city as is evident from the ever-increasing periphery of Calcutta.

Today, *bhadralok* Left politics that marked much of the post-partition period has not only disappeared (Bhattacharyya 1999) but in its stead the middle class has co-opted the right to the city through the discourse of bourgeois environmentalism, pushing migrants into tenuous relations with land and politics (A. Roy 2004). It is an unfortunate reminder that episodes of popular uprisings in support of subaltern claims are fleeting, but also perhaps hopeful of uprisings occurring from some of the most unanticipated corners.

NOTES

1. This is also evident from the fact that the *Namasudras* (low-caste Hindus) left much later from East Pakistan, as they shared much of the poverty and many of the grievances of their Muslim peasant neighbours.
2. Term used to denote genteel, educated class of people in Bengali. *Bhadralok* classes saw themselves as being the embodiment of Indian culture, nationality, and bearing values of social reform, progress, and modernity (Feldman 2003: 113).
3. The government tried to resettle many refugees out of the state of West Bengal, particularly in Dandakaranya, which became the most infamous project. Here the project entailed putting refugees in the forested Dandakaranya area that covers parts of several different Indian states including Madhya Pradesh, Orissa, Andhra Pradesh, and now Chhattisgarh in over 30,000 square miles. The arid, semi-rocky soil was ill-suited for refugees who were

formerly farmers. The project was also far removed from their familiar surroundings and ended up failing spectacularly as refugees left in droves in the 1970s.

4. Annual Report of the Department of Rehabilitation (hereafter ARDR), 1965–66.

5. The construction of the fence began in 1986. About 70 per cent of the fence has been constructed.

BIBLIOGRAPHY

Bandhopadhyay, H. 1970. *Udbastu*. Calcutta: Sahitya Sangsad.

Bayat, A. 2000. 'From Dangerous Classes to Quiet Rebels: Politics of the Urban Subaltern in the Global South', *International Sociology*, 15(3): 533–57.

Bhattacharyya, D. 1999. 'Ominous Outcome for the Left in West Bengal', *Economic and Political Weekly*, 34(46/47): 3267–269.

Chakrabarti, P. K. 1999. *The Marginal Men: The Refugees and the Left Political Syndrome in West Bengal*. Calcutta: Naya Udyog.

Chatterjee, N. 1992. 'Midnight's Unwanted Children: East Bengali Refugees and the Politics of Rehabilitation', PhD diss., Brown University.

Chatterjee, P. 2004. *The Politics of the Governed: Reflections on Popular Politics in Most of the World*. New Delhi: Permanent Black.

Chatterji, J. 1999. 'The Fashioning of the Frontier: The Radcliffe Line and Bengal's Border Landscape, 1947–52', *Modern Asian Studies*, 33(1): 185–242.

———. 2001. 'Right or Charity? The Debate over Relief and Rehabilitation in West Bengal, 1947–50', in S. Kaul (ed.), *The Partitions of Memory: The Afterlife of the Division of India*, pp. 74–110. Delhi: Permanent Black.

Chatterji, R. and D. Mehta. 2007. *Living with Violence: An Anthropology of Events and Everyday Life*. New Delhi: Routledge.

Cons, J. 2007. 'A Politics of Sensitivity: Ambiguity and Exceptionality along the India–Bangladesh Border', in *Sarai Reader 07: Frontiers*, pp. 20–29.

Das, S. K. 2000. 'Refugee Crisis: Responses of the Government of West Bengal', in P. K. Bose (ed.), *Refugees in West Bengal: Institutional Practices and Contested Identities*, pp. 7–31. Calcutta: Calcutta Research Group.

Dasgupta, A. 2001. 'The Politics of Agitation and Confession: Displaced Bengalis in West Bengal', in S. K. Roy (ed.), *Refugees and Human Rights*, pp. 95–129. Jaipur and New Delhi: Rawat.

Deb, A. 2000. 'The UCRC: Its Role in Establishing the Rights of Refugee Squatters in Calcutta', in P. K. Bose (ed.), *Refugees in West Bengal: Institutional Practices and Contested Identities*, pp. 65–79. Calcutta: Calcutta Research Group.

Feldman, S. 2003. 'Bengali State and Nation Making: Partition and Displacement Revisited', *ISSJ*, 175: 111–21.

Holston, J. 2008. *Insurgent Citizenship: Disjunctions of Democracy and Modernity in Brazil*. Princeton: Princeton University Press.

Holston, J. and A. Appadurai. 1999. 'Introduction: Cities and Citizenship', in J. Holston (ed.), *Cities and Citizenship*, pp. 1–18. Durham and London: Duke University Press.

Jones, R. 2009. 'Sovereignty and Statelessness in the Border Enclaves of India and Bangladesh', *Political Geography*, 28(6): 373–81.

Kudaisya, G. 1996. 'Divided Landscapes, Fragmented Identities: East Bengal Refugees and Their Rehabilitation in India, 1947–79', *Singapore Journal of Tropical Geography*, 17(1): 24–39.

Massey, D. 1994. 'Double Articulation: A Place in the World', in A. Bammer (ed.), *Displacements: Cultural Identities in Question*, pp. 110–21. Indiana: Indiana University Press.

Metcalf, B. D. and T. Metcalf. 2001. *A Concise History of Modern India*, 2nd edition. Cambridge: Cambridge University Press.

Pandey, G. 2001. *Remembering Partition: Violence, Nationalism and History in India*. Cambridge: Cambridge University Press.

Ramachandran, S. 1999. 'Of Boundaries and Border Crossings', *Interventions*, 1(2): 235–53.

———. 2005, 'Indifference, Impotence and Intolerance: Transnational Bangladeshis in India', *Global Migration Perspectives* No. 42. Geneva: Global Commission on International Migration.

Roy, A. 2004. 'The Gentleman's City: Urban Informality in the Calcutta of New Communism', in A. Roy and N. AlSayyad (eds), *Urban Informality: Transnational Perspectives from the Middle East, Latin America and South Asia*, pp. 147–70. Lanham: Lexington Books.

Roy, R. 1972. *The Agony of West Bengal*. Calcutta: New Age Publishers.

Samaddar, R. 1999. *The Marginal Nation: Transborder Migration from Bangladesh to West Bengal*. New Delhi: SAGE Publications.

Sen, S. 2000. 'The Legal Regime for Refugee Relief and Rehabilitation in West Bengal: 1946–1958', in P. K. Bose (ed.), *Refugees in West Bengal: Institutional Practices and Contested Identities*, pp. 49–64. Calcutta: Calcutta Research Group.

Van Schendel, W. 2005. *The Bengal Borderland: Beyond State and Nation in South Asia*. London: Anthem Press.

Afterword

In Other Words: The Indian City and the Promise of Citizenship

Janaki Nair

Is the contemporary Indian city a space of hope or a site of despair? To pose the question in these stark terms at the end of a volume which presents detailed descriptions of new institutional forms that are being forged for the governance of cities, and new strategies of protest and accommodation that are emerging, in particular among the urban subaltern classes, is not to invite the obvious response that the answer would depend on whose city we are talking about. Rather, it is to pointedly refer to both the methodological and political assumptions that may lead to one or another conclusion, and to the challenges posed by the very object of study—the heaving, undisciplined, incoherent beast that is the Indian city—to existing theoretical categories and frames of reference. We might begin by asking: Is it necessary to be resolutely pessimistic, and anti-utopian, in order to defy or disturb capitalist jubilation that plots its 'progress' on every large-scale building or planned enclave, blind to the squalor that is the lot of most urban dwellers? Or do scholars have an obligation to acknowledge and highlight the wide range of strategies by which the large populations that throng Indian cities negotiate or manipulate the emerging order which marginalizes them, while also simultaneously allowing them to survive?

Both of these intellectual strategies place intolerable strains on the already dented toolbox containing such categories as citizenship, modernism, planning, and democracy. Such strains, we must recognize at the outset, are a robust sign of the recent flourishing of enquiries into the predicaments of contemporary Indian cities. The status of urban studies as the somewhat neglected cousin in Indian scholarship has disappeared in the last two decades, as historians, sociologists, and geographers have joined planners and policymakers in recognizing the urgency of coming to grips with the massive (and galloping) presence of the urban in contemporary India. The genealogies of the modern Indian city are now investigated with great verve by those seeking to go beyond merely descriptive accounts of urban economies and societies. New programmes and research units focused entirely on the city, such as SARAI (Delhi) and PUKAR (Mumbai), fellowships, conferences, books, journals, and courses are all testimony to the huge and growing concern for an understanding of the modern Indian city, and, less frequently, to provide the resources for imagining a new urban future. In many cases, as in the present volume, the questions that interest scholars have emerged from the limited successes and stupendous failures of contemporary schemes and plans, practices and events, calling for either longer term or comparative perspectives, for new conceptual frameworks, or altered methodological approaches to capturing the baffling heterogeneities that constitute the festering mess that Indian cities are in today.

Rather than allowing such bewildering heterogeneity to paralyze either the intellect or the will, the essays in this volume are concerned with relating the new systems of governance, as well as the resistance to, acceptance of, or participation in them, to the question of citizenship. Citizenship and its increasingly challenged and multiplied meanings is the unifying theme of this collection. The term 'citizenship', which we can neither do without nor accept in the sense in which it was minted, has been used to refer simultaneously to a formal association with the larger moral community of the nation, along with the rights that it bestows, and to the more substantive local relationships that constitute the fabric of urban life. This collection of essays extends the now emerging orthodoxy that recognizes the city as not just the space for an unfolding of citizenship, but one vitally formed and reshaped by the contests over the making and meaning of what it means to be a citizen.

How has recent Indian scholarship challenged, if not refashioned, the conception of citizenship? Earlier optimism about 'citizenship-in-the-making', since formal political independence had done little for those 'not-yet-citizens', betrayed the hope that, given time, the process of 'becoming citizen' would be complete. Such optimism has given way to severe criticisms of the more abstract notions of citizenship forged in other geographical settings and at other times, and to conceptual clarity about those whose formal rights are trumped in a far more pervasive, structural sense (Chatterjee 2008). The debacles of planning, whether of the national economy or of urban space, have led to a sober and pragmatic recognition of the interdependence between the planned and the unplanned, between corporate and non-corporate capital, between, in short, the steel and glass face of 'India Shining' and the 'castaway economy' outside the domain of the transformatory capability of capital (Sanyal 2007). In this account, the

Indian city, while increasingly coming under the thrall of capital and under the hegemony of the bourgeoisie,[1] is fated to miss the 'creative destruction' and vigorous reinscription of city space that historically occurred during the realization of modernist dreams elsewhere (Harvey 2006; also see Chatterjee [2011]). Therefore, historians, sociologists, and geographers alike, such as Madhu Sarin (writing on Chandigarh) (Sarin 1982) and Amita Baviskar (writing on Delhi) have noted the intimate links between the planned and the unplanned, the inside and the constitutive outside of modernity; to use the latter's words, 'the development of slums...was not a violation of the plan, it was an essential accompaniment to the plan, its Siamese twin' (Baviskar 2002). Indeed, as leading political scientists and economists have long recognized, governmental policies (such as planning in the wider sense of the term) have been envisaged as a domain immune from, or outside, politics, as devices to insure against the more threatening reconstitution of the social order (see, for example, Chatterjee [1997]).

The modernist dream has been challenged on yet another register which calls into question the long-held hope of the state—the institution which dominated the imaginations of planners, capitalists, and subaltern groups—as the institution which can deliver economic growth and a modicum of social justice simultaneously. This points in a different direction from the current campaign of capital to limit the role of the state to a service provider while allowing a free reign to market forces. For there is, indeed, widespread middle-class recognition that the 'the management of public affairs is too important to be left to the government' alone (de Azevedo 1998: 261).

The observed 'shrinkage' of the state as the principal mode by which planning occurs or can succeed (that is, the emergence of gated enclaves) is a sign of an accommodation not only with 'corporate capital' but with those whose non-legal existence is systematically produced by the law, relieving public agencies of their obligations to provide housing (or education or health services), while simultaneously posing no threat to vested interests, and therefore to the system itself.[2] I refer, therefore, to the growing recognition, as in many instances in this volume, that there is a legion of non-state agencies, actors, and powers that have long been, and are continuing to be, accessed by the urban poor, thereby calling into question the narrative of a transition to the 'modern' enabled by the state[3] (for example, Chapter 3 by Liza Weinstein, this volume). Arjun Appadurai has recently used the category of 'redundancy' to describe 'the multiplicity of claims in the idiom of power: over particular spaces, particular resources, particular relations'. He says, 'You have social forces, social movements, non governmental movements, popular movements, municipal movements, city governments, state governments, federal governments, all exercising very complex power claims over groups and bodies, locations, resources, etc' (*Perspecta* 2003). In such a scenario, what are the resources for imagining alternative futures and what are the institutional spaces, other than those of either state or market, that might actually be used in fashioning a new urban order? What hope do these 'alternative' power centres and strategies offer the urban poor of a determined and irreversible change in the conditions of their existence?

Indeed, can the concept of citizenship bear the burden of proliferating suffixes—'insurgent citizenship' (Holson 1999), 'flexible citizenship' (Nyamjoh 2007; Ong 1998),[4] or 'vernacular citizenship' (Gandhi 2008)— and what set of relations do they clarify? Clearly, these are moves towards unbundling features which have usually been put together in the original definition of modern citizenship, that is, the nation-state as its principal form, modernity as its reigning motif, rule of law as its modality, and democracy as the process which achieves these. Indeed, is it a sign of the scepticism about any assumed braiding of citizenship and democracy that Lisa Weinstein emphatically asserts the emergence of an uneven but 'democratic citizenship' in Mumbai? The contributors of this book focus quite centrally on the processes of political life in which citizenship is a goal rather than a claim on the state, and use a wide range of terms to describe these processes: a 'politics of patience' (an empowering political engagement, Sapana Doshi), a 'quiet encroachment of the poor' (a pragmatic recognition of marginality, Romola Sanyal), to a 'politics of contract' (a disempowering political engagement, Malini Ranganathan).

Despite the attention that some of the chapters give to initiatives that hope to shape cities through new entrepreneurial dreams that stitch the city to the region (Renu Desai), systems of e-governance that result in thinning citizenship by producing individuated consumers in the place of group rights to public services (Malini Ranganathan), or privatized solutions to slum rehabilitation (Sapana Doshi), there has been a self-conscious attempt to outline a politics of hope, of individual strategies, and organizational strengths that draw on a variety of (sometimes international) agencies to strengthen the case of the poor. The methodological move here is to map out a new organic composition of power in the city, where the politics of dispossession meets, if not its match, at least stout resistance.

Has the obligation to be attentive to a possible space of democratic politics, however, obscured the emergence of new and dangerous divisions that are being engineered in cities? Has it, for instance, tended to see the tedious adjustments made by the poor, the manipulations, and even the small explosions, as paving the way to social justice in the city? The division of Ahmedabad city post-2002 into two ethnically defined zones has been chillingly described by Darshini Mahadevia (2007): how does that account fit with Desai's articulation of the new economic miracles that have been promoted by Narendra Modi in Gujarat and the smaller efforts to counter these divisions, except as a reality that is strenuously denied? Similarly, while there is no doubt a subtle shift in the strategies of those who seduce slum dwellers into participating in rehousing schemes, do the actions of the poor determine these outcomes? To turn the lens on micro-politics and infra-power while anchoring the work in the larger frame of effects other than mere survival is surely the challenge that has been taken up here (Jaideep Gupte). Thus, the raucous activities of (lawyer and trader) 'civil society' in Benaras compared with the more cautious strategies of the relatively pow-erless (weavers and boatmen) provide an empirical refutation of the more schematized divisions of civil/political society (Jolie Wood).

There is no doubt that the focus on micro processes and participative politics visibilizes not just certain sections of society, but the operation and limits of certain categories. Thus, women may be securing important con-cessions in their daily negotiations with local bureaucracies, as Ranganathan has shown for Bangalore, while being marginalized in emerging modes of grievance redressal; may be, with ambiguous consequences, centrally mo-bilized as in Mumbai as Sapana Doshi has shown; or may be defiant and far from being powerless in providing security to the vulnerable as Jaideep Gupte has shown. Similarly, Romola Sanyal and Sunalini Kumar sharply foreground the importance of class as a category in making sense of refugee and environmental policies. Yet the scales on which the operation of the politics of gender and of class are discussed here are markedly different, and draw attention to an important limitation of such studies.

The question of scale becomes important in analyzing issues which are increasingly taking on global ramifications, and not usually in any posi-tive sense. How much of the lot of the urban poor has been determined and decided by forces which may only deploy local agents for limited purposes and what effects does that have on the kinds of strategies that are generated by the poor? In a recent article titled 'The Right to the City', David Harvey (2008) provides a somewhat pessimistic view of the processes of urbaniza-tion that are underway in many parts of the world. Speaking of the necessity of launching 'a global struggle, predominantly with finance capital, for that is the scale at which urbanization processes now work', he says that 'the right to the city, as it is now constituted, is too narrowly confined, restricted in most cases to a small political and economic elite who are in a position to shape cities more and more after their own desires'.

This volume of essays provides the material to challenge this pessimism, and yet simultaneously points to the limits of taking these small signs for wonders. Indeed, if Indian cities survive despite the formidable array of problems they face, it is because the coalition of interests that now prevails is one that serves capital well enough while maintaining a tight rein on more explosive reconstitutions of the urban fabric. The vision of Haussmann without his despotic powers, namely the phantasmagoric vision of complete juridical control by the bourgeoisie, continues to haunt the imaginations of the middle class, as an ongoing number of dreams and schemes indicate. There is a simultaneous vision of Neighbourhood Area Committees, alliances with transnational connections, and other 'associational' strategies functioning as the real space of democracy and as watchdogs against the venalities to which electoral bodies are prone (Coelho and Venkat 2009). Indeed, there is a growing sense that real hope resides in the proliferating Resident's Welfare Associations, which have worked out ways of securing their entitlements (to power or water, for instance) from a state increasingly inclined to making citizens pay for an infrastructure which has not even yielded a service (Ranganathan 2011; Ranganathan, Kamath, and Baindur 2009). Other scholars who have studied smaller initiatives, such as the Alliance of three organizations working with the homeless and urban poor in Mumbai, believe there are crucial and valuable signs of the operation of 'deep democracy' which rework urban governmentalities (Appadurai 2002). Yet, if the poor are allowed to flourish only under conditions of relative anonymity, remaining beyond the eye of the state, what remains of that freedom so long and so loudly demanded? Can the mere refusal to be visibilized, by planning agency, law, census, and now in the pernicious plans for Unique Identity (UID), add up to social justice in the city?

In the current scenario, as some authors indicate, the market, rather than the state, is being made to perform a democratizing function. Do we take these collective 'emergent citizenships' as a sign of a continuous reworking from below, a counter to state power, or rather one that begins where it has left off? If the definition of 'citizenship' that these authors argue is emerging in the 'mutinies' or indeed 'adjustments' made by the urban poor shares no common political language with that of the state, what hope is there of recognition that this too is 'citizenship'? One wonders, therefore, and with a necessary scepticism, whether the forms of citizenship that are outlined here are doomed to a 'fugitive' existence. The prospects for the proliferation of such initiatives as an alternative to a (former) exaggerated reliance on the state (in fact and in analyses thereof) appear limited in the immediate future, since, unlike those who see the power of Capital as pitted against those more localized forms of power, which are fostered and rewarded by the electoral process—in short, as mutually incompatible forms of power—it is their very interdependence and systematicity that must be recognized before a larger politics of hope can be outlined.

NOTES

1. I have tried to delineate some of these processes for contemporary Bangalore in Nair (2005).
2. I have considered some of the meanings of the routine and structured violation of the law, and not just by subaltern classes, in contemporary Bengaluru in Nair (forthcoming).
3. Nikhil Anand and Anne Radamacher also discern a slow and more inclusive, though resolutely unequal, process of meeting housing needs in Mumbai; see their 'Housing in the Urban Age: Inequality and Aspiration in Mumbai' (forthcoming).
4. In addition to the argument for a transnational 'citizenship' in Ong (1998), see Nyamjoh (2007).

BIBLIOGRAPHY

Appadurai, A. 2002. 'Deep Democracy: Urban Governmentality and the Horizon of Politics', *Public Culture*, 14(1): 21–47.

Baviskar, A. 2002. 'Between Violence and Desire: Space, Power, and Identity in the Making of Metropolitan Delhi', *International Journal of Social Science*, 55(175): 89–98.

Chatterjee, P. 1997. 'Development Planning and the Indian State', in P. Chatterjee (ed.), *State and Politics in India*, pp. 271–98. Delhi: Oxford University Press.

———. 2008. 'Democracy and Economic Transformation in India', *Economic and Political Weekly*, 43(16): 53–61.

———. 2011. 'Democracy and Subaltern Citizens in India', in G. Pandey (ed.), *Subaltern Citizens and Their Histories: Investigations from India and the USA*, pp. 193–208. Delhi: Routledge.

Coelho, K. and T. Venkat. 2009. 'The Politics of Civil Society: Neighbourhood Associationism in Chennai', *Economic and Political Weekly*, 44(26/27): 358–67.

de Azevedo, S. 1998. 'Law and the Future of Urban Management in the Third World Metropolis', in E. Fernandes and A. Varley (eds), *Illegal Cities: Law and Urban Change in Developing Countries*, pp. 258–73. London and New York: Zed Books.

Gandhi, A. 2008. 'Vernacular Citizenship and Everyday Governance amongst India's Urban Poor', paper prepared for Roundtable Discussion 'Urban Planet: Collective Identities, Governance, and Empowerment in Megacities', Berlin, June 2008. Available online at http://www.irmgard-coninx-stiftung.de/fileadmin/user_upload/pdf/ urbanplanet/identities/ws1/041-Ghandi.pdf (accessed on 24 January 2011).

Harvey, D. 2006. *Paris: Capital of Modernity.* London: Routledge.

———. 2008. 'The Right to the City', *New Left Review*, 53(September–October 2008): 23–40.

Holston, J. 1999. 'Spaces of Insurgent Citizenship', in J. Holston (ed.), *Cities and Citizenship*, pp. 155–73. Durham and London: Duke University Press.

Mahadevia, D. 2007. 'A City with Many Borders', in A. Shaw (ed.), *Indian Cities in Transition*, pp. 341–89. New Delhi: Orient Longman.

Nair, J. 2005. *The Promise of the Metropolis: Bangalore's Twentieth Century.* Delhi: Oxford University Press.

———. Forthcoming. 'Is There an Indian Urbanism?'

Nyamjoh, F. 2007. 'From Bounded to Flexible Citizenship: Lessons from Africa', *Citizenship Studies*, 11(1): 73–82.

Ong, A. 1998. *Flexible Citizenship: The Cultural Logics of Transnationality.* Durham: Duke University Press.

Perspecta. 2003. 'Illusion of Permanence: Interview with Arjun Appadurai', *Perspecta*, 34(2003): 44–52.

Ranganathan, M. 2011. 'The Embeddedness of Cost Recovery: Water Reforms and Associationism at Bangalore's Fringes', in J. Anjaria and C. McFarlane (eds), *Urban Navigations: Politics, Space and the City in South Asia*, pp. 165–90. New Delhi: Routledge.

Ranganathan, M., L. Kamath, and V. Baindur. 2009. 'Piped Water Supply to Bangalore: Putting the Cart before the Horse?', *Economic and Political Weekly*, 44(33): 53–62.

Sanyal, K. 2007. *Rethinking Capitalist Development: Primitive Accumulation, Governmentality, and Post Colonial Capitalism.* London: Routledge.

Sarin, M. 1982. *Urban Planning in the Third World: The Chandigarh Experience.* London: Mansell Publishing Limited.

About the Editors and Contributors

EDITORS

Renu Desai is Research Fellow at the Centre for Urban Equity, CEPT University (Centre for Environmental Planning and Technology University), Ahmedabad. She was formerly a Research Associate at Durham University, UK. She has a PhD in Architecture from the University of California, Berkeley. Her research examines the politics of urban development and citizenship in Ahmedabad, and focuses on the practices that constitute its post-industrial remaking as well as their intersections with the remaking of the city by Hindutva politics. She is also involved in a joint research project on the politics of sanitation and water in Mumbai's informal settlements. Her research interests include urban informality, planning practices and new modes of urban governance, housing struggles, and questions around violence, identity, and urban space, particularly in India.

Romola Sanyal is Lecturer in Global Urbanism at the School of Architecture, Planning, and Landscape, Newcastle University. She has a PhD in Architecture from the University of California, Berkeley. Her research explores the urbanization of refugee spaces with a particular focus on the Middle East and South Asia. She has published in journals such as *Urban Studies, Social Identities* and *Traditional Dwellings and Settlements Review*. She is currently working on a book manuscript based on her doctoral dissertation and is also collaborating with other scholars as part of the Post-Conflict Environments Project at the Woodrow Wilson International Center for Scholars in Washington, DC.

CONTRIBUTORS

Sapana Doshi is Assistant Professor in the School of Geography and Development at the University of Arizona, Tucson. She has a PhD in Geography from the University of California, Berkeley. More broadly, she studies the nexus of cultural politics and political economy in cities of the global South. Her current research is on the politics of redevelopment in Mumbai, focusing on social mobilization among displaced slum residents. She has also written on water infrastructure development and colonial state formation in the 19th-century Mumbai. Outside of academia, she has several years of experience working in development and social justice initiatives in Nepal, India, Brazil, and the US.

Jaideep Gupte is Research Fellow at the Institute of Development Studies, University of Sussex, where his research is on violence, vulnerability, and conflict, with a particular geographic focus on South Asia. He was formerly a Research Fellow at the Urban Design Research Institute, Mumbai. His training is in Politics (University of Oxford, UK), Development Studies (IDS, University of Sussex, UK), and Economics (Simon Fraser University, Canada). His areas of specialization include policing and security for development, and vulnerability, violence, and informal justice in urban slums, and he has research experience in India, Bangladesh, and Nigeria. He occasionally contributes opinion pieces and reports to Indian national dailies.

Sunalini Kumar is Assistant Professor in the Department of Political Science, Lady Shri Ram College, Delhi University. She has a Master's in Social and Political Sciences from University of Cambridge and an MPhil from the Centre for Political Studies, Jawaharlal Nehru University, New Delhi. She is currently pursuing a PhD from the Department of Political Science, Delhi University on the politics of protest and urban space.

Malini Ranganathan is post-doctoral Research Associate in the Social Dimensions of Environmental Policy programme at the Beckman Institute for Advanced Science and Technology, University of Illinois, Urbana-Champaign. She earned a PhD in the Energy and Resources Group at the University of California, Berkeley with a designated emphasis in Global Metropolitan Studies. Her dissertation investigated the political ecology of urban water reforms in peri-urban Bangalore. In particular, she examined how practices of insurgent citizenship in informal areas challenge and renegotiate the implementation of neoliberal water policies. Her current research interests include ethnography, the politics of flood vulnerability, collective action, and citizen–state relations in metropolitan areas.

Liza Weinstein is Assistant Professor of Sociology at Northeastern University, Boston, and a Senior Research Associate at the Kitty and Michael Dukakis Center for Urban and Regional Policy, of the same university. She has a PhD in Sociology from the University of Chicago. Her research and teaching interests include cities and globalization, urban political economy, global and comparative urban development, and state–civil society relations, with a primary geographical focus on India. Her research on these topics has appeared in the *International Journal of Urban and Regional Research, Politics & Society, City & Community,* and several edited volumes. She is currently working on a book manuscript, tentatively titled *Governing Informality: Toward a Political Economy of Slums and Slum Redevelopment in Globalizing Mumbai.*

Jolie M. F. Wood is Assistant Professor and coordinator of the Politics, Philosophy, and Economics programme at the Asian University for Women, Chittagong, Bangladesh. She has a PhD in Government from the University of Texas, Austin, where she wrote her dissertation on patterns in contentious politics and political expression among occupational groups in Varanasi, India. Her research interests involve political participation, contentious politics, social movements, and civil society in South Asia, and she has conducted extensive fieldwork in Varanasi and Delhi.

FOREWORD BY:

James Holston is Professor of Anthropology at the University of California, Berkeley. His research examines the worldwide insurgence of democratic urban citizenships. He is the author of *The Modernist City: An Anthropological Critique of Brasília* (1989) and editor of *Cities and Citizenship* (1999), as well as essays on citizenship, law, democracy, violence, urban architecture and planning, critical ethnography, and new religions. His recent book, *Insurgent Citizenship: Disjunctions of Democracy and Modernity in Brazil* (2008), examines the insurgence of democratic citizenship in the urban peripheries of São Paulo, Brazil, its entanglement with entrenched systems of inequality, and its contradiction in violence under political democracy.

AFTERWORD BY:

Janaki Nair is Professor at the Centre for Historical Studies, Jawaharlal Nehru University. She has done research and writing primarily on the social, cultural, and political history of Mysore/Karnataka, with a strong interest in the fields of women and urban studies, questions of law and state, and visual cultures and practices. Her books include *Women and Law in Colonial India* (1996), *Miners and Millhands: Work Culture and Politics in Princely Mysore* (1998), and *The Promise of the Metropolis: Bangalore's Twentieth Century* (2005). A collection of essays entitled *Mysore Modern* is forthcoming.

Index